ECONOMIC HISTORY AND DEVELOPMENT OF SIKKIM

BEFORE AND AFTER INDEPENDENCE

ECONOMIC HISTORY AND DEVELOPMENT OF SIKKIM

BEFORE AND AFTER INDEPENDENCE

Jagadish Chandra Debnath

ABHIJEET PUBLICATIONS

DELHI 110094

ABHIJEET PUBLICATIONS
2/46 Tukhmeerpur Extension
Delhi-110 094
Phone: 011-22960492, 65698474
E-mail: abhijeetpublication@gmail.com

ECONOMIC HISTORY AND DEVELOPMENT OF SIKKIM

First Published 2009

ISBN 978-81-89886-89-9

PRINTED IN INDIA

Published by J.K. Singh for Abhijeet Publications, Delhi-110 094, Lasertypesetting by Gaurav Graphics, New Delhi and Printed at Himanshu Printers, Delhi.

Preface

My interest in the study of the Sikkimese economy, particularly its development under planning, was roused in early 1965 when I had the opportunity of going to Sikkim in connection with an educational tour. At that time I visited various places and institutions in Sikkim and also met many dignitaries and prominent persons with whom I had wide-ranging discussions regarding economic problems of the country. These dignitaries and prominent persons, specially the Chogyal* whom I met in his palace, urged that a serious study be made of the economic problems and prospects of Sikkim which had not hitherto been undertaken by any scholar. Being inspired I undertook a study entitled "Structure of the Sikkimese Economy" which was later on approved by the University Grants Commission. This study was subsequently enlarged into the present form under the title "Development of the Sikkimese Sconomy under Planning (1954-71)".

In my study I have, first of all, discussed different aspects of the country and economy of Sikkim in a historical perspective with special reference to economic change in the pre-plan period (Ch. I, II). Next I have discussed the growth of public revenues and expenditures in Sikkim which may be taken as the precursor of the later era of planned development (Ch. III). Then I have embarked on the topic of development by

---

* "Chogyal" is a Tibetan word meaning Dharma Raja.

introducing the salient features of the three plans (Ch. IV). The next three chapters deal with the three main sectoral divisions of the economy and their development during planning (Ch. V,VI,VII). The last chapter is devoted to a review of the plans in Sikkim (Ch. VIII).

In the study it has been seen that the economy of Sikkim has the twin characteristics of a traditional and a modern economy. So far as the former is concerned it is mostly shaped and influenced by natural, mainly geographical, and cultural factors. Being completely a hilly economy and having climatic conditions ranging from subtropical to Alpine zones within a span of 80 miles and having similar diversity in rainfall, the country has not yet been able to evolve a stable and viable economy. On the other hand, cultural factors also inhibited the growth of the economy. The Lepcha-Bhutia culture having its roots in the Tibetan brand of Buddhism is a culture of asceticism, abstinence and denouncement of the material world in pursuit of spiritual goals. The social and religious customs, land tenure system, political set-up as well as administrative machinery were all the byproducts of that culture and were intertwined in such a manner that the penetration of economic modernism was practically impossible until very recently.

So far as the modern economy of Sikkim is concerned it has not yet been able to wipe out the traditional one, but has rather emerged out of the latter and both are still living side by side. Though the seeds of modernism were sown long ago when the First British Political Officer was appointed to administer Sikkim in 1889 very little was done to break the vicious circle of the old traditional economy. Only after the introduction of development plans in 1954 was there a major blow to the existence of the old economic set-up and we can say that the "take-off" started at that time. At present the economy is pushing forward with great momentum and it is expected that within a few years Sikkim will have a completely modern economy. In this respect the *Government of India has played a great role in supplying the entire finance of all the development plans as well as other non-plan assistances.*

In assessing the development plans the eccnomy has been divided into three sectors:

(i) the agricultural sector,
(ii) the industrial sector, and
(iii) the services sector.

In the agricultural sector other allied occupations like forestry are also included, and in the industrial sector power and transport have been included. The services sector comprises mainly health and education.

Although development has occurred in all the sectors during the period under study, the most significant development has occurred in the industrial sector, mainly with regard to transport and communication as it is absolutely nedessary in a hilly and river-strewn country like Sikkim. The services sector has also developed tremendously because it was felt by the planners that people cannot go without services like health and education, and because there was practically no private organisation to provide them before the introduction of plans.

The study ends with the conclusion that there is little prospect for a significant development of the agricultural sector and more emphasis should be placed on the establishment of industries based on forest and agricultural resources electricity, and skilled labour.

There are also other potentialities but these three are the most promising of all. Whereas the first two can be acquired from the vast forests, agricultural fields and innumerable rivers and rivulets of Sikkim the third one can be acquired from training. Development along those lines seems to be the best solution for the problem of economic underdevelopment of Sikkim.

I like to mention in this connection that although I got assistance from various quarters in course of my work the collection of data was not very easy. Sikkim had yet to evolve a scientific system for the preparation and preservation of economic data. Very often data were not available with respect to certain vital aspects of the economy and even if available they were occasionally incomplete. Sometimes two sources gave conflicting data. In such cases I have either not accepted them at all, or if they were indispensable, I have cited both of them in the work. It has been tried in the study to confine to the available published data as far as practicable..

For the completion of my work I convey my thanks to the Sikkim Durbar, the Office of the Political Officer in Sikkim and various other institutions in Sikkim and India that provided me with published data and other materials. I also acknowledge my debts to the University of North Bengal and the University Grants Commission for granting me financial assistance during the period of my research. Lastly, I express my deepest regard and gratitude to my teacher Professor Dhires Bhattacharyya, of Calcutta University who supervised my work. It is needless to say that without his guidance, encouragement and meticulous correction the present work would not have been possible.

AUTHOR

Contents

PART I: ECONOMIC HISTORY OF SIKKIM

1

Introduction to Sikkim

To have a proper understanding of the economy of any country and its problems it is necessary, first of all, to acquire a fair knowledge of the country pertaining to its different aspects like geographical features, people, historical background, political set-up and cultural factors, and the influence of all these on the economy. This will be particularly true for an underdeveloped economy like Sikkim's where since antiquity non-economic factors have been playing a major role in moulding the economic pattern of the state until the initiation of planned economic growth in very recent times. While it is not possible to go into details of the interaction of these non-economic and economic factors within the short compass of the present study, it is still fruitful to indicate briefly the relevant factors to facilitate our understanding of the Sikkimese economy.

A. Geographical Features

The role of geographical features in shaping the economy of a country like Sikkim cannot be over-estimated. In fact, man's economy, like his other creations, is superimposed upon and meshed into the geographical environment which is not only a storehouse of source materials like water, electricity and minerals but also a physical and biological condition within which his economic activities like production, exchange and consumption occur. In this light let us discuss the geographical features of Sikkim.

The name "Sikkim" is derived from the word "Sukhim" meaning a place of peace and happiness.[1] In Tibetan and Bhutia languages it is called Denjong—originating from "Bay Yul Demo Jong" meaning "the hidden valley of rice". This signifies that at the beginning of the 14th century when the Bhutias started entering Sikkim from Tibet they found the Lepchas producing rice in the Tista and other valleys in Sikkim.[2]

The small but beautiful state of Sikkim is situated in the eastern Himalayas. It is bounded in the north by the vast Tibetan plateau and in the east by Bhutan and the Chumbi valley of Tibet. To its west lies Nepal and along its southern boundary stretches the Darjeeling district of West Bengal in India. It is situated roughly along longitudes 88° and 89° East and latitudes 27° and 28° North.[3]

The origin of the lofty Himalayan mountain range which cradles Sikkim is as fascinating as anything. Geologists say that millions of years ago the area now occupied by the Himalayas was the site of the shallow Tethys Sea. During the tertiary period in the earth's history powerful compressive forces folded and thrust marine deposits which arose out of the waters in the form of gigantic earth waves.

In the post-tertiary age, approximately one million years ago, further upheavals took place which raised the central portion and the foothills of the Himalayas into a vast mountain system. During the following millenniums natural forces still acted upon the system and as a result was formed the present complex of mountains and valleys which comprise Sikkim and other Himalayan states.

Sikkim has an area of 2,828 square miles and its shape is almost a rectangle 70 miles long from north to south and 40 miles wide from east to west. Sikkim is a land of varied elevations ranging from 800 feet above mean sea level at the southern foothills to over 20,000 feet along the northern and north-western frontiers. As such the climate of Sikkim varies between the tropical heat of the lower valleys and the icy cold of eternal snows.[4]

From a geographical point of view there are three major lateral divisions of the Himalayas:

(i) the Great Himalaya,
(ii) the Inner Himalaya, and
(iii) the foothills and the bordering sub-Himalayan "Piedmont Plain".

The plain is called Terai and Dooars to the south-west and south-east of Sikkim respectively. The state of Sikkim lies in the Great and Inner Himalayas, so that we can divide Sikkim into two broad geographical divisions: the Great Himalayan Sikkim and the Inner Himalayan Sikkim.

The first geographic division—the Great Himalayan Sikkim—is the northern part of the country and is adjacent to the plateau of Tibet and here the peaks rise up to 29,000 feet above sea level, the average being more than 20,000 feet. These mighty mountain chains have been a barrier to the country's development of communication, trade, agriculture and industry, and is a great obstacle to economic growth.

The second division—the Inner Himalayan Sikkim—is the southern part of the country and has a lower altitude. It is a complex area of forest-covered ranges and intervening fertile valleys, such as the Gangtok valley. While it is not as formidable as the Great Himalayan region, it has nonetheless served to isolate the fertile valleys of Sikkim from the Gangetic plains of India and the plateau of Tibet.

The state of Sikkim is geographically a basin. To its north lies the Great Himalayan Range and to the east and west, the Chola and Singalila Ranges respectively which gradually taper into lower altitudes and foothills towards the south. To the south there is no natural feature demarcating the frontier between Sikkim and West Bengal except in the middle where it runs along the Tista and the Rangit till they meet near Melli.

The important passes and peaks in the three ranges of Sikkim forming the natural boundary of the state in three directions may be mentioned. In the Great Himalayan Range the most important passes are Sesela or Dachila (17,343′), Kongrala (16,840′), Nakula (17,290′) and Chorten Nymala (19,000′). The Chola or Dongya Range is also pierced by several passes, the most important being Tangkarla, Nathula (15,200′) and Jelepla (14,000′). The main pass in the Singalila Range forming the border between Nepal and Sikkim is Chiabhangjangla. In this range is to be found the Kanchenjunga

(28,168′), the third highest peak in the world and other giants like the Tent Peak and the Kabru (24,076′). The highest peak within Sikkim is Siniolchum (22,620′).

The Tista river winds its way through Sikkim, the main tributaries being the Rangit, the Rongni-Chu, the Lachen and the Lachung rivers, all snow-fed torrents originating in the Great Himalayan Range. Essentially, the entire Sikkim basin is the catchment area of the Tista river which may be regarded as the main artery of the state's water distribution.

The rainfall in Sikkim varies between 30 inches and 140 inches and some places have even 240 inches per year. The rainy season is between May and November. Along the Tista basin the monsoon cloud penetrates through the deep valleys upto the foot of the highest mountains and hence the wet zone extends as far as the snows. In fact, the bowl-like, mountain-girdled basin of Sikkim has been formed by the erosive work of the Tista and its tributaries.

In Sikkim one finds settled conditions of weather and in this respect they are in sharp contrast with those obtaining in the neighbouring Tibet where they change even in the course of a day. Sikkim has only a few areas where such sharp weather changes occur. Practically speaking, there are only two seasons in Sikkim: monsoon from May to November and winter from December to April.

Economic life in Sikkim is mostly influenced by the state's geographical features, particularly the condition of its terrain and climate. The basis of economic life in any underdeveloped country is land-use and so we should know how land is used in Sikkim. The study of land-use in Sikkim is important more because the state is a completely hilly region and as such poses peculiar problems and obstacles for the use of land.

From the point of view of *land utilization* Sikkim can be divided into three zones:

(*a*) Alpine pastures zone,

(*b*) forests zone, and

(*c*) crops zone.

We can compare this division with a similar one made by Sir J.D. Hooker, the famous botanist who made extensive tours and study in Sikkim during the British days. As the *Imperial Gazetteer of India* says "Sir J.D. Hooker divides the country into three zones, calling the lower upto 5,000 feet above the sea, the tropical; thence to 13,000 feet, the upper limit of tree vegetation, the temperate; and above to the perpetual snow-line at 16,000 feet, Alpine."[5]

The Alpine pastures zone stretches from the forests zone to the perpetual snow-clad areas but vegetation here rapidly deteriorates as the altitude rises. This zone more or less corresponds with the Great Himalayan region discussed earlier. The snow-clad areas constitute a considerable part of Sikkim and are entirely out of any use. However, the high mountain pastures are an essential part of plant resources of Sikkim and they have made possible the raising of livestocks without the need of forest clearance or maintenance. Sheep breeding and rearing is an important means of livelihood here and formerly when there was free communication and trade between Sikkim and Tibet often herds of sheep would pass into the Tibetan grazing land during summer and return in the winter. This seasonal migration was necessary for providing adequate grazing facilities to the sheep throughout the year as well as for the up-keeping of the sheep in a cool climate which is helpful in improving the output of wool.[6]

Below the Alpine pastures starts the forests zone. Forests dominate land-use in Sikkim as well as in other Himalayan states. Here the forests zone can be sub-divided into two sectors:

(i) the "deciduous" forests in the lower altitude which have been greatly reduced by clearings, and

(ii) above this sector, the "coniferous" forests with either persistent or deciduous leaves.

Above the tree-line which varies from region to region there is vegetation composed mainly of prostrate mountain pines and rhododendrons marking the gradual transition from forests to the Alpine zone.

Below the forests zone lies the crops zone. The crops zone is very extensive but cultivation naturally diminishes as the altitude rises. Rice and corn are seldom cultivated beyond the altitude of 6,000 feet. At higher levels wheat, barley and potato are the common crops. However, in these higher levels soil and climatic conditions are seldom suitable for farming and consequently crop yields are lower. The existence of two distinct and long seasons has influenced the vegetation of the zone.

Table 1
Settlement Pattern in Sikkim: 1961

Tehsil	*Rural area in square miles*	*Rural population*	*Number of villages with population*				*Total number of villages*
			Less than 200	*200-499*	*500-999*	*1000-1999*	
Gangtok	363	49856	51	74	29	1	155
Namchi	715	95726	60	147	48	5	260
Mangan	1736	9759	28	13	4		45
Total	2814	155341	139	234	81	6	460

Note: i) Gangtok town has an area of 4 square miles which when added, gives the total area of Gangtok Tehsil as 367 square miles and the total area of Sikkim as 2,818 square miles.

ii) Gangtok town has a population of 6,848 which when added, gives the total population of Gangtok Tehsil as 56,704 and the total population of Sikkim as 1,62,189.

Sources: i) Govt. of India, *Census of India, 1961*, Vol. 16, Part 8, pp. 40-46.

ii) Govt. of Sikkim, *Sikkim Through Figures* (Gangtok: Planning and Development Dept., 1969), pp. 4-5.

During the monsoon season rice, maize and other crops are grown while during winter oranges, apples and potatoes are the main products.

B. Settlement Pattern

Divergence in geographical features and the consequent difference in land-use in Sikkim has influenced the settlement pattern of the state. In the almost barren Great Himalayan region there is practically no source of livelihood except pasturage. Formerly, however, limited trade took place through the high Himalayan passes. Caravans carried cloth, spices and small manufactured goods from Sikkim and the neighbouring countries into Tibet and brought back salt, wool and yak herds. Since ancient times these passes— Nathu La and the Jelep La in north-eastern Sikkim—were some of the few areas in the world where free trade and travel persisted across international barriers. But after the Sino-Indian border conflict of 1962 there has been a total stoppage of this age-old intercourse. As a result, the settlement in this region has been reduced to a great extent.[7]

Moreover, the harshness of living condition in the Great Himalayan region is incomparable and unbearable. Nowhere else in the world are the mountains so high on the average, nowhere else is there such a difference in level between valley bottoms and the mountain summits and nowhere else is there such a huge mass of steep rocks destitute of plant growth of any kind whatsoever. These extreme natural conditions limit man's economic activities and provide few opportunities for livelihood.

Even in the Inner Himalayan region of Sikkim where altitude is not so formidable a barrier, steep topography aggravates the effects of altitude. The steep contour of land influences the whole life-pattern of the Sikkimese. In Sikkim most of the cultivation is done on sloping ground where work is strenuous and takes up a larger time. The slope increases the effects of gravity on cultivated land, causing the soil to slide downward slowly. Tillage speeds up this process by depriving it of plant cover for some time until cultivated plants grow up and also by making the earth friable. Lastly, the slope causes an outstanding number of avalanches of great destructive power occasionally sweeping away large tracts of cultivated area and high-altitude settlements. As a result of all this we find that this region of Sikkim is also sparsely populated though compared to the former region the density of population here is higher.

The 1961 census revealed the population of Sikkim as 162,189. The average density of population is 59 persons per square mile and nearly 96 per cent of the population live in rural areas. The average density of 59 persons per square mile is nearly the same as that in the United States but it is considerably less than the corresponding figure for the neighbouring Nepal (174) and a little more than that for Bhutan (47).[8]

The higher density of population in Nepal might have been one reason, among other ones as described later on, for the large-scale Nepali migration into Sikkim during the 19th and early 20th centuries. The Nepali migration was not so large in Bhutan which perhaps explains the comparatively low density of population in that country.

The settlement pattern in different parts of Sikkim is not uniform. The relative distribution of population in the three Tehsils can be shown as in the following diagram:

Diagram I

Percentage Distribution of Population and Area in Different Tehsils

(White columns indicate population and black columns indicate area)

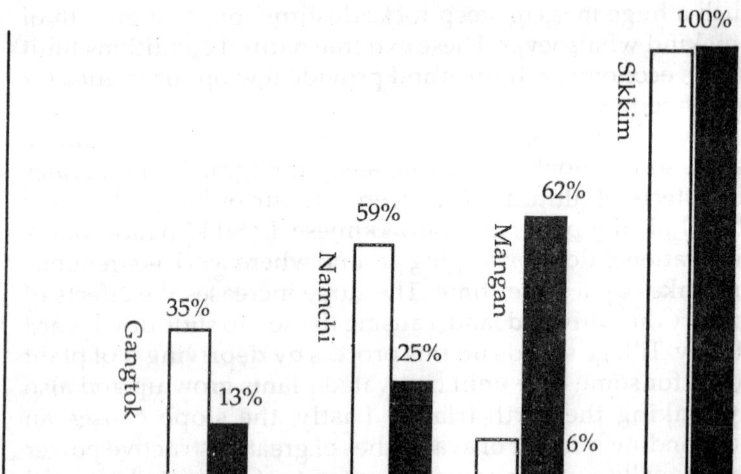

Sources: As in Table 1.

From the above diagram it is clear that Mangan Tehsil which occupies more than 50 per cent of the total area of the state has only 6 per cent of the total population while Gangtok Tehsil which occupies only 13 per cent of the total area has a population amounting to 35 per cent of the total. The reason for this uneven settlement pattern is that in the northern Mangan Tehsil the terrain is mostly barren and dominated by lofty snow-peaked mountains and glaciers which permit little habitation. The other two Tehsils are of lower altitude and both vegetation and communication facilities are available, and hence favourable to settlement.

Let us now discuss the settlement pattern in terms of the size and number of villages in different parts of the state. From the previous table it is seen that most of he villages in Sikkim consist of a population between 200 and 499. If the average number of members in a family is taken as 5, then it means that generally 40 to 100 families constitute a village. The size of the village population in Sikkim is, therefore, quite small compared to that in other states of India.

The size of the village population, again, is not the same everywhere within Sikkim. Most of the villages in Gangtok and Namchi Tehsils have a population between 200 and 499, while in Mangan Tehsil they have a population less than 200. Taking again the average number of members in a family as 5, this means that most of the villages in Mangan Tehsil have less than 40 houses. In general, we see that whereas in the lower valleys big settlements are common, in the upper hill-slopes they are relatively few. This may be explained by the fact that big settlements are more economical in the lower valleys than in the upper stratum of the state.

(a) Race, Religion and Language: Conflict and Consensus

The people of Sikkim, though small in number, is of a very intricate composition from the points of view of race, religion and language. Sikkim has a population composed mainly of three racial elements: the Lepchas, the Bhutias and the Nepalis.[9] The Lepchas and the Bhutias, who are more or less equal in number, jointly constitute about one-third of the total population while the Nepalis account for the remaining two-thirds.

According to popular belief, the Lepchas are the original inhabitants of the land. The local pronunciation of the word Lepcha is 'Lap-cha' or 'Lap-che' and is of a Nepalese derivation. Lap-cha is derived from a word in the Parbatiya dialect of Nepal, meaning 'lap'—speech, and 'cha'— unintelligible, i.e. the unintelligible speakers, a contemptuous term referring to the tribe not adopting the Parbatiya language.[10] The Lepchas call themselves 'Rong Pa' meaning the ravine folk which suggests that they might have lived before somewhere near a river.[11] It is said that they originally migrated from the Assam-Burma border in the 13th century but no authoritative proof of that has yet been established.[12] They ruled over Sikkim until the middle of the 17th century when the Bhutias established their kingdom there.

Due to the infiltration of the Bhutias since then and the immigration of the Nepalis towards the end of the 19th century the Lepchas gradully lost much of their land. Today the principal concentration of the Lepchas can be found only in the Tolung valley of north-western Sikkim. By circumstances the Lepchas have been accustomed to living in remote and inaccessible regions where they have developed a fondness for birds, beasts and flowers and an extensive knowledge of the mountains and forests.

The Bhutias started entering Sikkim from Tibet from the beginning of the 14th century.[13] However, they took absolute control of the country only in the mid-17th century when the Bhutia monarchy was established. The social customs of the Bhutias are generally similar to those of the Lepchas due to religious similarity and close contact for centuries and now the two communities inter-marry freely. The Bhutias are good traders and many of them are herdsmen looking after the valuable herds of yaks and sheep.

The third main community consists of the Nepalis. It is indeed curious that the largest group of people in Sikkim should be the Nepalis who migrated from Nepal slowly but steadily and pushed their way into the land. Today the Nepalis constitute about 72 per cent of the total population in Sikkim.[14] The Nepalis are divided into a number of tribes. They are a hardy and industrious people and make excellent cultivators. The Nepalis have been migrating into Sikkim since the last century and are concentrated mostly in the western regions of the country. Some of the social customs of the Nepalis differ from those of the Lepchas and the Bhutias and hence there is generally no inter-marriage with the latter two communities. Amongst the more orthodox of the Nepalis, even inter-caste marriage within a tribe is strictly banned due to the influence of the Hindu caste system. There are also two other smaller groups of people in Sikkim.

One such group is the small but distinct group known as the Tsongs. They were originally settlers from the Tsang-po valley in Tibet. In recent years attempts have been made to use the term 'Tsong' to denote persons other than the original Tsongs and this has led to much political dispute. The other smaller group consists of the traders and officials coming from other states of India who are numerically insignificant but socially and economically quite influential.

Previously Mahayana Buddhism of the Tibetan type was the religion of the monarch and as such it has assumed the status of a state religion. There was an Ecclesiastical Department of the Government of Sikkim which supported, financially and otherwise, the maintenance of the Buddhist monasteries of the land. Important religious ceremonies were attended by the Chogyal, as well as the members of the State Council* and other high officials; and even for the Indian Political Officer and his senior officials it was obligatory to attend such ceremonies.

Now Buddhism is professed by about 28 per cent of the population and most of the Lepchas and Bhutias are its adherents. There are about 67 Buddhist monasteries in Sikkim. The important monasteries from the historical point of view are located at Pemayangtse, Tashiding, Phensad, Phodang, Rumtek and Ralang. These are the most sacred religious centres in Sikkim.

There is no well-established religious centre for the Hindus in Sikkim even though Hinduism is professed by the majority of the people, mainly the Nepalis. This is perhaps because Hinduism has been brought into the country only in the recent past along with the influx of the Nepalis. Moreover, unlike the

* It was like a cabinet, but its members were landlords—not people's representatives. Its purpose was to assist the king in administration. In later years some people's representatives were inducted in the state cabinet.

former religion it did not get any state patronage. It is noteworthy, however, that there is no hostility between the Buddhists and the Hindus in Sikkim and the two religions exist side by side and often in a synthesised form.

There is also a small number of Christians in Sikkim. The Church of Scotland Mission and the Scandanivan Alliance Mission are the two main Christian missions in the country. Primitive Lepcha religion of the pagan type is also traceable in some quarters, but it is gradually dying out in the face of its more dominant counterparts.

During the British Raj English was the official language of Sikkim. But after the departure of the British from Sikkim in 1947 regional languages have began to compete with English. 'Sikkimese' which is the language of the Bhutias and Gorkhali, the language of the Nepalis, are now recognised also as official languages. At present most of the official declarations are made simultaneously in these three languages.

The Lepchas have their own language which is also called Lepcha. It is not an official language but that does not affect the Lepchas very much as they are generally proficient in either of the two other regional languages. The Lepcha language is not developed and has a very limited literature consisting almost entirely of translations from Tibetan religious books. The alphabet was invented in the 17th century but few people know it at present. A grammar was written by General Mainwaring in 1876. But since then no significant attempt was made for the development of the language.[15] Now the Government is attempting to publish some school text-books in it.

The 'Sikkimese' language belongs to the Tibeto-Burman family. It is written in the Tibetan script which is nothing but the ancient Indian Brahmi script that went to Tibet and was accepted there along with Buddhism. The language is very much akin to the dialect of south-eastern Tibet which is adjacent to Sikkim. The different Nepali tribes have their own separate languages or dialects, but almost all Nepalis now tend to speak in Gorkhali. It is a language derived from Sanskrit, written in the Indian Devanagari script and linguistically akin to the family of north Indian languages.

Of all the three regional languages Gorkhali is developing very fast and is tending to be the common language in offices.

In a rural area where the Lepchas, the Bhutias and the Nepalis inhabit, Gorkhali is used as the *lingua-franca*. Among the Lepchas and the Bhutias, 'Sikkimese' or the Bhutia language is understood by all and is used as a common language. But between the Lepchas and the Bhutias on the one hand and the Nepalis on the other, Gorkhali is used as the common language. The reason is that 'Sikkimese' is a complicated tonal language which is not easily mastered by the ordinary Nepali peasant, but the Lepchas and the Bhutias are much more successful in learning Gorkhali which seems to be easier to learn. Moreover, those who are accustomed to go to the Gangtok bazar or who have contact with the Government officials are, in fact, fluent in Gorkhali.

The presence of culturally diverse groups in Sikkim hinders the state's cohesiveness. For instance, the lack of a common racial background is responsible for the disunity of the Sikkimese people. The term "Sikkimese" indicates a resident of Sikkim and has little linguistic or ethnological implication. An urgent necessity is, therefore, to build closer relations between the Lepchas, Bhutias and Nepalis, and the relatively small, but politically and economically significant group made up of the Indian traders and officials.

The Lepchas have lost much of their land by the infiltration of the Bhutias and, above all, by the rapid spread of Nepali settlers. Conflict between the Lepchas and the Tibetan Bhutias led to considerable disturbances in Sikkim in the past. The Lepchas were pushed into the forest and lower vallyes below 4,000 feet by the Bhutias who settled at higher elevations. However, at present there is little conflict between these two ethnic groups and perhaps due to the heavy Nepali inroads into Sikkim the two have become much more cohesive, socially as well as politically. But cohesion has not yet been achieved between the Lepcha-Bhutias and the Nepalis.

Before the influx of the Nepalis the Lepchas derived their livelihood mainly from the bounty of the forest. The forest provided plenty of game, edible fruits and tubers, medicinal herbs and fibres that could be woven into fabrics. The Lapchas practised *jhum* or shifting cultivation in which they cultivated only small patches of the forest, cutting down the trees, burning the undergrowth, and planting the clearing with corn, buckwheat and millet.

The Nepali settlers, on the other hand, cut down wide areas of the forest for their paddy-fields. In consequence, the Lepchas' living space was continually reduced, the tribe became more sedentary, enlarging its fields and livestock. Hunting and gathering supplies in the forest lost in importance; the forest ceased to belong to them, and they had to pay dearly for the large amount of timber needed in the construction of their traditional houses.

As a people, the Lepchas are honest, peace-loving and unselfishly helpful. But their timidity and shyness, their naivety and tendency to individualism have proved poor weapons in the unequal struggle they had to wage for four centuries against the interlopers from the north and the west.

Relationship between the Bhutias and the Nepalis was also not very cordial. Neither the Bhutia King nor the Bhutias in general favoured the large-scale immigration of the Nepalis and they often tried to prevent the influx, though not always with success. Political rights were denied to the Nepalis and that was a veritable breeding ground of discontent among the largest section of the people.

(b) The Growth of Population

A few words may be said about the growth of population in Sikkim. The recorded statistics on population growth since the census was undertaken by the British for the first time in 1891 show remarkable variations. During the first decade (1891-1901) population increased almost two-fold while during the next decade (1901-1911) it increased less than one and a half times. During the next four decades (1911-1950) the increase was even lesser—population increased only one and a half times during this period. A detailed statistics is given in Table 2.

The British encouraged Nepali settlement in Sikkim in order to curb the Tibetan influence on the Bhutia monarchy as well as to have a large number of Sikkimese subjects more loyal to the British than to the Sikkim King. As H.H. Risley says:

> "The influx of these hereditary enemies of Tibet (i.e. Nepalis) is our surest guarantee against a revival of Tibetan influence. Here also religion will play a leading part. In Sikkim, as in India, Hinduism will assuredly cast out Buddhism, and the praying-wheel of the lama

> will give place to the sacrificial implements of the Brahman. The land will follow the creed; the Tibetan proprietors will gradually be dispossessed, and will betake themselves to the petty trade for which they have an undeniable aptitude. Thus race and religion, the prime movers of the Asiatic world, will settle the Sikkim difficulty for us, in their own way."[29]

It is very difficult to make a comprehensive study of Nepali immigration in Sikkim due to the lack of community-wise population data in the census reports. The Lepchas, the Bhutias and the Nepalis constitute three distinct communities of Sikkim—ethnically, culturally and socially; but it is surprising that the census authorities never took notice of it. It may, however, be presumed that the rate of influx of Nepali settlers gradually diminished but it never died out completely.

C. The History

(a) Pre-British History: The Era of Absolute Monarchy

Little is known about the early history of Sikkim. There is no authentic chronicle of the Lepchas who are regarded as the authochtones or original inhabitants of the country which is called after them the Lepcha Land. A much better account is obtained of the Bhutias and the Nepalis who entered the country in later periods successively. There are only a few and scattered references to the Lepchas in the chronicles of the Bhutia Kings of Sikkim. The Lepcha folk-lore and tradition also provide little historical information.

According to one Lepcha legend the first Lepcha chief was of divine origin and The-Kong-Tek was the sixth in direct descent.[19] If each generation is assumed to have an average span of 25 years, for six generations we have a total time-span of 150 years. The time of The-Kong-Tek and Khye-Bumsa is generally assumed to be during the first half of the 15th century, as stated in the royal chronicles. So, according to this calculation, the first Lepcha King reigned around the later half of the 13th century. It can be presumed then that the Lepcha society and kingdom were well-established by the 13th century A.D., but we have no information about the earlier period.

Another Lepcha tradition referrs to four Kings named Tur-ve, Tur-Sang-Pono, Tur-Ayek and Tui-Sung who reigned

Table 2
Growth of Population in Sikkim

Year	*Persons*	*Variations*	*Percentage variations in total population*	*Males*	*Females*	*Females per thousand males*	*Variations in males*	*Variations in females*
1891	30,458							
1901	59,014	28,556	93.7	30,795	28,219	916		
1911	87,920	28,906	49.0	45,059	42,861	951	14,264	14,642
1921	81,721	-6,199	-7.1	41,492	40,229	970	-3,567	-2,632
1931	109,808	28,087	34.4	55,825	53,983	967	14,333	13,754
1941	121,520	11,713	10.7	63,287	58,221	920	7,464	4,248
1951	137,725	16,205	13.3	72,210	65,515	907	8,921	7,284
1961	162,189	24,464	17.8	85,193	76,996	904	12,983	11,481

Sources: (i) Imperial Gazetteer of India (1908).
(ii) Census of India (for the above years).
(iii) Sikkim Through Figures, 1969, Tables 4 and 9.

apparently at the same time in different parts of the country. When the four died, their places were taken over by treasurers, secretaries and headmen.[20] It is clear that the above four Kings reigned Sikkim before the arrival of the Bhutia chief Khye-Bumsa. It seems that after acquiring their loyalty Khye-Bumsa and his successors tried to retain it by re-transferring the occupied lands to them and creating a feudal clan of the Lepcha chiefs subservient to the Bhutia supremacy. The reference to the secretaries, treasurers and headmen in the above tradition, perhaps, relates to this class.

The erstwhile Chogyal Ruling House of Sikkim trace their descent from a King named Indrabodhi who was ruler of what is today known as Himachal Pradesh in India. Eastward migration of the western Himalayan tribes under adventurous princes is well-known in history and this was particularly so when Buddhism declined in India—the motive being partly to escape religious persecution and partly to spread the faith. A prince from the far west in the line of King Indrabodhi is understood to have founded the Mynak kingdom in the north-eastern Tibetan province of Kham in the 9th century A.D.[21]

Twenty-five generations after the founding of the kingdom a scion of the Mynak House went on a pilgrimage towards the west with his five sons. This was in the first half of the 15th century. At a place named Sakya one of the sons, Khye-Bumsa, married the daughter of the Sakya hierarch and settled at Phari in the nearby Chumbi valley. This valley became the nucleus of the later kingdom of Sikkim in the early 16th century.[22]

While Khye-Bumsa was at Sakya a big building was under construction in the famous Sakya monastery. So heavy were the four main pillars of the building that none could raise them into place. Then Khye-Bumsa stepped forward and with a Herculean display of strength lifted the pillars into proper position. In fact, the name Khye-Bumsa means "the possessor of the strength of a hundred thousand men" and it was given by the grateful monks of the monsatery as a recognition of his great service.[23]

Years later, and apparently on the advice of the same lamas, Khye-Bumsa travelled to Sikkim in quest of the Lepcha-chief The-Kong-Tek and his wife Nye-Kong-Nal. While The-Kong-

Tek was a *"bong-thing"*, his wife was a *"mun"*. It may be mentioned in this connection that in the primitive religion of the Lepchas the place of the *bong-thing* was very important. He might be called a shaman, a medicine man or an exorciser. He was supposed to possess the power to prophesy and grant boons. His female counterpart was the *mun*, though of a much lower position.[24]

After strenuous search Khye-Bumsa met the legendary Lepcha chieftain who, forwarding the customary exchange of pleasantries and gifts, predicted that the childless Khye-Bumsa would have three children and that his descendants would become the future rulers of Sikkim. The prophecy came true as recorded history shows. Phuntsog Namgyal, a direct descendant of Khye-Bumsa, established himself as the first consecrated King of Sikkim in 1642. Here fact and legend converge.[25]

It is interesting to note how the Bhutia immigrants established a well-ordered kingdom with the support and co-operation of the local Lepchas. There is a description of how Khye-Bumsa established friendship with the Lepcha chief The-Kong-Tek by swearing blood-brotherhood:

"They agreed by this that all the males should be considered to be related to the sons and all the females to the daughters. This friendship was cemented by a ceremony at which several animals, both domestic and wild, were sacrificed and all the local deities invoked to bear witness to this solemn contract of friendship, binding the Lepchas and the Bhutias in an inseparable bond. They sat together on the raw hides of the animals, entwined the entrails around their persons, and put their feet together in a vessel filled with blood, thus swearing the blood troth to each other."[26]

The alliance between the Lepchas and the Bhutias is said to have been possible because Khye-Bumsa had, by this time, converted the Lepchas to Buddhism. But we must not also lose sight of the shamanistic rituals of the above covenant; and it might have been a common belief in these rituals and not Buddhism proper that was the main binding force between the two communities. In fact, the Lepcha religion had a great deal of similarity with the pre-Buddhist and shamanistic religion of Tibet called *Pon* or *Bon*.[27] This common cultural tie between Tibet and Sikkim was not an insignificant factor in the matter of racial integration between the Lepchas and the Bhutias.

The wise and diplomatic administration of the Bhutia chiefs also contributed to make that integration firmer and permanent. The Bhutia immigrants in co-operation with the local Lepcha chiefs established for the first time a central political power in Sikkim with the Bhutia control at the apex of the system. The local Lepcha chiefs who contributed to the formation of the kingdom were appointed as ministers, governors and high officials. With the regranting of lands the local Lepcha chiefs were transformed into an aristocracy of feudal lords who were subordinate to, but compared well with, the Bhutia aristocracy. There was, therefore, no feeling of being ruled by foreigners among the Lepchas who gradually mingled with the newcomers and adopted their religion and culture.[28]

The dynasty of Phuntsog Namgyal ruled Sikkim until the country was merged with India in 1975. A genealogical table of the successive rulers is given below:

The Consecrated Rulers of Sikkim

1. Phuntsog Namgyal (1604 - ?) Consecrated in 1642	
2. Tensung Namgyal (1644 - ?) Consecrated in 1670	
3. Chagdor Namgyal (1686-1716) Consecrated in 1700	Son of the second wife of Tensung Namgyal
4. Gyurmed Namgyal (1707-1733) Consecrated in 1717	Son of Chagdor Namgyal
5. Namgyal Phuntsog (1733-1769) Consecrated in 1733	Only son of Gyurmed Namgyal born of a nun—posthumously
6. Tenzing Namgyal (1769-1793) Consecrated in 1780	Son of the third wife of Namgyal Phuntsog
7. Tsugphud Namgyal (1785-1863) Consecrated in 1793	Son of Tenzing Namgyal
8. Sidkeong Namgyal (1819-1874)	Eldest surviving son of the second wife of Tsugphud Namgyal
9. Thutob Namgyal (1860-1914) Consecrated in 1874	Step brother of Sidkeong Namgyal and son of the fifth wife of Tsugphud Namgyal

10. Sidkeong Tulku (1879-1914) Consecrated in 1914	Second son of the first wife of Thutob Namgyal
11. Tashi Namgyal (1893-1963) Consecrated in 1914	Step-brother of Sidkeong Tulku and the first son of the second wife of Thutob Namgyal
12. Palden Thondup Namgyal (1923-82) Consecrated in 1963 was the Ruler of Sikkim until it was merged with India in 1975.	Second son of Tashi Namgyal

Source: Government of Sikkim, *Sikkim: A Concise Chronicle.*

(b) The British Penetration and Control: The Era of Dyarchy

Without going into details of the later history of Sikkim we may mention only the most important and relevant events since the beginning of the 19th century when Sikkim came in contact with the British. It was also during this period that the Nepalis, being encouraged by the British, settled in Sikkim in large numbers.

Sikkim came directly under British influence when she was involved in the Anglo-Nepali war of 1814-15. In this war Sikkim was allied with the British. In the Treaty of Titalia concluded in 1817 a new boundary was established between Sikkim and Nepal whereby Sikkim regained many parts of southern and western Sikkim that had been lost to Nepal following the Treaty of 1792 between Nepal and Tibet. In 1834-35 Sikkim sought British assistance to prevent an incursion into Sikkim by the Kotapas, the rebel Sikkimese, supported by the Nepalis. The rebels and the Nepalis were repulsed and in 1835 the district of Darjeeling, so long forming the southern part of Sikkim, was ceded to the British.[30]

The government of Sikkim in the pre-British era was always a Tibetan-type hereditary and absolute monarchy since 1642 when Phuntsog Namgyal was consecrated as the first Chogyal of Sikkim. The word "Chogyal" is a Tibetan word meaning Dharma Raja and it had been commonly used by various Tibetan kings and chieftains in the past. Like the Tibetan "Tsongdu" or National Assembly, the Chogyal of Sikkim also had a Council of Ministers consisting of the 'Kazis' or feudal landlords who assisted the King in the governance of the country. However, the King was the supreme authority and any action on the part of the subordinate authority was subject to the approval of the King.

During the British reign in India this absolute monarchy was gradually undergoing a change. Being threatened by her hostile neighbours Sikkim had been slowly coming within the fold of British influence and control. By and by the British acquired a position to have a say in the internal administration of the state and in the treaty of 1861 Sikkim virtually became a protectorate of the British. Clause 19 of the Treaty says:

> "The Government of Sikkim will not cede or lease any portion of its territory to any other State without the permission of the British Government." Furthermore, "the whole military force of Sikkim shall join and afford every aid and facility to British Troops when employed in the Hills", and "the Government of Sikkim engages that no armed force belonging to any other country shall pass through Sikkim without the sanction of the British Government."[34]

In the Convention between Great Britain and China relating to Sikkim and Tibet in the Year 1890 the Chinese recognised Sikkim as a protectorate of the British Government. Clause 2 of the Convention says:

> "It is admitted that the British Government, whose protectorate over the Sikkim State is hereby recognised, has direct and exclusive control over the internal administration and foreign relations of that State, and except through and with the permission of the British Government, neither the Ruler of the State nor any of its officers shall have official relations of any kind, formal or informal, with any other country."[35]

In 1889, just one year before the signing of the Convention, Claude White was appointed the First British Political Officer in Sikkim and had been invested with the authority of a *de facto* ruler. Henceforth the relation between the Sikkim Government and the British Government remained practically the same until the latter withdrew from India in 1947.

Only in 1905 did the Maharaja regain some of his authority as a ruler following a visit to Calcutta, where he was invited to meet the then Prince of Wales. Then in 1906 a significant change took place in the administration of Sikkim when control over all state affairs was transferred from the Government of Bengal to the Government of India.[31] But still the situation did not change very much. As H.H. Risley said two years later:

> "Sikkim, in fact, has been treated substantially as part of British India, subjected for political reasons to the nominal rule of a princelet of the Merovingian type."[32]

The Imperial Gazetteer of India (1908) gives a description of this dyarchical political set-up in Sikkim: "The Political Officer, who is stationed at Gangtok, advises and assists the Maharaja and his Council but no rules have yet been laid down for the civil and criminal administration. The landlords ... exercise a limited civil and criminal jurisdiction within the lands of which they collect the revenue, but all important cases are referred to the Maharaja or the Political Officer. Those referred to the Maharaja are decided by him in consultation with his ministers *(lompo)*, at present five in number, two of whom are always in attendance on him. Appeals are heard by the Maharaja sitting with one or more members of his Council, or by a Committee of the Council. Capital sentences passed by other authorities require the confirmation of the Maharaja. The annual budget estimates of income and expenditure are, in the first instance, approved by the Maharaja and his Council, and are then submitted for the sanction of the Government of India by the Political Officer."[36]

From the description of the *Imperial Gazetteer of India* (1908) it appears that a great amount of political and economic power had been usurped from the King by the Political Officer. The Political Officer had three types of power:

a) He would advise and assist the King in administration, thereby exerting his influence behind the curtain.

b) He would act as the final authority for the matters that were referred to him by the landlords.

c) He had the sanctioning authority of the state budget on behalf of the Government of India and as such exerted a great influence in the economic matters of the state.

In fact, the remaining powers in the hands of the King were only nominal as the British frequently over-ruled the royal decision and on occasions even imprisoned the King.[37] This was facilitated by the fact that there was no written constitution or law of the country, as the *Imperial Gazetteer* states: "*no rules have yet been laid down for the civil and cirminal administration*". In such a situation the British fully exerted their influence to attain their objectives.

In May, 1946, prior to the British withdrawal from India, Lord Wavell, the Viceroy of India, declared on behalf of the British Government that under the new Indian Constitution Britain would cease to exercise the powers of paramountcy in relation to the Indian states. *Sikkim, as an Indian state under the Indian Constitution of 1935*, came within the scope of the above declaration.

About the new position of the Indian states Wavell also declared: "*The void will have to be filled either by the states entering into a federal relationship with the succession Government or Governments in British India or, failing this, entering into particular political arrangements with it or them.*"[38]

In accordance with this formula Sikkim wanted a treaty relationship with independent India, but until that was concluded, she agreed to maintain the former relationship. Accordingly, a Standstill Agreement was signed on February 27, 1948 between the Sikkim Durbar and the Government of India according to which all agreements, relations and administrative arrangements as to matters of common concern existing between the British Crown and the Sikkim state on August 14, 1947 were deemed to continue pending the conclusion of a new treaty.

Negotiations for a new Indo-Sikkim Treaty started in 1949 and it was finally signed on December 5, 1950 in a climate of goodwill and friendship. The Treaty opened a new chapter of mutual collaboration and help in the history of Sikkim.[39]

The main provisions of the Treaty may be mentioned as the following:

(i) "Sikkim shall continue to be a protectorate of India and, subject to the provisions of this Treaty, shall enjoy autonomy in regard to its internal affairs." [Article 2]

(ii) "The Government of India will be responsible for the defence and territorial integrity of Sikkim. It shall have the right to take such measures as it considers necessary

for the defence of Sikkim or the security of India, whether preparatory or otherwise, and whether within or outside Sikkim. In particular, the Government of India shall have the right to station troops anywhere within Sikkim." [Article 3(I)]

(iii) "The external relations of Sikkim, whether political, economic or financial, shall be conducted and regulated solely by the Government of India, and the Government of Sikkim shall have no dealings with any foreign power."[Article 4(I)]

(iv) "If any dispute arises in the interpretation of the provisions of this Treaty which cannot be resolved by mutual consultation, the dispute shall be referred to the Chief Justice of India whose decision thereon shall be final."[40] [Article 12] [Vide Appendix II]

The end of the British rule in India not only ushered in an era or new Indo-Sikkimese relationship, but it also brought about a new political atmosphere within Sikkim. The independence movement in India had already created a great impact on the minds of the Sikkimese people. Moreover, the various reforms of Sir Tashi Namgyal, the then Chogyal of Sikkim, aroused a high level of political consciousness. As a result, we find for the first time in the history of Sikkim the formation of various political parties like Sikkim Rajya Praja Sammelan, Praja Mandal and Praja Sudhar Samaj. These parties launched political movements for the establishment of democratic rights of the people. Let us see now how far these new political forces were able to mould the traditional political set-up of the kingdom.

Previous to 1947, the Maharaja administered the state with the help of a number of secretaries and landlords and there was no people's participation in the Government. In 1947 when India shook off the British yoke and gained independence Sikkim also felt the first shake of political agitation, and in December that very year, the three political parties—Sikkim Rajya Praja Sammelan, Praja Mandal and Praja Sudhar Samaj—were all amalgamated into a single party, the Sikkim State Congress, with a three-fold demand of *"Abolition of Landlordism, Accession with India and an Interim Ministry as a prelude to the introduction of fully responsible government in Sikkim."*[41]

The Sikkim State Congress demand of accession to India was opposed by a section of the people and this led to the formation of Sikkim National Party which favoured only a treaty relationship with India.

The Chogyal had all along tried to keep up with the growing political demands of the people. In 1947 he included some members of the public in the State Council which was hitherto composed only of landlords. In 1948 three Congress members representing the Lepchas, Bhutias and Nepalis were appointed Secretaries to the Government. However, these members were expelled from the Party several months later and they had to resign.

In April, 1949 a demonstration was staged by the Sikkim State Congress. The Indian Political Officer in Sikkim mediated between the Durbar and the Congress and a Ministry under Sikkim State Congress was formed in May, 1949.

The Chogyal later dissolved the Ministry and requested the Government of India for deputing a Dewan* whose rank was that of a Prime Minister. Meanwhile the administration was taken over by the Political Officer until the arrival of the Dewan in August, 1949. Since then the position of the Dewan has always been held by Indian officials.

In 1951 an All-Party Agreement was reached whereby the State Council was to be composed of 17 members of whom 6 were to be reserved for the Lepaha-Bhutias, 6 for the Nepalis and the remaining 5 were to be nominated by the Chogyal. Another All-Party Agreement was reached in 1952 regarding the electorate and the method of election.

Based on these agreements a Proclamation was issued in 1953 defining the Constitution and the function of the State Council. According to this the State Council would be elected and an Executive Council formed to govern Sikkim. This Constitution was modified in 1958 following an agreement between the two parties and the Constitution of Sikkim stood as such until the popular uprising in 1973.[42]

---

* The Dewan was later on known as the Principal Administrative Officer and subsequently as the "Sidlon", a Tibetan synonym.

Sikkim, however, could not evolve a political unity during the period under review due to its lack of internal coherence and occasional misunderstanding as to its relation with India. Political problems in Sikkim were of two types. First of all, there was the social heterogeneity which hindered the growth of political unity and integrity. Secondly, the smallness and geographical position of the country made it dependent on India which generated various misgivings among the people.

Until 1961 the Nepali settler did not have the status of a citizen. But in that year the Sikkim Subjects Regulation came into force and this gave citizenship to the settlers. The regulation was, however, the subject of heated discussion in the Sikkim State Council and provoked considerable agitation outside. The regulation approved by the Indian Government was promulgated by the Maharaja but without the consent of the State Council.

The regulation divided the Sikkimese people into three distinct races — Lepcha, Bhutia and Tsong. The new term 'Tsong' was for the people other than the Lepchas and the Bhutias. Since the term Nepali denotes a citizen of Nepal, a new term for the Sikkimese Nepalis was necessary to distinguish them. The Sikkim National Party dominated by the Lepchas and the Bhutias, demanded that the new term be reserved for the people of Tibetan and Bhutanese origin and that the Nepalis settled in Sikkim be called Sikkimese Nepalis. The Sikkim State Congress and the Sikkim National Congress, dominated by the Nepalis, favoured replacing 'Nepali' with 'Tsong'. Thus the term Tsong became the bone of contention for the Lepcha-Bhutias as well as the Nepalis.

A section of the legislation further empowers the Government to deprive any subject of Sikkim of his citizenship if he has shown by act and speech to be guilty of dissatisfaction or disloyalty towards the King. This provision has been subject to much criticism as the political parties fear that it may be used to revoke the citizenship of the party leaders when they are in opposition.

All this indicates how racial heterogeneity of the Sikkimese led to disunity in the political field. To curb further complications the Government prohibited fresh settlement of the Nepalis. But still a great deal remains to be done before all internal differences and discords are eliminated and a united Sikkimese nation emerges.

Again, coming to its foreign policy, particularly its relation with India, Sikkim had not yet been able to evolve a unanimous public opinion. The protectorate status of Sikkim in the Treaty of 1950 had not satisfied all and everyone in Sikkim. There was often a clamour for greater autonomy and freedom in the external affairs of Sikkim. After the entry of Bhutan into the United Nations with the patronage of India this demand become much more vocal.

Moreover, even though some Sikkimese would allow India to control the external affairs of Sikkim, they were not ready to tolerate any intervention in the internal matters of the country. The Treaty vests full powers to the Government of Sikkim so far as internal matters are concerned. But in the discharge of duties and responsibilities for all external affairs of Sikkim "whether political, economic or financial," for defence and strategic communication India might seek the co-operation of the State Government which the Sikkimese may not like, or India might do something which may look like intervention in internal matters in the eyes of the Sikkimese.

Under these circumstances the position of the Indian Political Officer in Sikkim was a very delicate one. He was a representative of the Government of India and as such should look after Indian interests. But it was also his duty to see that Indo-Sikkimese relation is not embittered. Compared to the Political Officers in the British period, who were practically autocrats, the later incumbents in the post had to be much more tactful.

The position of the Sidlon is also no less delicate. Since its inception the post has become part of Sikkim's administrative machinery, and his role is as difficult as it is important. As the chief adviser to the Maharaja his interests must be those of Sikkim. Yet, no matter how much they are, he is a suspect — an Indian in Sikkimese clothing. As a result, however useful and sympathetic he may be, he is not given the full credit that he deserves.

Whatever may be the motivations and attitudes of the political parties the truth is that Sikkim cannot be a fully independent country simply because it must depend for its everyday necessities upon India, the only neighbouring country from which it can procure goods and services of all types and at the lowest transport cost. It is to be remembered in this connection that all the development plans of Sikkim have been entirely financed by India apart from other usual grants and subsidies, and without this help from India it would hardly have been possible for Sikkim to execute those plans.

Non-interference in Sikkim's internal affairs had been reiterated again and again by Mr. Nehru, the late Prime Minister of India, who once said: "If we bring a small country like Sikkim within our fold by using force, it would be like killing a fly with a bullet."[44] The subsequent Prime Ministers of India and the Indian Political Officers in Sikkim have also expressed similar views.

However, by a popular mandate through referendum Sikkim became a full fledged state of Indian Union in 1975.

It is necessary to emphasise this aspect because much of the country's present difficulties spring from an ambivalent attitude towards India.

D. The Society

The role of cultural environment is no less important in the making of the Sikkimese economy and, in fact, the economy of a country is but one aspect of the composite culture of that country. According to Thoman the term "culture" designates:

"the totality of a society's ideals and ideas, including such diverse features as mores, folk-ways, laws, arts, sciences, religious beliefs, highways and cities — in short, including the lasting accumulation of human learning and thought in that society. In this sense, a culture is a recognizable way of life of a group of people, regardless of the size of that group. It is a summary of what that group believes to be of positive and of negative importance, and includes the objectives, the problems, and the achievements of that group."[45]

Culture is pertinent to the study of any economic system specially because the different peoples of the world do not have identical objectives, nor do they have identical means of reaching their goals. Certainly most members of the primitive societies do not consider seriously the possibility of owning refrigerators or automobiles, nor are they able currently to produce and maintain such commodities. Their entire grasp of needs as well as the means of satisfying them is limited to the horizons of elementary cultures.

On the other hand, members of certain technically advanced societies specially in the West look upon refrigerators and automobiles as objects of want. The cultures of such societies obviously contain not only an understanding of how an automobile is produced and maintained but also an incentive for ownership of this costly gadget.

Still there are certain other societies, that may not regard ownership of an automobile as a worthy goal in this life. Most of the oriental cultures are of this type and economic underdevelopment of these countries does not necessarily mean cultural backwardness as compared with the technically advanced western countries. Cultural objectives of a society are thus very important in shaping that society's needs and wants as well as the means of satisfying them.

Let us now see whether and to what extent Sikkimese culture has contributed to the development of the economy. As culture is a very broad and general concept only the most salient features of it which materially affect the economy will be taken into consideration. The Sikkimese population can be divided into two distinct culture groups: the Lepcha-Bhutias professing the Tibetan-type Buddhism and the Nepalis professing Hinduism and our study will follow this division.

With regard to the Lepcha-Bhutia group we shall particularly mention the roles played by the marriage system and the village monastery in the economic life of the people.

The marriage system among the Lepchas and the Bhutias is in many ways related to the eoonomic fate of the people. One important feature of it is the custom of bride price. In a poor country like Sikkim this custom is quite unwarranted: often it proves to be too exorbitant for the groom. This necessitates a strenuous saving for a long time on the part of the bride-groom and very often he has to work in the fields of his would-be father-in-law to cover the bride-price. On the other hand the strenuously saved bride price is channelised into unproductive expenditures, mostly in the form of feasts in which the entire village people are invited.

This custom of bride price eats into the very vitality of the society and is one of the prime factors for the degeneration of economic welfare of the people. If the entire amount of bride-price collected from all the marriages in a village could be utilised for economic development of the village, the villagers might have had the experiences of some of the most essential amenities of the modern world such as village roads, water supply, electricity, sanitation and better housing facilities.

It is very difficult, however, to break any tradition which is deep-rooted in the psychology of the people—but it seems to be unavoidable in the context of the extreme poverty of the Sikkimese people. Moreover, the custom of bride price is not a cherishable element of culture and as such there should be no hesitation in doing away with it. On the one hand the Government should take legal steps to stop this practice and try to enforce them effectively, on the other hand the people should be given modern education and enthused to work for the economic uplift of the people.

The existence of the custom of polyandry among the Lepcha-Bhutias is another important factor which has affected the economic life of the people to a great extent. This custom is a direct result of the custom of bride price. When several brothers can save money that is enough only for a single bride. They think it reasonable to go for polyandry. First of all, it has led to a reduction in population. It is one of the reasons why the Lepcha-Bhutias who settled in Sikkim long before the Nepalis are now numerically smaller than the latter.

Secondly, polyandry has increased the immobility of the members of the family which means also the immobility of labour. This has led to the concentration of the Lepcha-Bhutia community in a few small areas in the north of the country.

Thirdly, it hinders the incentive to work. While a brother earns, other polyandrous brothers may sit idle or even work within the family.

Let us now consider the role of the village monastery in moulding the rural economy. Since the time of Bhutia migration into Sikkim the Gonpa* or the village monastery has become the pivot of community life as well as the prime bond of unity between the two ethnic groups, the Lepchas and the Bhutias. The geographical location of the Gonpa in a typical Sikkimese village+ can be demonstrated by the following diagram:

Diagram II. A Sikkimese Lepcha-Bhutia Village

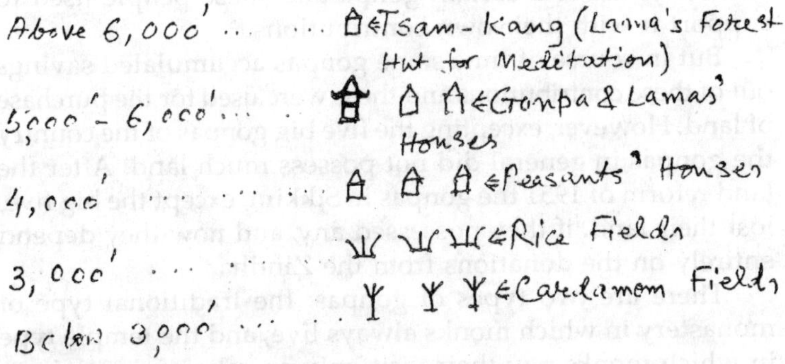

From the above diagram we see that the gonpa is situated at the highest point in the village, normally at the height of 5,000′ to 6,000′ feet from the sea level overlooking the valley and backed by the forest. Still higher in the forest is the lama's* hut for meditation called Tsam-Kang. Outside the precincts of the gonpa but around it there is a hamlet or cluster of households of the lamas who serve the gonpa. Further below there is another hamlet at the height of near-about 4,000 feet inhabited by the peasants. Below that there lie the rice fields and pastures until at 3,000′ feet one finds the beginning of the cultivation of cardamom. Apart from the gonpa, within each hamlet there is at least one Buddhist shrine of some kind unless the hamlet is entirely inhabited by the Nepalis.

* In English it is often spelt as 'Gonpa'. The Tibetan spelling, when transliterated, is 'd Gompa'.

\+ In Sikkim a distinction is made between a village and a hamlet. While the former is a composite structure as shown in the following sketch, a hamlet is a part of the village representing a cluster of households often on a racial basis.

All the households within the jurisdiction of the gonpa are called "Zindha". Generally the Zindha supports the gonpa but sometimes a gonpa possesses its own land which may be a source of its income. But originally the gonpas did not possess any land but were simply authorised to receive gifts and donations from certain villages over which they had their respective religious authority. Actually, certain villagers were made laymen of a certain gonpa and these people used to support it with their own contributions.[46]

But in course of time some gonpas accumulated savings out of these contributions and these were used for the purchase of land. However, excepting the five big gonpas of the country the gonpas in general did not possess much land. After the land reform of 1951 the gonpas in Sikkim, except the big five, lost their land, if they possessed any, and now they depend entirely on the donations from the Zindha.

There are two types of gonpas: the traditional type of monastery in which monks always live, and the temple type in which monks pay their visit only on religious occasions. The monks of the Geluk sect observe celibacy and reside solely within the gonpa—and here the gonpa takes the shape of the traditional monastery. But the monks of the Kagyu sect normally have their wives and children and generally reside outside the gonpa — and there the gonpa takes the shape of a temple. When the monks of the Kagyu sect are not engaged in prayer or meditation they cultivate and live outside the gonpa. But there are occasions of festivals when they stay in the dormitory of the gonpa being engaged in prayer day and night; and temporarily the gonpa looks like a monastery.

There is no restriction on the basis of descent, status, wealth or occupation of the father for a boy to become a lama, though on the whole there are more lamas among the Bhutias than among the Lepchas. The only exception is the Pamiongchi gonpa which is the biggest monastery in Sikkim where admission is open only to the sons of the Bhutia aristocrats. Fourteen major noble families of Tibetan origin have the right

---

* The priests in the monasteries of Sikkim are generally called 'Lamas' though the term is applied in Tibet only to those who have achieved the highest religious status and learning.

to be admitted to the monastery without payment of entry fee. Eight other minor families of the Bhutia nobles have also the right of admittance, but only on the payment of a heavy entry fee.[47] There are a few nunneries attached to some gonpas. As in the case of boys, entry into the nunneries depends on the desire of the girls rather than that of their parents. Training in the nunneries is not very severe and no specific discipline is observed.

The relationship between the gonpa and the peasants is an age-old one and it has remained intact even when there has been major changes in the upper strata of the society. Before the abolition of landlordism in Sikkim the peasants used to contribute to the gonpa through their landlords, apart from their own personal contributions. Often there were changes in the ownership of land which meant changes in landlords, but never was the peasant ousted from his ancestral land of cultivation, nor was there any change in the relationship between the gonpa and the peasants.

Even now the influence of the gonpa over the peasants has not diminished. The factor behind this is the fact that the activities of the peasants are greatly regulated by the gonpa: the rituals at birth, death, illness or the agricultural rites are all performed by the lamas of the gonpa. In short, the priests are the intellectual elite whom the peasants consult for guidance. For a Buddhist peasant hardly a day passes without any contact with the lamas.

Economically speaking, the lamas are a parasitic class of the society and they, along with the expensive religious rites and customs, cause a huge drainage of savings of the people. Moreover, the lamaistic culture has also influenced the attitude of the people towards the modern world. The Lepchas and the Bhutias are generally averse to modern education and much more eager to educate their sons in lamaistic training.

Lamaism seems to be an important factor behind economic backwardness of the Lepcha-Bhutias. In this connection we may refer to the hypothesis of Max Weber which proclaims that the rise of Protestantism was a major cause of Industiral Revolution in Europe.[48] According to him Protestantism kindled the light of courage and initiative among the people that had so long remained passive. This spirit was conducive to economic ventures.

The Weber hypothesis highlights the role of religion in the economic development of a country. In this respect lamaistic Buddhism is not very congenial to economic prosperity. The Buddhist Lepcha-Bhutias of Sikkim are basically introvert in nature and to a devout Buddhist spiritual advancement is more important than economic prosperity.

The Nepalis, on the other hand, are extrovert in nature and more interested in mundane matters. As a result, we often see the Nepalis succeeding the economic ventures where initiative and perserverence are essential. We can hardly see the Lepcha-Bhutias in those fields. This will be evident from the story of Nepali immigration into Sikkim as told by Namgyal and Dolma:

> "Since the year 1871 ... there was an influx of Gorkhalis from the neighbouring state of Nepal.... They settled down for good, and began digging, hoeing, smashing and overturning rocks, felling down trees, and turning the courses of streams at such a rate that all jungles were turned into fields, in a very short time."[49]

One characteristic of these colonists was that once they had succeeded in establishing a local community of their own, they gradually expanded to other neighbouring areas dominated by the Lepchas and the Bhutias. From the Nepali point of view, these areas, though inhabited by the Lepchas and the Bhutias, were considered to have much unused land. In fact, the latter two communities cultivated only the most fertile lands of the area leaving aside the less fertile ones. These waste lands were enough to attract the land-hungry Nepali colonists. While converting such barren lands into arable lands the Nepalis usually worked as casual farm labourers for the Lepcha-Bhutias. The latter hired the labourers because many members of their families occasionally lived outside the locality to lead a religious life in the gonpas or other institutions. The entry of the Nepalis was not, therefore, opposed but welcomed in such cases.

An outstanding feature of the Nepali settlement was that though initially the colonists were economically handicapped, particularly with regard to the availability of land, ultimately they became successful. A Nepali who had come from Nepal with empty hands could, within two decades, succeed to such an extent that economically his standard became comparable to or even higher than that of the Lepchas or the Bhutias who had been settled there for generations.

The basic reason for such an outstanding achievement of the Nepalis compared to the others is to be found in the differences in cultural pattern of the two communities. These differences have, in turn, led to different rates of capital accumulation as between the two communities. A higher rate of capital accumulation is generally found among the Nepalis. The cultural factors that influence the rate may be mentioned as follows:

(i) First, given the same labour force with the same resources, the productivity of the Nepalis is much higher than that of the rest due to an intensive use of their labour.

(ii) Secondly, the consumption of the Nepalis is much lower than that of the Lepcha-Bhutias due to the former's lack of and the latter's indulgence in conspicuous religious expenditures.

Regarding the productivity of labour force it may be noted that whereas many Lepcha-Bhutias engage in priestly activities thereby reducing potential productive labour, almost all the Nepalis devote their labour to the economic pursuits of life. For the Nepalis, entry into priesthood is entirely regulated by birth: unless one is born a Brahmin one cannot be a priest. So a non-Brahmin Nepali thinks it incumbent to climb up the ladder of social prestige, success and economic prosperity through his own perseverance.

For the Nepalis, wives are an important source of labour and to them marriage means the acquisition of more labour for productive purposes rather than the responsibility to feed a dependent. Again, Nepali children over the age of five are often put to work and those above ten may even earn more than their own requirements. This is not so among the Lepcha-Bhutias. Moreover, the Nepalis are versatile labourers: they can act as coolies in the bazar, construct roads and buildings, collect various kinds of fruits, roots, herbs and other materials from the forests for their own consumption as well as for sale in the bazar and so on, whereas the Lepcha-Bhutias hardly engage themselves in any type of work other than cultivation, even when they are extremely poverty-stricken. Due to all these, naturally, the productivity of the Nepalis is higher than that of the other communities.

Coming to the consumption pattern of the two communities we may first refer to the custom of bride price and feast on the occasion of marriage among the Lepcha-Bhutias as referred to earlier. This often exhausts the entire accumulation of savings of the family concerned and may even lead to a life-long debt. In contrast, the marriage of a Nepali couple is very simple and no conspicuous consumption or expenditure is made therein.

Another drainage of savings among the Lepcha-Bhutias is that they often have to feed some members engaged in monastic activities. Almost every household has one or more monks to support. Even when a monk earns in his profession his support is maintained by the society. In that case the Buddhist population has to perform the following activities as part of their religious duties:

(i) occasional donations to the gonpa either *(a)* in kind or *(b)* in money — and these being particularly heavy during festivals;

(ii) free labour service for the *(a)* construction or *(b)* repair of the gonpa; and

(iii) payment of high fees for various sorts of services rendered by the lamas.

On the other hand, the amount spent by the Hindu Nepalis for religious purposes is negligible. The Nepalis have no obligation to the gonpa — neither have they any institution like that. There are, of course, a few Hindu festivals but the expenses for these are very low compared to that of the Buddhists.

Another important point to note is that alcoholism is a widespread practice among the Lepcha-Bhutias whereas a Hindu Nepali hardly drinks. This means that the Nepalis can save a lot which their counterpart might have spent for drinking. Moreover, aversion to drinking is congenial to hard work and physical fitness which increase the productivity of labour.

The diet, clothing and housing of the Nepalis are quite simple and inexpensive. A Nepali can do away with rice that is expensive in Sikkim and be satisfied with the consumption of maize grown on his own kitchen garden. But, for the Buddhists, rice in a must and it is often taken along with meat which is also another expensive item. The materials as well as tailoring of Nepali costumes are simple and cheap and can be obtained in any market of Sikkim. On the other hand, the Tibetan-style Bhutia costume, which has also come to be the Lepcha costume, is much more expensive and requires a great deal of special tailoring. The difference is perceptible even in the case of housing. A Nepali house is easily built by a man himself out of mud and straw while a Lepcha-Bhutia house is built of timber which is expensive and requires expert handling by hired carpenters.

We see, therefore, that in contrast with the Buddhist Lepcha-Bhutias who are basically introvert and accept any situation as given, the Hindu Nepalis are basically extrovert and challenge any situation that confronts their economic interests. A Nepali believes that the limitations imposed by a particular situation are not insurmountable but requires to be tackled tactfully and diligently. A Lepcha-Bhutia on the contrary, simply by-passes those limitations while journeying to the spiritual world.

REFERENCES

1. A. Kakodkar, *Bhutan and Sikkim* (Gangtok: Office of the Political Officer in Bhutan and Sikkim 1955), p. 7.
2. *Ibid.*
3. Govt, of Sikkim, *Sikkim: A Concise Chronicle* (Gangtok: Publicity Deptt.), p. 6.
4. Govt. of Sikkim, *Sikkim: The Land and Its People* (Gangtok: Publicity Deptt.), p. 1.
5. *Imperial Gazetteer of India,* New Edition, Vol. 22 (Oxford: Oxford University Press, 1908), p. 366.
6. S. Bose, "The Bhot of Northern Sikkim", *Man in India,* 46, No. 2 (April-June, 1966), 169.
7. *Ibid.,* p. 168.

8. P. P. Karan and M. Jenkins, *The Himalayan Kingdoms: Bhutan, Sikkim and Nepal* (New York: Van Nostrand Co. Inc. 1963), p. 41.
9. Govt. of India, *Bhutan and Sikkim* (Gangtok: Office of the Political Officer in Sikkim), p. 12.
10. C. B. Stocks, "Folk-lore and Customs of the Lapchas of Sikkim", *Journal and Proceedings: Asiatic Society of Bengal*, New Series, 21, No. 4 (1925), 322.
11. Govt. of Sikkim, *Sikkim: The Land and Its People*, p. 4.
12. Kakodkar, p. 8.
13. Govt, of Sikkim, *Sikkim: Her Faith and Future* (Gangtok: Dept. of Information and Publicity), p. 7.
14. V. H. Coelho, *Sikkim and Bhutan* (New Delhi: Vikas Publications, 1971), p. 3.
15. G. B. Mainwaring, *A Grammar of the Rong (Lepcha) Language: As It Exists in the Darjeeling and Sikkim Hills* (Calcutta: Baptist Mission Press, 1876).
16. C. Nakane, "A Plural Society in Sikkim: A Study of the Inter-Relations of Lepchas, Bhotias and Nepalis," *Caste and Kin in Nepal, India and Ceylon*, ed. C. V. Furer-Haimendorf (Bombay: Asia Publishing House, 1966), p. 261.
17. *Imperial Gazetteer of India*, p. 369.
18. *Ibid.*
19. Stocks, p. 331.
20. *Ibid.*, p. 330.
21. Govt. of Sikkim, *Sikkim: A Concise Chronicle*, p. 5.
22. P. Carrasco, *Land and Polity in Tibet* (Seattle: University of Washington Press, 1959), p. 186.
23. "Portrait of a Country," *The Statesman* (Calcutta), June 2, 1960, p. 1.
24. Stocks, p. 338.
25. *The Statesman*, p. I.
26. T. Namgyal and J. Dolma, *History of Sikkim*, trans. Lama Dewa Kazi Samdup, MSS, Part I, p. 21, cited in Nakane, p. 217.
27. W. D. Shakabpa, *Tibet: A Political History* (Yale University Press, 1967), p. 334.
28. Nakane, p. 216.
29. *The Gazetteer of Sikkim* (Calcutta: Bengal Secretariat Press, 1894), p. xxii.
30. Coelho, p. 17.
31. *Ibid.*, p. 21.
32. *The Gazetteer of Sikkim*, p. xvi.
33. Coelho, pp. 105-9, 115-17.

34. *Ibid.*, p. 108.
35. *Ibid.*, p. 110.
36. *Imperial Gazetteer of India*, p. 321.
37. Govt. of Sikkim, *Sikkim: A Concise Chronicle*, pp. 18-20.
38. Cited in Coelho, p. 25.
39. Govt, of Sikkim, *Sikkim: A Concise Chronicle*, p. 31.
40. Coelho, pp. 115-17.
41. K. R. Pradhan, "Whither Sikkim?", *United Asia*, 12, No. 4 (1960), 492.
42. Govt. of Sikkim, *Sikkim: A Concise Chronicle*, pp. 29-30.
43. Karan and Jenkins, p. 63.
44. *The Statesman*, p. I.
45. R.S. Thoman, *The Geography of Economic Activity: An Introductory World Survey* (McGraw-Hill, 1962), p. 14.
46. Namgyal and Dolma, p. 154.
47. *The Gazetteer of Sikkim*, p. 27.
48. H. Weber, *From Max Weber: Essays in Sociology* (London: Kegan Paul, 1948).
49. Namgyal and Dolma, Part 4, p. 37.
50. Nakane, p. 255.

2

Economic Changes in Pre-Plan Sikkim

To understand properly the significance of economic development in Sikkim under planning it is necessary to probe into the country's economic change during the pre-plan period. This will not only help us to have a continuity in our study but also facilitate a comparative assessment of economic growth during the two periods.

In this chapter an attempt will be made in that direction. First we shall make a general survey of the evolutionary process of the economy. Then the land tenure system of Sikkim will be taken up as it is intimately connected with the agrarian sector of the economy. Lastly, we shall consider the question of occupational pattern and its gradual change over time.

Our study of the economic change in pre-plan Sikkim may be broken up into three parts relating to the three main periods in Sikkim's history, viz., the Lepcha period, the Bhutia period and the British period. The Lepcha period ended in 1642 when the first Bhutia King was consecrated, the Bhutia period ended in 1889 when the first British Political Officer was appointed and the British period ended in 1947 when the Indian subcontinent became free of British rule. In between the British period and the commencing of the plan era there were only 7 years (1947-1954) which though not belonging to the British period were economically more or less akin to the latter. As such the British period may be deemed to cover these years as well.

Two points must be borne in mind in this connection. First, the above historical division should not be thought to mean that the economy jumped from one stage to another in a particular year. Evolution is intrinsically a continuous process, and to divide the process into water-tight compartments is artificial, although we have taken recourse to it for the sake of analytical convenience.

Secondly and as a corollary to it, we must note that the earlier economic setups have not died out completely and we can still find their remnants here and there even within the modern economy.

A. The Economy

It is interesting to study the evolution of the Sikkimese economy. Little is known regarding the earliest economic set-up of the country. It seems that the earliest Lepcha society of Sikkim was semi-nomadic and tribal in character due to the primitive mode of acquisition of food. In such circumstances some sort of a primitive communal society can be expected. One characteristic of such a society is that all production and means of production are equitably distributed in accordance with the decision of the society taken collectively. In the accounts of some British writers we find, however, the existence of private property among the Lepchas, but that might be a later development.[1]

When the Bhutias came, they brought with them Tibetan ideas and customs and gradually tried to instal in Sikkim a Tibetan-type feudal society with the monarch at the apex of the system. This was not, however, feudalism in the western sense of the term. As Thorner says: *"A feudalism without manors, serfs of the manors, feudal contract, vassals and fiefs based on feudal contract, is simply not feudalism...."*[2]

Still we hold that the Bhutia society and economy were basically feudal in character. In the Bhutia Sikkim land was the grand pillar of the socio-economic structure, just as it is in any feudal society. The King was the sole proprietor of land in the country and below him were the feudal lords such as the Kazis who had a definite territorial jurisdiction and collected revenues within it with the help of officials such as the village headmen called "Mandals". Land, the prime factor in a feudal society, was thus also the prime factor in Sikkim's socio-economic set-up and its evolution.

Regarding feudalism in India Kosambi says that it shared with European feudalism a low level of technique, simple instruments, individual production, primitive labour division, production for immediate need, limited market, political decentralisation, conditional holding by landlords on service-tenure and possession by landlords of quasi-judicial functions.[3] We can point out that the Bhutia feudal society of Sikkim also shared these points of similarity.

According to Bhowani Sen, in any feudal system the following relations are to be found: *(a)* the producer possesses his own means of production (plough, cattle etc.) other than the land itself; *(b)* the producer works independently of his lord; *(c)* the producer is unfree — he cannot leave his master of his own volition and in the case of a serf, he is tied to the land by law; *(d)* the producer has to render surplus labour to his master, for example, in the form of tribute, or of forced labour — this surplus being extracted from the producer by non-economic means; and *(e)* in feudalism all landownership carries obligations to the state, either in the form of land revenue or of services.[4]

In the case of Sikkim, except the third relation all other relations were present during the Bhutia period. Available records do not show any proof that the peasants were tied to the land. Until very recently, the Sikkimese custom was that anybody could cultivate any unoccupied piece of land.

There seem to be three reasons for the free employment of the peasantry in Sikkim:

(a) First, the custom of shifting cultivation prevented the peasants from being tied to a particular piece of land.

(b) Secondly, agricultural production at that time was quite meagre and, in fact, the proportion of state revenue contributed by agriculture was so small that the feudal state machinery did not consider seriously the prospect of tying peasants to land.

(c) Thirdly, the Tibetan theory of land-holding was such that the monarch had absolute ownership of land and

as such the intermediate feudal lords could not tie the peasants to the "land of the monarch".

Significant advancement in Sikkim's economy began after the establishment of British control, particularly after 1889 with the appointment of Claude White as the first British Political Officer in Sikkim to look into the affairs of the state. The British period in the evolution of the Sikkimese economy is important for various reasons. Let us examine them one by one.

The initiation of the post of the Political Officer in Sikkim opened up a new chapter of co-operation and collaboration between Sikkim and India not only during the British rule but also in the post-independence period. At present the Indian Political Officer acts as the representative of the Government of India and he is the main channel for the flow of economic aid to Sikkim.*

After the appointment of the first Political Officer Sikkim's budgetary system underwent major changes. Prior to 1889 there was no systematic revenue system in Sikkim and the Maharaja collected in taxes "what he required as he wanted it from the people."[5] The British Political Officer laid the basis for taxation and consequently a better revenue system was established. The new system was not, however, very scientific and often recourse had to be taken to the earlier method of ad-hoc taxation.

Due to a sounder budgetary system and stringent administrative measures the revenue of the State increased, and as more revenue became available, for the first time in the history of Sikkim, construction of public works was undertaken. In this category falls mainly the construction of roads — the purpose being not so much related to public welfare but to the interests of the British in Sikkim and beyond; and the British Government bore the larger share of the cost of construction. Within a few years it was possible to ride on mule-back from one end of Sikkim to another and in 1906 for the first time Gangtok was linked with India by wheeled traffic.

---

* This has changed after Sikkim's merger with India as a full-fledged state of India in 1975.

In a country like Sikkim the importance of *transport and communication* cannot be overestimated and the British did a lot for their improvement. This led to the easy movement of factors and goods from one region of the country to another as well as from the country to the outside and vice versa. A natural corollary to this was the development of trade ana commerce, both internal and external. The British were particularly interested in the Indo-Tibetan trade and in it Sikkim became a partner as the trade route ran through the country.

The development of trade and commerce had a great impact on the evolution of the economy as it brought about the concept of *private property*—the cornerstone of capitalism. As Edgar says: "Among some of the ruder tribes on the North-East frontier, there seems to have been absolutely no true conception of private property until the idea was learned from contact with Bengali traders."

The development of trade and commerce during the British rule was thus an important factor for the introduction of capitalist elements in the economy of Sikkim.

The contact with the outside world that developed during the British rule was also an important guiding force in the evolution of the Sikkimese economy. Some writers like Frank hold that in determining an economic and social system as feudal or capitalist, the crucial aspect to consider is *whether the system is closed or not.* On that account it can certainly be said that the British heralded the growth of capitalism in Sikkim by making the country open.

In analysing the growth of capitalism in India D.D. Kosambi has said: "The impetus had to come from outside. It was in England, not India, that the bourgeoisie developed out of Indian gold." In the case of Sikkim also this view held good, with modification that here the impetus came from British India. In Sikkim there were many *Indian businessmen* who contributed to the capitalist development of the country. After the independence of India and the subsequent treaty between India and Sikkim this contribution has increased much more.

Before the British took over the administration of Sikkim the economy had been purely in a primitive form. It was rigidly traditional in its pattern and was devoid of any sign of modernism whatsoever. Rudimentary technology forming the basis of agriculture, the people had to gather their food from jungles during the slack season. *Absence of any surplus product limited all other economic functions.* Trade was irregularly carried on between different sections of the community by bartering articles of habitual needs.

Due to the underdeveloped nature of the economy no *indigenous currency system* could develop in Sikkim. Occasionally Tibetan, Nepalese, Bhutanese or Indian coins were used for exchange purposes, but the extent of that exchange was quite small. When the British supremacy in Sikkim was established, Indian Rupee was introduced as the *de facto* currency of the country.

The introduction of Indian Rupee gave a great jolt to the stagnant economy of Sikkim. So long money was practically a non-entity in the whole economy, except that some currencies of the neighbouring countries were used for transactions with the traders of those countries or that some silver coins were used by women as ornaments. Side by side, there was the existence of primitive media of exchange like mithuns, pigs, hens and other livestocks as is evident from the folk-lore of the Lepchas and other accounts of the past.

Along with the introduction of a full-fledged money a new economic class emerged. They were the people who earned some money through their association with different government projects as contractors or wage-earners. Money now being the major factor in the economic scene, the people were tending towards developing some "private property" which was in sharp contrast with the traditional mode of life and in conformity with the modern economic outlook.

The concept of private proerty was, of course, not quite unknown in the primitive society as it had its origin in the formation of the habit of cattle-rearing; but it could not take a definite shape in the barter economy of Sikkim. The idea of possessing and developing wealth without actually being associated with property was so far unknown. The function of money as a "store of wealth" gave a new impetus to economic enterprise. *The new money not only facilitated exchange but was also conducive to more secure savings which could easily be channelised into productive lines.* The introduction of money in Sikkim was thus a great phenomenon sowing the seed of the modern economic system.

Economic self-sufficiency is said to be a fundamental characteristic of the traditional society. Though not actually self-sufficient in the modern sense it was the traditional mood of acceptance which made the people content with whatsoever they could get. But due to a greater contact with the outside world, mainly through the Britishers and the Indian traders, the Sikkimese people gradually became aware of *further needs* and wants; and it was quite difficult for them to remain contended with what they had. New demands sprang up and these were met from the markets now within their reach. Consequently the prerequisites of a market economy were satisfied and the age-old traditional economy of Sikkim gave place to the modern market economy.

Another major event that shook the Sikkimese economy during the British period was the heavy *influx of the Nepalis*. Namgyal and Dolma give a good description of the Nepali influx during the later part of the 19th century and there we find how the Nepalis turned jungles and waste lands into cultivable fields within a very short time.[11]

The first impact of the settlement was the introduction of *competition*. For the first time in Sikkim's economic history the people felt competition in earning their livelihood. It had not been the case when the Bhutias conquered the country. So far as agriculture was concerned, land was quite abundant at that time and as such there was no pressure on land. As regards other occupations, the Bhutias primarily resorted to pasturage and trade which were new occupations introduced by them and so there was no competition with the Lepchas, the original inhabitants of the country.

One important consequence of this competition was that instead of extensive cultivation intensive cultivation was resorted to. As land had to produce more to feed the enlarged population it had to be cultivated more frequently and more intensively. This led to the introduction of *permanent cultivation* in Sikkim.

With the introduction of permanent cultivation peasants gradually became attached to land and a new sense of ownership in land evolved. Land was now looked upon as a property. Consequently, it took the appearance of a commodity which could be transferred or sold.

The government also sponsored wet rice cultivation for keeping the fertility of land intact as well as for increasing production; but in the process it contributed, perhaps unknowingly, to the growth of private ownership in land. Land, the prime "factor" of production, now took the appearance of a *"commodity"* which is the basic characteristic of capitalism.

During this period labour, another primary factor of production, also took the form of a commodity. This fact is much more important from the point of view of the evolution of the economy because *the buying and selling of "labour power" is said to be the sine qua non of capitalism.* As Sweezy remarks, it is *"the differentia specifica of capitalism."*[12] Takahashi has also clearly pointed out that the distinguishing features of feudalism and capitalism are the absence or presence of labour power as a commodity:

> "In feudalism, since the immediate producers appear in combination with the means of production, and hence labour power cannot take the form of a commodity, the appropriation of surplus labour by the feudal lords takes place directly, by extra-economic coercion without the mediation of the economic laws of commodity exchange. In capitalism, not merely are the products of labour turned into commodities, but labour power itself becomes a commodity."[13]

When the British took over the administration of Sikkim they had to spend heavily on the construction of roads, buildings and other establishments, and as such they employed a large number of wage-labourers. The Lepchas and the Bhutias were initially reluctant to offer their labour, partly because of their age-old inhibitions and partly because of their better economic position. But the Nepalis neither had such inhibitions nor could they find a better alternative to earn their livelihood. In fact, the Nepalis had migrated from their native country in search of jobs and the opportunity provided by the British in Sikkim was quickly availed of. Labour now became a commodity which was sold by the Nepalis and bought by the English. Gradually the Lepchas and the Bhutias also offered their services, but their proportion in the total labour force was quite negligible.

It is, however, not true that prior to the British administration there was no employment of labour. But that employment was unilateral without any reciprocal payment for it — in other words, it was forced labour and here the point raised by Takahashi is pertinent. The feudal lords including the King and his subordinates extracted this labour as a matter of right. The payment for the labour services in money during the British period was something new in the history of Sikkim.

Apart from the introduction of paid labour the British also tried to abolish the old feudalistic custom of forced labour. By the end of the 19th century they were able to abolish it. A correspondence from the Chief Secretary to the Government of Bengal to the Commissioner of the Rajshahi Division dated July 23, 1898 shows that the Political Officer in consultation with the Maharaja and the Council decided: *(i)* that forced labour should be commuted as much as possible into money payments, and taken in kind only in special cases, and *(ii)* that the Kazis should not be entitled to any forced labour.[14]

The introduction of paid labour and abolition of forced labour helped the *monetisation* of the economy which is essential for the development of capitalism. Monetisation proceeded also through other activities of the Government. The elaborate bureaucratic setup established by the British created a class of salaried officials, clerks and workers. This was contrary to the feudal system and it increased money flow within the economy. Side by side the revenue system was standardised and in 1889 we find the first budget prepared in accordance with the procedure followed in capitalist countries.

But in spite of the existence of all those elements of capitalism Sikkim could not develop into a full-fledged capitalist economy. It was still predominantly a feudal society with the old class relations and little entrepreneurial activity. Sikkim's economy during the British period can thus be termed *"a feudal economy with increasing capitalist elements"*.

The economy during this period was also chracterised by underdevelopment though not stagnation. Various reasons may be cited for this. First of all, Sikkim's peculiar geographical features coupled with inadequacy of natural resources was the main bottleneck for any significant development of the country. The British, of course, tried to exploit the existing natural resources like forestry, water-power and minerals but their attempt was not commensurate with the needs of development.

Moreover, Sikkim being an agricultural econony, its development should have been initiated in the agricultural sector. But during this period agricultural development did not receive much attention. There was, of course, some improvement, particularly with respect to the transition from shifting to permanent cultivation, but the lot of the peasants did not improve very much. Infertility of land, lack of manuring, unscientific cultivation and rural indebtedness were the prime factors behind the underdevelopment of the agricultural sector. But, of all these, the main culprit was the vicious circle of *rural indebtedness*. The governmental attempt to curb this was only partially successful.

The first major governmental measure to resist the evils of rural indebtedness was the introduction of Sikkim Debt Law in 1910 whereby the rate of interest to be charged on the peasants was limited and money-lenders were prohibited from lending money to be repaid in grain. A special court was also appointed for the trial of cases between money-lenders and cultivators and this court punished breaches of the law.

The money-lenders in Sikkim at that time were mostly the Marwaris and some of them attempted to evade the law by obtaining decrees at higher rates in the Darjeeling Court and having them sent to Sikkim for execution. These attempts were, however, frustrated due to the refusal by the Political Officer to execute such decrees unless they conformed to the Sikkim Debt Law. There was also the unwritten law that Marwaris and Modis would not be permitted to possess land in Sikkim or to have any control over such land.[15] As a result of the above measures several Marwari money-lenders left Sikkim as their business declined.[16] Another important measure was the institution of co-operative credit societies which provided easy loans to the agriculturists.[17]

Before the introduction of the Sikkim Debt Law in 1910, Rs. 20 lent to the peasants was frequently repaid in grain to the value of Rs. 30 or Rs. 40 six months later[18] which means a rate of interest of 100% or 200% per annum. But after the introduction of the law no creditor was allowed to charge as interest more than 12% of the principal per annum. This rate was, however, subsequently raised to 12.5% or 2 annas in the rupee. At the same time it was decided that no creditor would be allowed to give *dadani* (loan) for cardamom or other crops or to take the produce of the fields as interest on debt.[19]

These governmental measures to save the peasants from excessive indebtedness were not, however, quite successful and we find as late as in 1938 gross violations of the law. In the accounts of Morris there are references to two types of credit prevalent among the Lepchas of Zongu at that time: the indigenous system and the moneylenders' system. In the indigenous system "if the borrower repays the loan (of grains) within one year no interest is charged: otherwise fifty per cent is added to the principal when the loan is repaid — in kind, of course. In return for the use of plough oxen it is usual to give the lender eight pounds of grain per day, but if a bullock is required for a sacrifice or ceremony it is usual to repay the loan in kind. If this cannot be done for some considerable time the borrower usually takes a chicken and some *chi* (country liquor made of millet) to the lender, but apart from this no interest is charged."[20]

Coming to the money-lenders' system Morris says that the money-lenders were first established in Mangan in about 1908 and for the first ten years or so everyone thought it was a great convenience to be able to meet his outside requirements on the spot. At the time of Morris there was no one in the Zongu area who was not in debt.

Most people at that time obtained their seed from the moneylenders, in payment for which they had to set aside a certain definite proportion of the cardamom crop without regard for what the current rate for that particular year might eventually be. It made no difference what kind of seed was taken; the repayment was always in the form of cardamoms. The people also obtained advances in the form of cloth, salt, kerosene oil and so on.

A further cause of debt was that the money-lenders took every opportunity of foisting unwanted goods upon the Lepchas who had not the strength of mind to refuse, especially when no payment was demanded at the time. Morris noted that this usually took the form of cotton materials of the very poorest quality, as a result of which most of the people, and particularly the children, were then clothed in materials ill-suited to the climate.

These money-lenders also violated the Sikkim Debt Law and extracted exorbitant rates of interest. From Morris's account we find that for eighty pounds of rice worth seven rupees on an average, the borrowers had to pay back a like weight of cardamoms which was worth fifteen rupees. Often the price of cardamoms fluctuated and in the boom years it was as high as sixty rupees, so that the rate of interest actually turned into 100% to 750% per annum. Similarly, cloth to the value of ten rapees was paid for with eighty pounds of cardamom. The ignorant Lepchas knew practically nothing about these matters and the money-lenders also would never allow them to repay their debts in cash, even if this was available.

Moreover, should a man be unable to liquidate his debt at the time of the cardamom harvest interest was charged at the rate of half the principal per annum; that is to say, 50 per cent compound interest and, of course, in kind. In terms of money this interest rate was, therefore, much higher. The interest charged on cash loans was a bit lower: it was at the rate of six annas in the rupee per annum, which works out at 37.5 per cent per annum.

All these indicate gross violations of the Sikkim Debt Law. Morris gives some causes for the violations. He says:

> "... but who can control this in a district where the moneylender himself is the only one who can read and write? People are required to give a receipt when they take a loan, but all they can do in actual practice is to affix their thumb-impression to the account written out by the money-lender himself: they neither know nor care what he has written."

Another important reason for the violations was that the Government had practically no control over the moneylenders. As Morris says: "Cardamoms are a State monopoly, and the right to trade in them has been sold to the official State Bankers, an outside concern which, in turn, also controls all the money-lenders in the State."[22] No doubt, this was a convenient arrangement for the authorities and saved the provision of numerous extra officials, but at the same time this was instrumental to the practical nullification of the Sikkim Debt Law.

The people also were compelled to cultivate cardamom not only to meet the demand of the money-lenders, but also to pay taxes, as the new system of taxation required payment in cash and the peasants could secure cash only by selling cardamoms, no other agricultural produce having any market whatsoever. The cultivation of cardamom, however, was not in itself the cause of misfortune, because in many parts of Sikkim where people were much more sophisticated and better able to safeguard their own interests, it proved to be a source of extra profit. Ignorance of the people, cunning of the money-lenders and inaction on the part of the Government were the primary reasons for rural indebtedness in Sikkim.

In the field of industry also Sikkim did not show any substantial growth during the British period. The main reason for this was the lack of an entrepreneurial class to undertake industrial ventures. The emergence of capitalist elements in the feudal set-up of Sikkim was thus practically frustrated due to a lack of entrepreneurship in the industrial field.

In Sikkim there were, however, the traditional Bhutia traders trading between Sikkim and Tibet mainly on barter There were also the Indian traders, mostly Marwaris, trading between Sikkim and India, and often engaging themselves simultaneously in lending operations. *But these commercial and financial entrepreneurs never thought of an industiral undertaking which could increase the physical output of the country.* There are various reasons why this commercial and financial entrepreneurship could not evolve into industrial entrepreneurship during the British period.

First of all, the talents required to guide an industrial enterprise differ substantially from those needed for successful commercial or financial entrepreneurship. An industrial entrepreneur must have a wider set of personal abilities than a trader or a money-lender. Even more important than being venturesome and profit-oriented, he must be a person who can lead others in a common enterprise. He must also have extensive technical skills and knowledge of his branch of production, along with the economics of production and sale.

In the second place, the risks and uncertainties of

transforming a given amount of capital into industrial assets are much greater than in trading or financial operations. This is so because there is less flexibility in an industrial operation and once capital is transformed into fixed assets it must wait and follow its destined course, whatever may happen in the mean time. The profitability of an industrial enterprise is more directly influenced by changes in tastes and fluctuations in demand than in the case of capital invested in trade, commerce or finance.[23]

As regards the definition of industrial entrepreneurship it is still an unsettled question in economics. There has not yet evolved a uniform definition of the concept. Some economists think of industrial entrepreneurs primarily as innovators, others think of them as bearers of risks and others still place their emphasis on the entrepreneurs' function as mobilizers and allocators of capital.

According to Schumpeter industrial entrepreneurship is defined in terms of "creative response" and "innovation". Generally, if confronted with a change, an economy, a sector of it or an individual reacts by doing what the existing practice suggests. But if the reaction is outside the realm of existing practice, it can be called a "creative response" or "innovation". According to Schumpeter this "creative response" or "innovation" is the *sine qua non* of economic development which implies the doing of new things or of old things in a new way.[24]

The foregoing discussion has brought out the fact that the growth and development of industrial entrepreneurship in any country depends on the existence of persons with a certain psychological make-up favourable to entrepreneurial activities. It is quite understandable that in the traditional society of Sikkim these persons were rare. At the same time the environment which nurtures these persons was also absent there, neither was there an attempt to change the existing environment.

The most essential pre-requisites for an environment conducive to the growth of entrepreneurship in any country may be examined now with particular reference to Sikkim.

We may first mention what Max Weber calls "psychological atmosphere" which rests on the presence of social sanctions sufficiently strong to ensure general acceptance of entrepreneurial functions as "good". A healthy environment for innovating enterprises is out of the question without a popular faith in economic enterprise. In this context the roles played by religious feeling, nationalism, legalism, tradition, custom and even education in creating the faith are highly important.

In the case of Sikkim religion, custom and traditional education were such that they turned the attention of the people from mundane affairs to the spiritual world and, therefore, initiative and enterprise for economic gains could not be expected in such a social set-up. The basic precept of Buddhism which was adhered to by the Lepchas and the Bhutias was the abandonment of desire which was diamentrically opposite to any urge for economic enterprise. Like Buddhism the Hindu religion also through its doctrine of retribution (Karma) dismissed economic progress as an object *non desideratum* while heralding spiritual progress as the highest and most noble form of advancement; and the Nepalis who adhered to this religion were influenced thereby. However, in Hinduism denouncement of the material world was less pronounced and perhaps this was one of the reasons why the Nepali settlers, even though initially handicapped, were ultimately economically more successful than the native Lepchas and Bhutias.

The second environmental element conducive to the growth of entpepreneurship is the freedom of the businessman to take the ordinary and legitimate risks of doing business. These risks are mainly of four types as enumerated by Simons: the risk of investing in the wrong place, of demand changes, of technical obsolencence and of guessing badly because too many others guessed the same way.[25]

In Sikkim during the British period there was certainly no restriction imposed on any of the above risk-takings. For the Sikkimese people it was rather the other factors like dearth of raw materials and capital, lack of technical know-how and communicational bottlenecks that were the main reason for not availing themselves of the freedom. So far as the Indian businessmen were concerned, they were, of course, not so much free in their activities even though they were better equipped with capital and technical know-how. For example, Indian traders in Sikkim were debarred from owning any landed property within the state—and this prevails even today and often they had to pay a very high rent to the feudal aristocrats for hiring a shop or a piece of land. This evidently hindered entrepreneurial activities.

Finally comes the role of the state to encourage and enhance entrepreneurial activities. The primary function of the state in this regard is, of course, the political security of the state, both internal and external so that economic activities are not hampered by political upheavals. In this respect Sikkim during the British period was quite secure and the economy provided scope for enterprise.

The state has also some corrective and promotional roles to play in the growth of entrepreneurial activities. The corrective role is mainly in the nature of eliminating the obstacles to freedom of enterprise and the promotional role is in the form of the state taking part in the economic activities of the country so that the government enterprises become not only complementary to the private ones but also promote the activities of the latter.

It may be pointed out that the promotional function of the state is of the gratest importance in underdeveloped countries. The promotional function may include private undertakings through subsidy or incentive, and a minimum provision of legal and legally enforceable institutional rules according to which private economic decisions can be made and implemented. But the most important among the promotional activities of the state is the task of providing social overhead capital which influences the development of entrepreneurship in a positive direction.

The most important among the different types of social overhead capital are the provision of power and transport facilities. The existence of these two vital facilities is essential for industrial development. The government may also provide various forms of information to the risk-bearers regarding sources of supply, markets, technical know-how and so on which the small and medium-scale industries cannot obtain so easily of their own. Moreover, technical education and training of personnel are also important aspects of economic growth where governmental help is necessary.

The Government did practically nothing in these respects. The British certainly opened up the country to the outside world by improving the transport and communication system. But this was done for administrative purposes as well as for opening the Indo-Tibetan trade route through Sikkim and as such the Sikkimese were not provided with adequate communicational infrastructure for undertaking big economic ventures. The Government also did not take up any public enterprise nor did it encourage or help the establishment of private firms in any way.

On the other hand, the British Government's attitude towards economic development of Sikkim was rather passive or even negative. This is well illustrated in a passage from H. H. Risley:

> "The peculiar position of Sikkim renders it impossible for us to ignore it as we ignore Bhutan, or to treat it on terms of comparative equality as we treat Nepal. Sikkim cannot stand by itself and if we withdrew our support, it must ultimately fall either to Tibet or to Nepal. But for our treaty obligations the latter consummation would hardly be one to be deeply regretted...."[26]

Obviously, the above statement betrays complete passivity on the part of the British administrators towards the interests of Sikkim. Another reason why the British yet held Sikkim in their control was the need of protecting British interests in the bordering district of Darjeeling which is clear in the following statement:

> "Once let our hold be relaxed, and Sikkim would become the Alsatia of the Eastern Himalayas, and such a state of things would react most formidably on the security of life and property in the great European settlement of Darjeeling."[27]

B. Land Tenure System

The land tenure system of Sikkim has been, as elsewhere, a by-product of the social and economic transformation of the country. We have no written account or evidence regarding the earliest form of land-holding in Sikkim; but from some sources written in later years we get a glimpse of the earlier period when the Lepchas were the only inhabitants of the country.

These accounts written mostly in the 19th and early 20th centuries not only give us a picture of the Lepcha land system in those years but also help us to arrive at a reasonable inference as to the earlier past. This is due to two reasons:

First, it is seen from these accounts that the Lepchas still continued to practise the old land system or part of it even though the contemporary state authority advocated a foreign system. It would be reasonable to suggest, therefore, that the distinguishing features of the Lepcha land system at that time were the remnants of the past and that these had been practised in a much more pronounced manner during the Lepcha period.

Secondly, the Bhutia monarchy in Sikkim also was not absolutely opposed to the continuance of the old Lepcha tradition and practice. In fact, and as will be clear later on, it tried to preserve the essential features of the old Lepcha land system. The attempt on the part of the monarchy to preserve the Lepcha land system may be taken as another reason why the later descriptions of it might be accepted to represent some features of the earlier system.

Gorer, writing on the 19th and the early 20th century Sikkim points out that not communal, but individual ownership of land was the traditional custom among the Lepchas and this practice persisted even when it was confronted with a state power which advocated a diametrically opposite system.

From the account of Gorer we find that it was according to the native Lepcha tradition that the more protected valley ground was divided into pieces of private property, though, the higher ground was common property for all. Gorer further points out that this common ground was also divided into private lands by the year 1840.[28] In the late 19th and the early 20th century Sikkim, therefore, private ownership of land was the most predominant feature of land-holding among the Lepchas. This was perhaps an outcome of the growth of private property during the period as discussed in the earlier section.

We presume that the above practice also held good in ancient times as it was the "native Lepcha tradition". We find a remarkable resemblance between this practice and the ancient Indian land system. As Dr. R.K. Mookerji says:

> "Since the beginning of history, society in India has been based on the principle of private property in land.... There is no trace in Vedic Literature of communal property in the sense of ownership by community of any sort, nor is there mention of communal cultivation. The extent of communal control and ownership of land probably applied to what was "no man's land", the grass land which served to separate one plot from another and was used as village common for purposes of pasture for cattle."[29]

It is difficult to ascertain the relationship between the individual proprietor of land and the sovereign of the country during the Lepcha period. Perhaps the Lepcha chief or king exacted taxes from these proprietors as and when necessary. As Sikkim then was a small country inhabited by a small race comprising, perhaps, only a few thousand people, it is probable that there were no intermediaries between the sovereign and the actual land-holders. In India, however, the king granted villages or lands to the applicants in the later Vedic period and these grants created land-lords and depressed the position of the actual cultivators of land who were thus turned into tenants.[30]

One corollary to the fact that land was privately owned is that land was a property and possessed the characteristics of a commodity in the sense that it could be transferred through sale or inheritance. It could not, however, evolve into a full-fledged commodity in the modern sense of the term in the absence of money and a monetised economy during the Lepcha period.

Some distinguishing features of the Lepcha land system during the later periods may be mentioned. In the Lepcha theory of inheritance, as we find in the description of more recent writers, *property descends from the elder to the younger brother,* and then when all of the first generation are dead or too old, to the *sons of the elder brother according to seniority* and this process goes on thereafter. In the Lepcha custom of land-holding, theoretically speaking, there should, therefore, be no *subdivision of land* through inheritance.

In practice, however, this is not strictly followed. If a son wishes to settle on his own during his father's life-time, the father assigns him, with the consent and co-operation of the village headman, his share of the land. If the sons wish to separate after their father's death, the property is divided by the village headman. The house is given to the eldest son, and the animals, movable property and land are divided up equally. The eldest son has always the first choice. If there are different sizes of the fields, he takes the biggest one. If the number of fields is not exactly divisible by the number of the sons, the biggest fields are split into two, thereby facilitating division. Should two or more brothers wish to continue to live together they will be given the adjoining fields.[31]

As land can be inherited only by the males, a Lepcha family without a male offspring occasionally takes a son-in-law to reside with his bride in his father-in law's house and inherit her parents' property. But this arrangement is not popular and often people prefer to adopt a young male child, usually the child of a relative or else to let the property pass at their death to a substitute tax-payer known as 'ke-tsop' to be named by the village headman.[32]

When a person dies without heirs or the heirs are too young, the village headman appoints a substitute tax-payer or 'ke-tsop', as a rule the younger son of a large family i.e. not the eldest son as he will inherit his father's property. If there are no direct heirs, the *ke-tsop* will keep the property permanently. If the heir is too young, the *ke-tsop* hands over the property when the heir attains adulthood. During his guardianship the *ke-tsop* is responsible for the payment of taxes. He cultivates the land of the heir and supports his ward, but if he can make a profit he keeps it for himself.[33]

This concept of landed private property, though still prevalent in some Lepcha enclaves, was radically challenged by the intrusion of the Bhutia immigrants and the consequent Bhutia rule and cultural domination. The new concept said that *land was not a private property* and as such it could not be sold, transferred or sub-divided at the will of the land-holder. *The sole ownership of land rested now on the sovereign* of the country and *the land-holder enjoyed only the privilege of usufract,* but not outright ownership.

We can make a contrast between the Lepcha and the Bhutia land-holding systems which existed side by side in Sikkim from the time of establishment of Bhutia monarchy in 1642. The nature of land-holding in any country is intimately related to the prevalent sociopolitical philosophy behind it as well as the contemporary economic background that warrants a particular land-holding system. These two aspects are equally important in the explanation of the Bhutia land-holding system in Sikkim.

Historically, culturally and to a great extent ethnically Sikkim lies within the realm of Tibetan influence; and in examining the nature and implication of land-holding and the related land-revenue systems of Sikkim special mention must be made to that.

Since time immemorial and until very recently in the Tibetan system of land-holding all land was considered to belong to the ruler. Individuals could hold land only from their ruler who had the right to resume it at will. There was no private property in land in the western sense of the term.[34]

Since the establishment of Bhutia monarchy in Sikkim the Sikkimese theory of land-holding also maintained that all land belongs to the King, and only usufract, not outright ownership devolves on the residents of the land. In Sikkim it was customary for the King to give land for its use. Indeed, in most of the Tibeto-Burman culture-areas this was the tradition.[35]

Below the Sikkim King there was a host of personnel to supervise land holdings and collect revenues. There were the feudal lords named Kazis, the village headmen named Mandals and various other officers whose jurisdiction comprised certain specified tracts of land. These personnel enjoyed authority and privileges so long as they were not in conflict with the King's sovereignty. The Kazis, for example, had some kind of hereditary title to their office although they had no proprietory right in their land.

The activities of these personnel were manifold: *(i)* they exercised some authority over their jurisdiction, *(ii)* they adjudicated minor disputes within their territories, *(iii)* they referred to the King matters of import for which they were not competent to take final decisions, and *(iv)* finally, they assessed the revenue payable by the people settled within their jurisdiction.

A description of the land tenure system prevalent in Sikkim in the middle of the 19th century is available in the writings of Campbell. His account, however, does not deal with the entire country but a part of it which had just been annexed by the British but was still known as the Sikkim Morung. The total area of this territory was reckoned at 4,000 square miles and its boundary was "from the Mechi on the West to the Teesta on the East, with Purneah and Rungpore to the South".[36] This area comprised, more or less, the present-day Siliguri-Naxalbari block in the Darjeeling district of West Bengal.

The Sikkim Morung was traditionally a part of Sikkim in the plains of Terai below the foothills of the Darjeeling district. In the treaty between Nepal and Tibet in 1792 this tract of land was ceded to Nepal. In the Anglo-Nepali war of 1814-15 Sikkim allied with the British and in the subsequent Treaty of Titalia concluded in 1817 Sikkim regained this territory. It was, however, annexed by the British in 1850 after which Sikkim has never been able to regain it.[37]

Campbell in his *Papers on the Sikkim Morung* published in 1851 gives a description of the land tenure system prevalent in that region which was a part of Sikkim till 1849 and where the British had not yet introduced any new system. It is curious to note how the Tibetan land-holding system was modified here as a result of proximity of this territory with India having a different land tenure system.

For example, the four different classes connected with land in the Sikkim Morung were: Jotedar, Bhagidar, Thikadar and Praja—all of them corresponding to similar classes in India at that time. In fact, the terms themselves were of Indian origin. Moreover, we find that an officer named Chaudhuri was responsible for the collection of revenue there, but that was also a wide-spread practice in India. Incidentally, we may mention here that in the first Mughal land settlement at the time of Akbar conducted by Raja Todar Mal in 1652 Bengal proper was composed of 19 Sarkars divided into 682 Parganas each of which was administered by a Chaudhuri.[38] Evidently the Mughal system persisted till 1851 when Campbell wrote.

We may give an account of the land tenure system in the Sikkim Morung during the mid-19th century in the words of Campbell:

"A jote in the Morung is a portion of unmeasured land, there is no land measure in use, bearing a jumma varying from 1 rupee the lowerst per annum to rupees 253, which is the highest. The Jotedar holds it by a pottah which has never been granted for a longer period than 4 years. He cannot sell or mortgage the land, such a proceeding has never been effected, and would not have been allowed by the former Government. If he desires to quit the jote, it reverts to Government. It goes by succession from father to son, and to heirs in general. A jote is sometimes abandoned for uncleared rent-free land.

"The Bhageedar is a share holder in a jote; there may be one, or more. He has no pottah from the Government nor written agreement with the Jotedar, but his right is upheld by Government. The extent of his share is specified in fractions of a rupee of the jumma. The specification is verbal between him and the Jotedar. The share descends by succession, but cannot be alienated by sale or mortgage. If the Bhageedar quits, the Jotedar falls into the whole of his share, and can assign it in whole or part to another Bhageedar, without the consent of the remaining Bhageedars on the jote. He pays his share of the Government due to the Jotedar, who settles all accounts of the jote with the Choudery. He is liable to Government for his share of balances if the Jotedar is not forthcoming, and sometimes, by agreement between the Choudery and Jotedar, he pays his share of dues direct to the Choudery. The Choudery or even the Government cannot put in a new Bhageedar without consent of the Jotedar.

"The Teekadar is a contract farmer. His contract is not hereditary; the Jotedar may, at the death of a Teekadar during the currency of his contract, assign it to any other person. Bhageedars often employ Teekadars, their contracts are not under the authority of the Jotedar at all, nor do they require his sanction.

"The Purja differes from the Teekadar. He is not a farm servant, but rather a contract cultivator. He gets half the produce of the land he cultivates, and runs no risk. The Jotedar, Bhageedar or Teekadar, for all three have Purjas, furnish the bullocks, ploughs, seed, etc., can dismiss the Purja at pleasure, move him to another portion of the jote, add to, or diminish the land he cultivates; in short, can treat him much as they like. He is always kept in debt to his principals, and is more a serf of the Jotedar than a free agent. He has no claim whatever to property in the soil."[39]

From the above account we get the following hierarchy of land-holders in the Sikkim Morung at the time of Campbell:

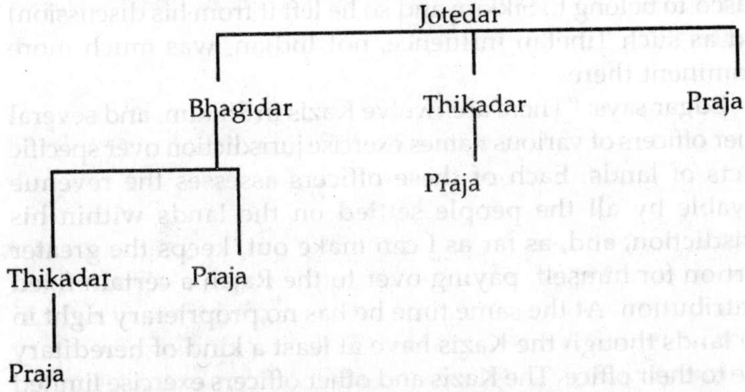

(Standard spellings for the terms have been used in the above chart.)

From the above chart we see that the general hierarchy was like this: Jotedar — Bhagidar — Thikadar — Praja, but sometimes the intermediary land-holders, viz, Bhagidars and Thikadars, were absent, either or both.

After describing the land tenure system in the Sikkim Morung, Campbell comes to the question of ownership of lands:

"From the above particulars it will appear that the Jotedar and Bhageedar alone can be said to possess rights of property in the soil. The Teekadar and Purja have none. The property, therefore, in the widest sense of the term lies conjointly in the Government, the Jotedar and the Bhageedar. If it is allowed that all three are possessed of some rights of property in the soil, it remains to shew the proportion held by each. If the proprietary right is established to the Government exclusively, the rights of the other two will be restricted to the usufract only, and this is the view taken of the matter by the people. Under the late Government, by general consent and usage, the Raja was considered the owner of all the land, whether under primitive forest, or occupied, and cultivated".[40]

A similar account is obtained from the writings of Edgar

in 1873. We have seen in the account of Campbell that the Indian land tenure system had a great influence in the case of the Sikkim Morung. But we do not find any such influence in the account of Edgar, perhaps because the areas dealt with by him were closer to Tibet (the Sikkim Morung since 1850 ceased to belong to Sikkim and so he left it from his discussion) and as such Tibetan influence, not Indian, was much more prominent there.

Edgar says: "There are twelve Kazis in Sikkim, and several other officers of various names exercise jurisdiction over specific tracts of lands. Each of these officers assesses the revenue payable by all the people settled on the lands within his jurisdiction, and, as far as I can make out, keeps the greater portion for himself, paying over to the Rajah a certain fixed contribution. At the same time he has no proprietary right in the lands though the Kazis have at least a kind of hereditary title to their office. The Kazis and other officers exercise limited civil and criminal jurisdiction within the lands the revenue of which they collect, all important cases being referred to the Rajah and decided by Changzed and the Dewans, who are at present three in number.

"The cultivators have no title to the soil, and a man may settle down on and cultivate any land he may find unoccupied without going through any formality whatever, and when once he has occupied the land, no one but the Rajah can turn him out. But the Rajah can eject him at any time; and if he should cease to occupy the land, he would not retain any lien upon it. There is a kind of tenant-right however, under which cultivators are enabled to dispose of unexhausted improvements. Thus, as it was explained to me, a man who has terraced a piece of hill-side could not sell the land, but is allowed to sell the right of using the terraces. This custom is acknowledged not to be absolutely a right, but more of the nature of an indulgence on the part of the Rajah, by whom it was allowed to grow up for the sake of convenience."[41]

Apart from this socio-political philosophy of land there were also some economic factors behind the absence of tenant-ownership in contemporary Sikkim. One such factor was the practice of jhum or shifting cultivation. The widespread custom of shifting cultivation required continued movement of the peasants from one plot of land to another. This practice prevented the growth of any sense of ownership in the minds of the cultivators.

In the case of the lands where permanent cultivation with the help of terraces etc. was carried on, the rights of the cultivators were a bit pronounced, although those rights were not conceived of in the modern sense of the term. It was only in the sense of an 'allowance' on the part of the ruler as pointed out by Edgar.

The *Imperial Gazetteer of India* gives a description of the system of land tenure as prevalent in the beginning of the 20th century. The collection of land revenue then was in the hands of various types of landlords, viz., the Lamas, the Kazis and the Thikadars. At that time there were 71 landlords divided into the following categories:

1.	Lamas	13
2.	Kazis	21
3.	Thikadars	37
	Total	71

Under these landlords were the village headmen called "Mandals" who actually collected the revenue from the ryot (tenant) and paid it to the landlords who in turn paid a fixed amount to the state treasury, the amount having been determined at the commencement of his lease. The Lamas were an exception and they did not pay dues of any kind, nor were they bound to render labour for the King as in the case of others.[42]

An important landmark in the land revenue system of Sikkim was the introduction of 'elaka' leases in 1925. These were issued by the Durbar for a period of 15 years. An elaka was a revenue-collecting unit under the superintendence of a collector. In the event of the death of a lessee during the term of his lease, the Government had undertaken to renew the lease in favour of his heir only in the male line of descent and failing that to the duly recognised adoptee of the lessee.

According to the *Administration Report of the Sikkim State for the year 1929-30* there were 104 elakas in Sikkim in that year. The different categories of revenue-collectors for those elakas were as follows:

Categories of Revenue-Collectors	*Number of Elakas*
1. Private Estates of the King	29
2. Kazis	21
3. Five Big Monasteries	15
4. Nepalis	13
5. Managers Appointed On Commission	11
6. Lepchas	8
7. Bhutias	6
8. Domiciled Plainsman	1
Total	104

Source: Ad. Report for 1929-30, Ch. 4.

In the beginning of the thirties of the 20th century attempts were made for the measurement of wet, dry and garden lands, as possessed by different classes of people inhabiting Sikkim. The Government also did not encourage the acquisition of vast holdings and had set a limit of the maximum acreage a proprietor might possess. Ordinarily, a tenant was not permitted to acquire more than 20 acres of cultivable land. In the case of Mandals the maximum was 30 acres, and for the lesees it was 100 acres. The son or brother of a lesee separate in interest from the latter, could have a maximum holding of 50 acres. Members of family not separate in interest from the head of the family were not deemed to be able to acquire landed property in their own name in excess of the limit fixed for the head of the family. We find, therefore, that the Government of Sikkim at that time assumed a progressive outlook in limiting the sizes of the land-holdings for different categories of people.

But the Government failed to show a progressive outlook in the treatment of land sales to racial groups other than the Lepchas and the Bhutias. The Lepchas and the Bhutias were regarded as "hereditary State subjects" and there was a law prohibiting land alienation by hereditary State subjects in favour of non-hereditary subjects such as the Nepalis or the domiciled plainsmen. It was said that this law acted "as a very useful check on the former class which is proper and improvident being steadily replaced by the latter who are more subtle and shrewd." Civil Courts were also debarred from sanctioning sales of land belonging to hereditary subjects in favour of non-hereditary subjects in execution proceedings (whether money or revenue suits) without the express sanction of the Durbar.[43]

Another interesting point to note here is that even during the thirties of the 20th century the old Tibetan philosophy was prevalent and formed the backbone of the land tenure system in Sikkim. Land was still the royal property and any other proprietorship was deemed as an allowance on the part of the King. To quote from the *Administration Report of the Sikkim State for the years 1931-32, 1932-33 and 1933-34:*

"Every inch of the land in the State, broadly speaking belongs to the Sirkar i.e. the Government of the country. The rights of the raiyots are fixed and secured and are governed by State Notifications and custom. The raiyot, deriving his title from the Sirkar i.e. the Ruler, regards his lands fully as private, heritable and saleable and otherwise transferable property. The complexity of the land revenue system of the State and the nature of the leases issued to various Elakhadars in the working of that system can be appreciated only when it is fully realised that the theoretical owner, viz. the Sirkar may be presumed to have demised the land to individual proprietors of different holdings, subject to the land laws of the State."[44]

Gorer also points out in 1938 that at that time private ownership of land was prevalent among the Lepchas, but it was because the King allowed the continuance of that native custom. He also points out that even in that case royal sanction was necessary for any transfer of land.

Thus Gorer Says: "All the land of Zongu (a Lepcha enclave) belongs to the Maharajah and cannot be owned by anybody not of Lepcha blood. Transactions of land between residents inside Zongu need the consent of the Mandal, and if necessary, the confirmation of the court."[45]

There were some provisions for new settlers which also clearly show the paramount rights of the monarch. If a Lepcha from outside Zongu wished to settle there, he had to apply to the headman in whose village he wised to live and the headman then forwarded the case to the court. If the request was granted, the headman summoned all the villagers and instructed them each to give a strip of land to the newcomer; he himself would give a piece of uncleared forest. It was extremely rare, however, for immigrants to arrive in this way. From the account of Gorer it is seen that in a period of thirty years only one such case was reported in the Lingthem village in the Zongu area. New settlers usually joined the community either through marriage or adoption.

Another important feature of the Tibetan land tenure system that followed from the absolute authority of the King was that land could not be sub-divided even in the case of inheritance. Accordingly, the Tibetan custom was that the eldest son should inherit the property as a whole and the Lepchas were also expected to follow this custom. But in practice, as we have seen, the Lepcha brothers, often inherited the property equally and as such the property was sub-divided. This deviation also was allowed by the King.

However, so far as the Bhutias were concerned the Tibetan system was strictly followed. They could not transfer land either by sale or gift. In the case of inheritance, if there were many sons in a Bhutia family, polyandry generally made a place for the younger brothers within the household, or else the younger brothers who had no right of inheritance left the household and in that case monasticism provided the best shelter and recluse. If there was a lack of males, the adoption of a son-in-law insured the continuity of the household as a unit and, therefore, in any case there was no question of subdivision of land.[47]

The term of the lessee system was to expire in 1940 but it was extended until 1948. At the end of the Second World War in 1946 land reforms were taken in hand by Sir Tashi Namgyal. A trigonometrical survey of all lands was made and gradually the powers and functions of the landlords were being clipped. The landlords' courts and their powers of registration of lands and deeds were abolished in 1948. The same year the lessee system was abolished and the people were given the privilege of paying taxes direct to the Government.[48]

In the land reform of 1951 the land-holding unit of an elaka was abolished. Now instead there was the local unit called 'block' which comprised one large hamlet, or two or more small hamlets with one headman called 'Mandal'. Wider than this there was the unit called 'area' which was also a polling constituency for the election to the State Council. A block or an area, however, often coincided with the former unit of an elaka.

Another major aspect of the land reform of 1951 was that the estates of the Kazis as well as of other big landlords were taken over by the State and the land thus acquired was distributed among the poor cultivators. The feudal lords like the Kazis were transformed into a class of salaried officials with a much lower economic and social position.[49] However, many of them have since been able to maintain their previous status, at least partially, by owning big houses and properties in Gangtok as well as by holding important positions in the political parties, the State Council and other social organisations.

C. Occupational Pattern

An important characteristic of the occupational pattern in a primitive society is the preponderance of activities for the procurement of food as compared with other economic activities. Sikkim is no exception and until recent past most of the occupations of the people were meant for food procurement.

Let us begin with the occupational pattern among the Lepchas, the original inhabitants of the country. Three distinct occupations of the early Lepchas may be mentioned in this connection: hunting, gathering and shifting cultivation. These are still the major sources of food in some of the Lepcha enclaves in Sikkim. However, as modern civilization penetrates into the country these are gradually being subordinated to more advanced means of food procurement.

Miss C. de Beauvoir Stocks describes the occupational pattern of the Lepchas in 1925 as follows: "The Lepchas live chiefly on agriculture and on plants and roots in the jungle. Rice, Indian corn, wheat, barley, millet, etc., are cultivated, giving three or four harvests every year.... Hunting and fishing are practised with primitive implements, poisoned arrows being used, or nets and traps made of bamboo."[50]

In Gorer (1938) we find a good description of how hunting

as an occupation was gradually being abandoned during the early years of the 20th century due to changes in the Lepcha society and economy. In his words:

"In former times and still today in the less fertile regions, the Lepchas relied on hunting for a great deal of their food; but in Lingthem and most of the other villages of Zongu game is hunted less and less. There are a number of reasons for this which interact on one another; the stigma which the Lepcha interpretation of lamaism places on the killing of animals excludes some of the community entirely from this pursuit, and even those who are not lamas feel a certain disclination to killing animals. The settled houses and greater amount of ground under cultivation and increasing domestic herds make the necessity for wild animals less urgent, and the growing commitments of agricultural life give less time for hunting. Indeed, nowadays if a young man wants to go hunting ... he usually has to sneak away when his elders are not looking, and is liable to get a good scolding when he does return for withdrawing his labour from the fields."[51]

Gathering as a source of food has also declined with the opening up of new occupational opportunities and deforestation of the countryside. Previously the Lepchas gathered edible plants, fruits, roots, tubers and leaves from forests which covered a large portion of the country. It has been stated that the word Kalimpong is of Lepcha origin meaning "a gathering place".[52] This indicates the importance of gathering in the life of primitive Lepchas.

Shifting cultivation was the most important source of food for the primitive Lepchas. There were several reasons for this:

(i) The technique of production was very simple.

(ii) As hunting and gathering required movement from one place to another agriculture of a shifting type was most suitable.

(iii) Due to the abandance of land in comparison with population, the amount of harvest was quite significant.

Shifting cultivation has a long history in Sikkim. The method of cultivation during the middle of the 18th century has been described as follows:

"A new patch of jungle would be cleared every year, and when dried set fire to. On the cleared space, paddy, codo and bhutta, as well as various other white and black grains would be sown. Next year another patch of jungle would be cleared. The virgin soil of course yielded a very rich crop, and people used to gain their living very easily, and also enjoyed a good many sorts of fruits and herbs which they cannot get now. As they had not much call on them for free labour contribution nor much of tax of pay, they were very happy."[53]

This method of cultivation dominated agriculture until the later half of the 19th century when the change from shifting cultivation to permanent wet rice cultivation occurred.[54] In some areas like Zongu, however, it was introduced as late as the twenties of the 20th century.[55] Today in most parts of Sikkim shifting cultivation has been substituted by permanent cultivation.

Gorer in 1938 gives a description of shifting cultivation or what he calls "cultivation in temporary fields". These temporary fields consisted of clearings made in the forest, for the purpose of cultivation for one year, and then allowed to lie fallow for seven years before being cultivated again. All suitable land was divided up into private holdings, the landmarks consisting of big trees or streams or stones set up at irregular intervals. On the whole, these clearings were not isolated — three or more households had all their portions next to one another and travelled round together every year. But related households did not usually have adjacent grounds. When the land was originally distributed care was taken that nobody should be especially favoured and as such related households were not assigned adjacent grounds.

The clearing of land was started in the early spring; the women cut down the lower growths with their sickles while the men climbed and lopped the bigger trees and saplings. Previously the trees used to be cut down if possible, but at the time of Gorer there was a court order forbidding the destruction of trees. When all the debris had been collected the straight sticks were sorted out and the rest was put into heaps and set fire to, the ashes acting as a loosener and fertilizer of the soil. After burning, the ground was cleared of charred wood and remaining weeds by hand, and was then sown with the main crop. This was done in the simplest manner possible—holes were made in the ground with a pointed stick and the seed dropped into and around them.

The principal crops of these temporary fields were millet and "dry rice" (dry rice was the name given to some varieties of wild rice which did not require irrigation). For each household only one field of maincrop millet and one of dry rice were made every year. Sometimes other grains or plants were grown among these crops, generally a certain amount of maize and vegetables when their yield in the field garden was insufficient. Along with these a small amount of buckwheat was also sown for seed purposes. The main sowing season for buckwheat was the autumn when harvests of the above crops were made. The buckwheat sown in the autumn ripened in about five months' time when again the spring sowing was resorted to in another temporary field.[56]

Shifting cultivation was the traditional technique of agricultural production, but gradually it gave place to permanent cultivation. There were several reasons for the introduction of permanent cultivation in Sikkim. Before the influx of the Nepalis during the later half of the 19th century the inhabitants of Sikkim used the technique of shifting cultivation that provided them sufficient food, at least so far as the cereals were concerned. But the influx of the Nepalis necessitated a much better utilization of land and permanent cultivation was the obvious course of action. The British also encouraged this technique of production, particularly wet rice cultivation through terraces and in that matter the Nepalis were expert.

The extent of better utilization of land due to the introduction of this technique was enormous. A piece of land under permanent cultivation could yield 8 times or even more production than under shifting cultivation. This was possible because under permanent cultivation the same land was used each year during the period when it would have remained fallow according to the other method of cultivation. Moreover, in permanent cultivation it was possible to pay greater attention to agriculture as the cultivator no longer moved from place to place but resided beside his agricultural plot. This new technique also made it possible to ensure better irrigation and manuring through the introduction of terraces in the hill slopes.

Permanent cultivation was of two types: dry and wet. The dry variety was again of two types: one, resorted to in the field gardens called "sing" to supplement the produce of shifting cultivation and the other for the cultivation of cardamom. These two types of dry permanent cultivation did not require irrigation. On the other hand, the wet permanent cultivation required irrigation, specially through terraces, mainly for rice.

Of the different types of permanent cultivation, the one resorted to in the field gardens was introduced first — however, the exact time of introduction is not known. About the other two types Gorer says that in the Zongu area they were introduced quite recently. Gorer says in 1938:

"The two latter types of cultivation, which are now of very great importance in Lepcha life, are both very modern: cardamom was introduced at the beginning of the century, rice terraces for wet paddy less than twenty years ago."[57]

The Imperial Gazetteer of India gives an account of the major crops of cultivation at the beginning of the 20th century:

"By far the most important crop is maize, which occupies a larger area than all other crops together; it is estimated to cover 94 square miles. After maize, the largest areas are under marua, buckwheat, rice, wheat, and barley, which are estimated to cover from 4,000 to 12,000 acres each. Cardamoms, grown on about 6,000 acres, are a valuable crop. Cultivation has rapidly extended in recent years, but a large quantity of cultivable waste still remains. Plantains, oranges and other fruits are grown in the gardens, and the Government apple orchards started at Lachung and Lachen are proving a success."[58]

By the time of Gorer the major portion of agriculture in Sikkim was dominated by permanent cultivation and the extent of shifting cultivation was very negligible. He gives a description of how the different types of crops were raised by the different types of permanent cultivation. To quote him:

"Two main crops are raised in the field garden annually; first a mixture of barley and wheat, and subsequently maize. These grains are chiefly raised as stop-gap crops, and for fermenting; maize is thought little of, and to eat much of it is the surest sign of poverty. A number of fruits and vegetables are also raised on the edge of the field garden to give a variety of flavourings to the main rice dish; the greater number of these are importation from India, such as various varieties of pulse, tomatoes and chilli; some of them however are wild plants found locally and domesticated.

"Cardamom is grown in small clearings all over the lower slopes of the valley. It is a perennial plant propagated by cuttings which are taken in the early spring; the plant reaches its full bearing period within three years; at the end of ten years it starts to decline and new plantings have to be made; this can however be done on the same ground as the plant does not exhaust the soil. The plants need a good deal of care, and have to be hand-weeded at least three times a year. When the fruit is gathered, the old growth is cut down and burned.

..."Almost every household has at least a couple of terraces and some considerably more. These terraces are scattered all over the valley, and it is rare for two contiguous strips to belong to the same owner. It is theoretically permissible to exchange plots so that they shall be better grouped, but nobody considers doing so. The rice terraces are turned with a rough single pointed wooden plough drawn by a pair of oxen, as is the sing or field-garden near the house. Except on these artificially levelled places the ground is too precipitous for the use of a plough to be possible."[59]

Gorer has given a Lepcha agricultural calendar for the Talung valley of Sikkim which may also be taken as representative of the general agricultural practices in Sikkim throughout the year. We reproduce the calendar below:

TANGBU (February)	Clear the ground and finish sowing buckwheat.
NTBU (March)	Finish clearing ground and sow dry paddy in temporary fields. Sow maize and early millet in the valley. Weed cardamom in flower and strike new plants. This and the following months is the time of rain and hailstorms.
SUMGU (April)	Harvest barley and wheat. Clear ground for main-crop millet. Weed

	cardamom again round new-found fruit.
ZIBU (May)	Harvest buckwheat. Sow main-crop millet. Sow maize in garden burning the wheat straw for fertilizing. This and the three following months are the period of constant rain and heat.
NAPU (June)	Plant rice. Weed dry rice. This is the leanest month when people may go hungry.
TIKPU (July)	Harvest early millets in valley. Weed main-crop millet.
DENGBU (August)	Harvest the earliest variety of wet rice. Make a shade to dry cardamom fruit. Make a small sowing of buckwheat for seed.
GEEBU (September)	Harvest dry rice. The women start harvesting the millet, the men the cardamom. This and the two following months are relatively dry.
GOOBU (October)	Cardamom picking continues. Wet rice is harvested. Barley, wheat and onions are sown in the 'garden'.
CHOOPU (November)	The seed-buckwheat is harvested. Cardamom is sold. This and the next two months are the prosperous period, the time of little work and much feasting, of shopping and trading expenditions. Most marriages are celebrated now.
CHUCHIKPU (December)	The harvested temporary fields must be made ready for buckwheat. This and the two following months are the period of intense cold. Taxes are paid in this month.
CHUNIPU (January)	The big sowing of buckwheat.

Source: Gorer, p. 94.

Note: The Tibetan year which is followed in the above calendar begins in February and the first day of the Tibetan month falls on about the tenth of the English. So, the months 'February' etc. in the above chart should be interpreted as 'February 10th to March 10th' and so on.

Apart from agriculture the Sikkimese also carried on other occupations to maintain their livelihood. These occupations were not, however, very widespread and were sometimes confined within particular racial groups. One such occupation was the pasturage carried on by the Bhutias of northern Sikkim. It was introduced by the Bhutias and no account is available to indicate that any other social group resorted to that profession in Sikkim prior to the Bhutias. Livestock breeding and rearing within the boundary of the homestead land was, however, quite common and age-old.

The Bhutias also introduced the transfrontier trade of Sikkim with Tibet and they played an important role in it. To them the three occupations of agriculture, pasturage and trade were equally important. Talking about the occupational pattern of the Bhutias of northern Sikkim Bose says:

"Before the Chinese invasion, they used to make a good income from pasturing as well as trade with Tibet. They say that about a third of their demand was met by agriculture while the remaining needs were met by pasturing and trade."[60]

One characteristic of the Bhutia people was their migratory nature and it was reflected in their occupational pattern. As the Bhutias originally came from Tibet which is cooler than Sikkim, they could not stand the sultry summer of Sikkim and during this time they often migrated to the regions of higher altitude in Tibet.

Sometimes places of high altitude within Sikkim were also used as summer resort. This was particularly true for the people of Lachen. In the month of April each year all the young men and women of the valley would go to the higher places like Zemu, Talem, Samong, Yathang, Kalep and Thanggu and engage themselves with sowing potatoes. They would then come back to Lachen and in the month of May the whole people of the valley, including children and the aged, would migrate to the higher summer residence. From May to September they would stay there and engage in different kinds of activities like agriculture, pasturing and trade. In the month of October, after the completion of harvesting they would come down to Lachen to stay there for the remaining months.[61]

Of all the economic activities the grazing of sheep, goats and yaks was the most important occupation of the Bhutias who lived near the border of Tibet, because they could avail themselves of the grazing facilities in Tibet during their seasonal stay in that country. They used to send their sheep, goats and yaks during the monsoon to Tibet and bring them back to the lower altitudes in Sikkim before the onset of winter.

In the month of May when the Bhutias of northern Sikkim migrated to higher altitudes, they took with them their flocks of livestock. Sometimes they did not go to Tibet but to other high-altitude regions within Sikkim and in that case they used to hand over their flocks to the hired Tibetan shepherds for grazing in Tibet during the monsoon.

On the way to Tibet they used to pass about two months, i.e. May and June, in the higher and drier parts of northern Sikkim such as Dankung, Phakhulung, Yumthang, Sambong, Cholamo, Muguthang, Goma, etc. which were called "gots" or grazing centres. In reaching these grazing centres they had to cross several mighty passes within Sikkim such as Sebula (17,560f), Bongkyala (19,030f), Khorala (17,100f), etc. Thereafter during the months of July, August and September they used to graze in Tibet and come back to Sikkim in October.

Pasturing provided meat, fur, milk and milk-products to the people. So far as meat was concerned all the animals were equally important. But as regards fur, the most important source was sheep, and next came yak. Yaks were of two types: Pheyonoh and Lhonoh. Pheyonoh was the Tibetan yak, smaller in size, but with heavy fur and Lhonoh was the Sikkimese variety, bigger in size but with less fur. Traditionally Tibet was a supplier of wool and therefore the Bhutias were experts in the production of wool and woolen goods.

Monsoon was the best season for the manufacture of butter from the milk of sheep, goats or yaks. However, yaks' milk was the most important source of butter. It is said that for the production of one Kilogram of butter 8 Kilograms of yak's milk (or 12 Kilograms of cow's milk, or 6 Kilograms of sheep's milk) is necessary. Normally one yak yields about 3 Kilograms of milk per day during the monsoon. During the five months of the monsoon from May to September when the yaks grazed in higher altitudes, each yak yielded, therefore, an amount of about 56 Kilograms of butter. This butter, apart from being an item of food, was an important article of trade for the Bhutias.

Even now the Bhutias maintain their traditional live-stocks but after the closure of the Sikkim-Tibet border it is no longer possible to send the animals into Tibet for grazing, and at present some members of the family generally graze their animals in the high-altitude regions of northern Sikkim. They keep with them portable tents made of yak's skin as shelter in those high and cold regions. However, the importance of pasturing has decreased and the people are now adapting themselves to the new situation by assuming new vocations.

Let us now consider the place of art, craft and industry as occupations in the life-pattern of the Sikkimese. Sikkim was a primitive economy there being practically no scope for or inducement to the growth of other occupations. Among the primitive Lepchas, when they were the sole occupants of the country, there were very little art and craft and no industry worth mentioning.

In course of time, however, an element of buoyancy and renovation was infused in these occupations through contact with the Tibetans with the establishment of Bhutia rule in Sikkim. These Bhutias (Tibetans) were in turn influenced by the Chinese civilization and custom and as such we find remarkable Chinese influence in the art, craft and industry of Sikkim in the ensuring period. The Nepalis overran the country in the second half of the 19th century, but they could not substitute Chinese influence with their own; and we see that the Tibetan influence remained supreme even at the beginning of the 20th century. As White says:

> "The art and industries of Sikkim and Bhutan have an intimate connection with those of China, as from their earliest days these countries were in touch with China and its civilization, long before the people had any intercourse with India. With the spread of Buddhism a certain amount of Indian influence was brought in, but it is not very apparent."[62]

We may note, however, that White's division of the Sikkimese history into the pre-Buddhist and Buddhist phases in this connection seems unreasonable. *Recorded history of Sikkim traces the spread of Buddhism from the very time when the Bhutia monarchy was established in 1642. Prior to that we have no knowledge of any intercourse with Tibet or China — although it might be a possibility. The reason why even after the spread of Buddhism which was of Indian origin, Sikkim was in the fold of the Chinese culture and civilization is that Buddhism came to Sikkim via Tibet which had close connection with China. Moreover, the Bhutia Kings of Sikkim maintained close ties with Tibet and encouraged the propagation of Tibetan — and hence Chinese — culture and civilization.*

The Bhutias who came from Tibet naturally excelled in the Chinese-oriented arts and crafts. But towards the beginning of the 20th century the Nepalis overtook the Bhutias and practically monopolised in these occupations. White says:

> "In Sikkim the arts are now almost entirely carried on by Nepalese craftsmen, who excel in gold, silver and brass work".[63]

From White's description we find the process of manufacturing these articles of art. Articles made in gold, silver and brass were generally beaten into shape, backed with a kind of lac got from the roots of the sal tree, and the pattern was hammered out with blunt tools. They also cast exceedingly well in brass and bronze. The method they followed was to first model in wax the object they wished to make; they next coated the model with successive layers of cowdung, clay, and a little finely chopped straw; this was allowed to dry very slowly, and when thoroughly dry the wax vas melted out, leaving an excellent mould, into which the molten metal was poured. The casting obtained in this way was marvellous.

Very good knives were manufactured in Sikkim. They used to be made from indigenous charcoal iron, but at the time of White as steel bars could be bought quite cheaply, workmen entirely abandoned the old method of extracting iron direct from the ore.

Cotton cloth was also manufactured but the yarn was almost entirely made locally. The workmen weaved at small looms set up in different houses where the dying of the thread was also done.

Vegetable dyes, to be found in abundance in the forests and jungles of Sikkim, were traditionally used in the manufacture of cloth. But in the beginning of the 20th century aniline dyes were introduced in the bazars and the people, finding their cheap price and brilliant results took to them. In order to protect the traditional dying industry, Mr. White, the then Political Officer in Sikkim, prohibited the sale of aniline dyes throughout Sikkim and thereby forced the weavers to return to natural vegetable dyes which produced soft tints and lasted longer.

Carpets and woollen cloths were also manufactured in Sikkim. Mr. White started a few weaving schools in Lachung and these schools turned out excellent tweeds under the guidance of a Scandinavian missionary. Later on a carpet factory was also established at Gangtok under the control and supervision of the Maharani. But the great difficulty was to place the output on a proper commercial footing in the absence of a good market for high-quality woollen cloths and carpets.[64] We come to know that even in the twenties of the 20th century this picture remained practically the same. *Administration Report of the Sikkim State for 1922-23* says that in spite of strenuous efforts the sale of tweeds and rugs was dull during that year, as there were no big demands worth the name from outside. The revenue derived from the sale of tweeds and rugs sold locally during the year amounted only to Rs. 4,304 -3 -0.[65]

The Lepchas, however, led their traditional life and even in 1925 they did not show sufficient interest in these occupations. From the account of Miss Stocks we find that bamboo was the cheap material for the construction of various implements in Lepcha life such as mats, vessels, pins and there was no sign of decorative art in their make. Various types of ropes, baskets, etc. were made from jungle creepers. Spinning and weaving was done by women with the simplest types of implements like spinning rods and spindles which were held in their hands. There was also pottery-making but it was very crude plates of black mud; and articles of pottery having a better quality were imported from Nepal. Some villages manufactured a kind of thick white paper out of nettle plant. There was also the prevalence of the art of painting of skins which had been introduced from Tibet. In this painting the skins were first heated before being painted to enable the colours to be made fast. With the advance of modern civilization, Stocks observed, these local arts became rarer and gave place to more sophisticated articles imported from outside.[66]

Apart from these occupations, the establishment of British rule in Sikkim opened up a new occupation to the Sikkimese people—that of government service. Very few, however, got any permanent job and most of the employments were on the basis of temporary contract. This was particularly true for the construction of a large number of roads and highways undertaken by the British in their efforts to establish trade relations with Tibet. A good number of the Sikkimese earned their living by offering their labour services as day labourers in those construction works. Some people got employment in the construction of government buildings like office premises, residential quarters and dak bungalows, some were employed in the preservation and extraction of forest resources, some in the police force and some again in the social services like health and education. The number of government servants increased with the gradually expansion of public works.

Now let us take up the place of trade as an occupation among the Sikkimese. So far as internal trade was concerned it was quite insignificant in the non-monetised Sikkimese economy. Most of the internal trade was in the form of barter which facilitated the exchange of day-to-day necessities. During the British period with the expansion and monetisation of the economy the scope of internal trade, of course, increased. But the Sikkimese could not avail themselves of the opportunity. Morris has pointed out that even in the 1930's the barter system was prevalent among the Lepchas and only occasionally they sold their goods for money — and that also in order to pay direct taxes which were to be paid in money.[67] The above account may also be taken to hold good for other sections of the people as we do not get any reference to the contrary.

Coming to external trade we find that Sikkim initially developed her trade relations with Tibet with whom she had closer ties than with any other neighbouring country. But gradually as Sikkim came in greater contact with British India her trade with the latter increased. There seems to have been little trade between Sikkim and Bhutan, because apart from geographical barriers the two countries were similar in their economic pattern and as such one could provide very little of what the other required. There might have been some border trade between the two countries but not worth mentioning. Trade with Nepal was also insignificant due to the insurmountable Singalila range which formed the boundary between Sikkim and Nepal. Even today Sikkim's trade with these two countries is negligible.

Trade between Sikkim and Tibet during the later part of the 19th century can be gauged from the account of Edgar who visited Sikkim and the Tibetan frontier in 1873 for exploring the possibilities of Anglo-Tibetan trade across Sikkim. Edgar describes:

"While we were at the Pass, a man from Gungtuck, with his wife, came up with *murwa* of their own growing to the value of about six rupees, which they were taking to Choombi for sale. They said that they meant to take the proceeds to Phari, where they could buy salt, which they would bring in to Darjeeling, where they might probably lay out the proceeds of its sale in an investment for the Tibet market, if they found time to do so before next year's sowing season. I mention this case, as it is a typical one. There was scarce a day during my stay in East Sikkim that I did not meet people either coming from, or on their way to, Darjeeling with goods, the value of which at first sight seemed quite disproportioned to the labour that had to be undergone in taking them to market; but I have no doubt they find the traffic pays them. These *murwa*-sellers expected to get six rupees for their *murwa* at Choombi, and with this sum to be able to buy at Phari four maunds of salt, which they could sell in Darjeeling for Rs. 32, while the value of their *murwa* at Guntuck was only Rs. 4 - 8."[68]

Report on the Administration of Bengal for the year 1874-75 gives a list of items that were exported to or imported from Tibet by Sikkim. The items of export were mainly millet, rice, oranges and madder. The items of import were mainly ponies, blankets, salt, jewellery, yak's tails, China caps, musk, silk, tea and sheep. It is obvious from the above list that while Sikkim exported only a limited number of articles, she imported a good variety of goods. This suggests that Sikkim had an adverse balance of trade with Tibet.

In the above report it has also been stated that Tibet earned British rupees by selling their cattle, salt and other produce in Assam and Nepal. In the absence of any statistics on Sikkim-Tibet trade it cannot be ascertained definitely whether Tibet had a net earning from Sikkim. Most probably Sikkim also had an adverse balance of trade as Assam and Nepal had with Tibet.

The suggestion that Sikkim had an adverse balance of trade with Tibet is strengthened by the fact that during the entire period (excepting four years) for which data are available (from 1876-77 to 1922-23) Sikkim had a favourable balance of trade with Bengal, the only other country with which she had substantial trade. As British rupee was the international currency, the deficit in the Tibet trade was presumably bridged by the surplus in the Bengal trade.

A point to note in the description of Edgar is that the traders carried on their trade with Tibet and Bengal simultaneously. In fact, they were often traders between Tibet and Bengal — Sikkim being only the route. This also suggests that the two trades were complementary in nature — the deficit in one being filled up by the surplus in another.

Morris says that until 1918 most of the Lepchas in the Zongu area used to take forest dyes to Lachen in north Sikkim and then exchange them for Tibetan salt and wool. They kept a certain amount of this salt for their own use, but the bulk of it was taken to Darjeeling where they exchanged it for raw cotton which their women spun into cloth. This trade was, however, ultimately taken over by the moneylenders and traders from India who steadily wormed their way into Sikkim and ousted the local traders.

Morris also says that before the Indian money-lenders arrived, most of the Zongu people had a number of "ingzongs" which were some sort of blood-brothers. This fraternal relationship obviated the need for borrowing for trading purposes. Afterwards, with the presence of Indian money-lenders and the absence of trade among the local people, the institution lost its significance. Some people, however, had their ingzongs even in the 1930's but it was now only a means of cementing a close friendship.[70]

Although the Lepchas gave way to the Indian traders the Bhutias continued their trade in the traditional way. Some of the erstwhile Bhutia traders were, however, employed by their Indian counterparts as "carriers of goods" thereby practically being converted into wage-earners. As has already been stated, the Bhutias used to migrate to the Tibetan plateau during summer each year with their flocks of grazing animals, and in course of their journey to and from Tibet they carried on trade as a complementary profession. They carried manufactured articles from the plains of India to Tibet and during their return journey brought articles like salt, dried meat, wool, butter and other foodstuffs. In this trade ponies, and to some extent yaks, were used for transportation.[71]

But the Bhutia trade has stopped now. After the Sino-Indian border dispute in 1962 the Sikkim-Tibet border was sealed and the Bhutias have since been forced to seek alternative occupations.

Coming to trade between Sikkim and Bengal we see that prior to the arrival of the British it was quite negligible. The British were not, however, so much keen on developing trade with Sikkim as with Tibet, but in their attempt to foster the latter the former also developed.

In 1774 the Bogle Mission was sent to Tibet for investigating the prospect of an Anglo-Tibetan trade. In 1783 another mission under Turner was sent for similar purposes. In Bogle's report we find that the principal exports of Tibet to Bengal at that time were gold dust, musk and cow-tails, while the imports were broadcloth, otter skins, indigo, pearls, coral, amber, conch shells, spices, tobacco, sugar, Malva striped satins and a few white coarse cloths.[72] In Turner's report we find tincal as an additional export item. The additional import items were snuff boxes, smelling bottles, knives, scissors, spectacles, cloves, nutmegs, sandalwood, emeralds, sapphires, lapis lazuli, jet, cottons and leather.[73] *In those accounts Sikkim was deemed as part of Tibet* and as such the above descriptions may be taken as partially representative of Sikkim's trade with Bengal.

A land-mark in the development of trade between Sikkim and the British territories was the conclusion of the Anglo-Sikkimese treaty of 1861 whereby free trade was established between the two countries. The relevant portions of the treaty may be mentioned in this connection:

> *"The Government of Sikkim from this date abolishes all restrictions on travellers and monopolies in trade between the British territories and Sikkim. There shall henceforth be a free reciprocal intercourse, and full liberty of commerce between the subjects of both countries; it shall be lawful for British subjects to go into any part of Sikkim for the purpose of travel or trade, and the subjects of all countries shall be permitted to reside in and pass through Sikkim, and to expose their goods for sale at any place and in any manner that may best suit their purpose, without any interference whatever, except as is hereinafter provided." [Article 8]*
>
> *"No duties or fees of any sort shall be demanded by the Sikkim Government of any person or persons on account of goods exported into the British territories from Sikkim, or imported into Sikkim from the British territories." [Article 10]*

Detailed statistics on trade between Sikkim and Bengal are available for the period between 1876-77 to 1922-23 after which no such statistics were maintained. We may refer to the trade in some select years during this period. In the year 1876-77 the following were the main items of trade.

Sikkim's Trade with Bengal, 1876-77

Main Exports To Bengal	*Rs.*	*Main Imports From Bengal*	*Rs.*
1. Timber	7,08,708	1. Indigo	66,000
2. Cattle	19,710	2. Cattle	23,220
3. Miscellaneous Rain Crops	14,457	3. Brass & Copper	14,520

Source: Report on the Internal Trade of Bengal for the Year 1876-77, p. 270.

Coming to 1889-90 when the first Political Officer of Sikkim was appointed and the British hold in the country firmly established, we find a variety of items in the export-import list:

Sikkim's Trade with Bengal, 1889-90

Main Exports To Bengal	*Rs.*	*Main Imports From Bengal*	*Rs.*
1. Rain Crops	45,859	1. Cotton Piece Goods	33,775
2. Brass & Copper	14,500	2. Husked Rice	13,477
3. Gram & Pulse	13,417	3. Tobacco	7,271
4. Vegetable Oil	9,650	4. Intoxicating Drugs	6,480
5. Fruits & Vegetables	9,519	5. Provisions	6301
6. Silver	4,300	6. Cattle	5,194
7. Cattle	2,721	7. Salt	4,799
8. Hides of Cattle	2,509	8. Fruits & Vegetables.	2,888
9. Spices	2,489	9. Brass & Copper	2,470

Source: Report on Trade of Bengal with Nepal, Sikkim and Bhutan, 1889-90.

From the above lists it is clear that Sikkim's exports during the late 19th century were mainly the products of forestry, agriculture and minerals. On the other hand, she imported mainly industrial products like cotton piece-goods and agricultural products that could not be produced in Sikkim. Some items like brass and copper, fruits and vegetables, and cattle appeared in both the export and import sides of the trade.

But as the 20th century approached, some changes in the expert-import pattern were observable. These were mainly due to Tibet's trade with Bengal which passed through Sikkim. For example, brass and copper were initially used to be imported from Bengal (as in 1876-77) but later on they were exported to Bengal, although a small amount still continued to be imported (as in 1889-90). This change in trade pattern was not due to the discovery and exploration of these minerals in Sikkim, but to the fact that in the later years Sikkim began to import these minerals from Tibet and then export them to Bengal.

Similarly, in 1895-96 Sikkim exported yak tails worth Rs. 3,000s to Bengal. Most probably these also had been imported from Tibet which was famous for yak tails.[75] In fact, this situation prevailed even during the 1920's as the *Administration Report of the Sikkim State for 1922-23* says, *"the greater portion of Sikkim's exports to Bengal were really the 're-export' of livestock and raw wool imported from Tibet."*[76]

Another change in the trade pattern was that initially (as in 1889-90) Sikkim imported a large amount of foodgrains, especially husked rice, from Bengal. But in the early years of the 20th century there was a scarcity of foodgrains in Bengal which led to large-scale export of foodgrains from Sikkim.[77]

The development of Sikkim's trade with Bengal during the period of 47 years for which data are available can be seen from the following table:

Years	*Sikkim's Exports to Bengal Rs.*	*Sikkim's Imports from Bengal Rs.*	*Remarks*
1876-77	8,02,657	1,41,647	Probably includes Tibetan Trade (for the years 1876-77 to 1884-85)
1877-78	18,222	16,589	
1878-79	1,20,841	60,184	
1879-80	2,51,491	48,085	
1880-81	1,67,960	80,898	
1881-82	1,67,533	86,011	
1882-83	2,00,148	1,16,294	
1883-84	2,21,523	1,12,711	
1884-85	3,75,987	2,04,735	
1885-86	75,855	78,641	Deficit Balance
1886-87	52,497	40,071	
1887-88	1,74,835	76,035	
1888-89	1,24,636	75,723	
1889-90	1,17,847	1,10,070	
1890-91	1,50,580	1,23,226	
1891-92	2,20,157	1,26,989	
1892-93	2,43,591	1,80,919	
1893-94	2,83,111	2,07,068	
1894-95	4,18,879	3,06,006	
1895-96	4,66,555*	4,33,856	*Rs. 5,03,681 according to Report for 1897-98
1896-97	7,55,906	4,17,902	
1897-98	4,94,039	3,64,963	
1898-99	5,68,642	4,22,976	
1899-1900	5,69,623	3,86,988	
1900-01	4,21,579	2,55,546	

1901-02	5,06,386	3,19,707	
1902-03	3,43,396	2,73,716	
1903-04	3,09,872	3,10,770	Deficit Balance
1904-05	2,35,108	3,61,144	Deficit Balance
1905-06	4,07,725	4,74,691	Deficit Balance
1906-07	6,78,813	5,24,798	
1907-08	8,23,822	7,97,562	
1908-09	9,29,263	7,62,232	
1909-10	8,30,351	9,24,443	
1910-11	9,83,498	8,06,623	
1911-12	11,96,579	10,89,656	
1912-13	15,07,327	13,67,441	
1913-14	30,89,466	16,00,530	
1914-15	28,56,427	15,76,151	
1915-16	26,79,635	16,28,425	
1916-17	27,22,685	16,73,013	
1917-18	28,67,677	11,24,341	
1918-19	32,74,747	12,60,044	
1919-20	51,34,716	16,66,543	
1920-21	56,22,56	15,26,605	
1921-22	68,59,420	13,29,872	
1922-23	69,35,711	15,51,532	

Sources: 1. *Report on the Internal Trade of Bengal, 1876-77 and 1877-78* (for those years)

2. *Report on Trade of Bengal with Nepal, Sikkim and Bhutan: 1880-81 to 1912-13* (for the years 1878-79 to 1912-13).
3. *The Frontier Trade of Bengal? 1913-14 to 1920-21* (for those years)
4. *The Trade of Bengal with Nepal, Tibet, Sikkim and Bhutan in 1921-22* (for that year)
5. *Administration Report of the Sikkim State for 1922-23*, p. 17 (for that year).

Some sources say that the trade figures for the years 1876-77 to 1884-85 were related to Sikkim and Tibet combined, and those for 1885-86 and onwards were related to Sikkim proper.[78] We see from the above table that there was a sharp fall in exports from Rs. 3,75,987 in 1884-85 to Rs. 75,855 in 1885-86. During the corresponding years imports also fell from Rs, 2,04,735 to Rs, 78,641. Assuming the two years as normal, this fall is explained by the exclusion of Tibet trade in the figures for 1885-86.

From the above table we see that during the later years of the 19th century both exports to and imports from Bengal rose appreciably. But excepting 1885-86 there was always a surplus balance of trade for Sikkim. Taking 1885-86 as the base year, as the statistics of the earlier years probably included Tibetan trade, it is seen that by the end of the century Sikkim's exports increased 7.5 times and imports 5 times.

During the early 20th century also both exports and imports continued to increase. As before there was always (excepting 1903-04, 1904-05 and 1905-06) a surplus balance of trade and it went on increasing year after year. Thus in the recorded years of the 20th century exports rose 16 times while in the same period imports rose only 6 times. This means that as time passed on Sikkim earned more and more export surplus from her trade with Bengal. In fact, excepting 4 years in the whole period of 47 years there was a rising trend in export surplus. This corroborates our earlier hypothesis that Sikkim had a deficit balance of trade with Tibet which she paid up out of her earnings from Bengal.

As we have seen earlier, British power was attracted to Sikkim and established itself there to keep open the most direct trade route to Lhasa which led ultimately to Peking. The prime function of the British Political Officer, until the eclipse of British power in the Indian subcontinent, was to guard the trade officials at Yatung, Gyantse and Lhasa and keep communications alive.[79] The provision of free trade between Sikkim and the British territories in the treaty of 1861 had, in fact, been made in order to ensure free flow of trade between Tibet and the British territories.

After the departure of the British this ulterior motive was no longer there. The relation of free trade, however, still continued and it was later incorporated in the treaty of 1950 between Sikkim and India.[80] The motive was now solely the mutual benefit for the signatory countries. This had undoubtedly a great impact on the ushering in of the era of co-operation between the two countries and the initiation of development plans in Sikkim. The relevant portions of the new treaty may be cited as below:

"The Government of Sikkim agrees not to levy an import duty, transit duty or other import on goods brought into, or in transit through, Sikkim; and the Government of India agrees not to levy any import or other duty on goods of Sikkimese origin brought into India from Sikkim." [Article V]

(2) "Subject to such regulations as the Government of Sikkim may prescribe in consultation with the Government of India, Indian nationals shall have:-

(a) the right to carry on trade and commerce in Sikkim; and

(b) when established in any trade in Sikkim, the right to acquire, hold and dispose of any property, movable or immovable, for the purposes of their trade or residence in Sikkim.

(3) Subjects of Sikkim shall have the same right —

(a) to carry on trade and commerce in India, and to employment therein, and

(b) of acquiring, holding and disposing of property, movable and immovable, as Indian nationals." [Article VII]

As will be evident to anybody the provisions regarding trade between Sikkim and India were almost the same in both the treaties of 1861 and 1950. In 1970-71, the last year of the Third Plan of Sikkim Indo-Sikkim trade relation was practically the same as it had been 110 years ago — the volume of trade, of course, increased manifold by this time.

REFERENCES

1. See G. Gorer, *Himalayan Village: An Account of the Lepchas of Sikkim* (London: Michael Joseph, 1938); and C. Nakane, "A Plural Society in Sikkim: A Study of the Inter-Relations of Lepchas, Bhotias and Nepalis", *Caste and Kin in Nepal, India and Ceylon*, ed. C.V. Furer-Haimendorf (Bombay: Asia Publishing House, 1966).
2. D. Thorner and A. Thorner, *Land and Labour in India* (New Delhi: Asia Publishing House, 1962), pp. 11-12.
3. D. D. Kosambi,. *An Introduction to the Study of Indian History* (Bombay: Popular Book Depot, 1956), Ch. 7-10.
4. B. Sen, *The Evolution of Agrarian Relations in India* (New Delhi: Peoples' Publishing House, 1962), p. 150.

5. J. C. White, *Sikkim and Bhutan: Twenty Years on the North-East Frontier 1887-1908* (London: Edward Arnold, 1909), p. 26.
6. J. W. Edgar, *Report on a Visit to Sikkim and the Tibetan Frontier in October, November and December, 1873* (Calcutta: Bengal Secretariat Press, 1874), p. 62n.
7. A. G. Frank, *Capitalism and Under-development in Latin America* (New York: Monthly Review Publications).
8. See Kosambi.
9. C.B. Stocks, "Folk-lore and Customs of the Lap-chas of Sikkim", *Journal and Proceedings, Asiatic Society of Bengal*, New Series, 21, No. 4 (1925).
10. R. Choudhury, "Changing Pattern of NEFA Economy", *Amrita Bazar Patrika* (Calcutta), February 8, 1971, p. II.
11. T. Namgyal and J. Dolma. *History of Sikkim*, Trans., Lama Dawa Kazi Samdup, MSS, 1908, Part 4, p. 37.
12. P. M. Sweezy, *The Theory of Capitalist Development* (London: Dennis Dobson Ltd., 1946), p. 56.
13. P. M. Sweezy, et al., *The Transition from Feudalism to Capitalism* (Patna: Peoples' Publishing House, 1957), p. 33.
14. Correspondence No. 1783 p. dated Calcutta, the 23rd July, 1898 from the Chief Secretary to the Government of Bengal to the Commissioner of the Rajshahi Division.
15. Govt. of Sikkim, *Administration Report of the Sikkim State for 1913-14* (Calcutta: Bengal Govt. Press), p. 2. Hereafter referred to as *"Ad. Report for (Year)"*.
16. *Ad. Report for 1914-15*, p. 7.
17. *Ad. Report for 1916-17*, p. 2.
18. *Ad. Report for 1914-15*, p. 7.
19. *Ad. Report for 1913-14*, p. 2.
20. C. J. Morris, *Living with the Lepchus: A Book about the Sikkim Himalayas* (London: William Heineman, 1938), p. 279.
21. *Ibid.*, p. 281.
22. *Ibid.*, p. 282.
23. B.F. Hoselitz, "Entrepreneurial Element in Economic Development", *The Economic Weekly*, Annual Number, February, 1963, pp. 165-66.
24. J. A. Schumpeter, "The Creative Response in Economic History," *Journal of Economic History*, November, 1947, pp. 149-59.
25. H. C. Simons, *Economic Policy for a Free Society* (Chicago, 1948), p. 196.
26. *The Gazetteer of Sikkim*, (Calcutta: Bengal Secretariat Press, 1894), P. XV.
27. *Ibid*.
28. Gorer, pp. 70, 110.
29. R.K. Mookerji, "Indian Land System: Ancient, Mediaeval and Modern (with Special Reference to Bengal)," Govt, of Bengal.

Report of the Land Revenue Commission Bengal, Vol. 2 (Calcutta: Bengal Govt. Press, 1940), pp. 129-30.

30. *Ibid.*, p. 132.
31. P. Carrasco, *Land and Polity in Tibet* (Seattle: University of Washington Press, 1959), p. 56.
32. Gorer, pp. 105-6, 156.
33. Carrasco, p. 55.
34. *Ibid.*, p. 209.
35. H. Namgyal, "The Sikkimese Theory of Land-holding and the Darjeeling Grant", *Bulletin of Tibetology* (Gangtok), 3, No. 2 (July 21, 1966), 47.
36. A. Campbell, *Papers on the Sikkim Morung, Bengal Selection* No. 5 (Calcutta: Military Orphan Press, 1851), p. 4.
37. V. H. Coelho, *Sikkim and Bhutan* (New Delhi: Vikas Publications, 1971), pp. 16-18.
38. Mookerji, p. 207.
39. Campbell, pp. 9-10.
40. *Ibid.*, p. 11.
41. Edgar, p. 62.
42. *Imperial Gazetteer of India*. New Edition, Vol. 22 (London: Oxford University Press, 1908), p. 371.
43. *Ad. Report for 1931-32*, pp. 11-13.
44. *Ibid.*
45. Gorer, p. 109.
46. *Ibid.*
47. Carrasco, pp. 56, 210.
48. Govt. of Sikkim, *Sikkim: A Concise Chronicle* (Gangtok: Publicity Deptt), p. 28.
49. Nakane, p. 218n.
50. Stocks, p. 476.
51. Gorer, pp. 84-85.
52. Derived from Lepcha words.
53. Namgyal and Dolma, p. 36.
54. Nakane, p. 216n.
55. Gorer, p. 86.
56. *Ibid.*, pp. 92-3.
57. *Ibid.*, p. 86.
58. *Imperial Gazetteer of India*, p. 370.
59. Gorer, p. 91.
60. S. Bose, "The Bhot of Northern Sikkim", *Man in India*, 46, No. 2 (April-June, 1966), 168.
61. *Ibid.*
62. White, p. 294.
63. *Ibid.*
64. *Ibid.*, p. 297.

65. *Ad. Report for 1922-23*, p. 16.
66. Stocks, pp. 476-77.
67. Morris, p. 279.
68. Edgar, p. 32.
69. Govt. of Bengal, *Report on the Administration of Bengal for the Year 1974-75* (Calcutta: Bengal Secretariat Press) p. 27.
70. Morris, p. 278.
71. Bose, p. 169.
72. C. Markham, *Narratives of the Mission of George Bogle to Tibet; and of the Journey of Thomas Manning to Lhasa* (London: 1876), pp. 124-9.
73. S. Turner. *Account of an Embassy to the Court of the Tashoo Lama in Tibet* (London: W. Bulmer, 1800), pp. 381-4.
74. Coelho, pp. 105-9.
75. Govt. of India, *Report on Trade of Bengal with Nepal, Sikkim and Bhutan: 1889-90* (Calcutta: Bengal Secretariat Book Depot), p. 13.
76. *Ibid*, p. 17.
77. *Ad. Report for 1918-19*, p. 9.
78. See Govt. of Bengal, *Report on the Internal Trade of Bengal 1877-78*; and A. Lamb, *Britain and Chinese Central Asia*, pp. 342, 344.
79. Coelho, p. 50.
80. *Ibid.*, pp. 115-17.

3

Growth of Public Revenues and Expenditures in Sikkim

In the previous chapter we have traced out different aspects of the Sikkimese economy in a historical perspective. But we have not so far discussed the growth of public revenues and expenditures in Sikkim which may be called the precursor of the later development of the public sector. In today's Sikkimese economy the public sector, along with its plan undertakings, is no less important than the private sector and as such it will be pertinent for us to probe into the growth of this sector in a historical perspective.

In this chapter we shall be mainly concerned with the growth of public revenues and expenditures in the pre-plan period. Some discussion of the "internal" revenues and expenditures during the plan period will also be undertaken as these are complementary to the "plan" expenditures which are financed entirely by the Government of India. The latter will be taken up in the next and subsequent chapters.

No account is available on the revenue-expenditure process of the state during the Lepcha period. About the early part of the Bhutia period also we know very little. Our sources of information regarding the later Bhutia period indicate that the revenue - expenditure process at that time was mainly related to the maintenance of the King's establishment. Presumably, that was also the case in earlier periods.

In the following sections we shall first discuss the revenue system prior to 1889 when the British introduced the modern budgetary system in Sikkim for the first time. Then we shall take up the revenue system since 1889 where it will be seen that initially there was an admixture of the old and the new revenue systems but gradually the former gave place to the latter. Lastly, we shall discuss the question of public expenditures in Sikkim.

A. Revenue System Prior to 1889

An important aspect of the early Sikkimese revenue system was the absence of any type of "land revenue" even though in most primitive economies land is the primary source of maintenance and as such also the primary source of revenues. The reason for this unusual phenomenon should be sought in the land tenure system of the country which was a prototype of the Tibetan system and introduced in Sikkim by the Bhutia Kings. According to this land tenure system land did not belong to the subjects but to the King and, therefore, it could not be a basis of taxation. Let us now discuss the Tibetan revenue system and see how far it influenced the Sikkimese system.

As Pedro Carrasco says about the Tibetan revenue system:

> "The household of the land-holding peasant is then the basis of taxation; land is *not* taken into account at all, or only very roughly by classifying holdings into full, half or quarter allotments."[1]

There was, however, no clear-cut and precise system of revenue in Tibet. There were many taxes, some in money but mostly in kind or labour services, all of which were levied to meet specific needs of the state organization. There were thus duties levied in grain, butter, animals, transport, farm labour and so forth.

One great difficulty in reviewing the Tibetan revenue system is that taxes and services were usually named after the product or labour they provided, but the unit that was taxed and the rate of assessment were rarely stated in the sources. The lack of these informations may be due to the fact that in Tibet no theory of taxation developed, as is probably the case in most of the oriental economies, and taxation was mainly on an ad hoc basis, to meet some specific needs. The only consideration behind any taxation was the *ability* of the tax-payers to pay. In Tibet, therefore, each area paid in whatever goods or labour it could best provide and to facilitate this assessment was often made of the *village community* as a whole and the determination of the load on each peasant was left to the community.

During the recent period in Central Tibet three types of taxes were noticed: *(i)* "household" or head taxes, usually levied *in money, (ii)* "land" taxes *in grain* assessed in terms of the amount of seed sown in the land, and *(iii)* "extra" taxes *in kind and labour services,* levied on each household, apparently not at a fixed rate but varying according to the needs of the state.[2]

Strictly speaking, all these taxes were household taxes, because the "land" tax in grain was not actually a land tax but a tax on the ability of the houselhold measured on the basis of the harvested crops which again were measured in terms of the amount of seed sown; and in the case of other "extra" taxes, they were levied on an ad-hoc basis and were often imposed on animals as a substitute for the "land" tax where agriculture was meagre and pasture was the main source of livelihood.

The early Sikkimese revenue system introduced by the Bhutia Kings was practically a prototype of the above-mentioned Tibetan system, and that prevailed until the introduction of the modern budgetary system in the late nineteenth century. Campbell wrote in his account of 1849 that there was a "house or family tax, which takes the place of land-rent in Sikkim."[3]

Campbell, however, also refers to the existence of "land revenue" in the Sikkim Morung territory which was annexed by the British in 1850. The reason for the existence of such a revenue was perhaps that this region was in the plains of the Terai and contiguous with the British Indian and Nepalese territories where the custom of land revenue was long-established. About land revenue in the Sikkim Morung Campbell says in 1851:

> "The annual jumma is rupees 23,630 — 5 — 0 assessed on 549 jotes, under similar number of pottahs issued

> without any exception to the holders under the late Government. The collections are made by officers called Chouderies, eleven in number, who are remunerated by a commission of 8 to 45 per cent on their collections. These officers have always been employed in the Morung, and have had an hereditary tenure of office. They were Judicial as well as fiscal officers, but have no judicial functions now. They have no rights of property over the mouzahs in which they collect. They are all Jotedars, however, in their own districts, and all of them hold Jotes in other portions of the Morung, but without any privileges or exemptions."[4]

The annexation of the Sikkim Morung was a heavy blow to the royal exchequer of the country which is evident in a letter from the Maharaja of Sikkim to the British Viceroy and Governor-General of India dated 25th March, 1863:

> *"I am a poor Rajah, my maintenance depended solely on the Sikkim Morung, which Your Lordship is well aware of.*
>
> *In an evil hour ill-disposed and ignorant people, my servants, destroyed the long established friendship and alliance with the British Government, for which the Morung was confiscated and annexed to the British Territory. Hence I was reduced to poverty and distress, and my sorrows were frequently represented by Petitions to Government. It has been my good fortune last year that the British Government very favourably granted me a life pension of Rupees 6,000 per annum, which sum, I beg humbly to state, is too small for a Rajah, whatever may be his position. But yet I consider myself fortunate enough that I have obtained the favour of the British Government, which favour, I cherish my hope, will continue to be displayed to me. I am solely solicitous of the kind patronage, and am the humble and obedient servant of the British Government. Whatever may fall upon me, whether good or bad, I consider it right to represent to the British Government, and therefore I take the liberty to state as follows:-*
>
> *"Since the confiscation of the Sikkim Morung I have been reduced to great distress, and have contracted a debt of Rupees 35,000 for the maintenance of myself and family.*

> *It is beyond my means to repay this sum. As I have already stated I am a most humble and obedient servant of the British Government. My creditors having importuned me for the repayment of the debt, and finding it to be quite out of my power to do so, I anxiously and most submissively pray that the British Government will graciously be disposed towards me, and will cause my debt to be satisfied."*[5]

The British consented to the prayer of the Sikkim King, but the payment was made in instalments on the condition of the King's good conduct and co-operation in the construction of a road to the Tibeten border through Sikkim for the promotion of Indo-Tibetan trade.

From the above accounts we can guess the amount of total annual revenue of Sikkim at the time of annexation of the Sikkim Morung. Campbell points out that the annual revenue from the Sikkim Morung from the same area when annexed amounted to Rs. 23,904—6—9.[6] The annual revenue from the Sikkim Morung at that time was therefore, about Rs. 23,000. In his letter the Sikkim King says, "my maintenance depended solely on the Sikkim Morung" which means that more than 50% of the state revenue accrued from that area and if so, the total revenue of Sikkim in the mid-nineteenth century just before annexation of the Sikkim Morung was between Rs. 23,000 and Rs. 46,000, probably round-about Rs. 30,000.

Another source says that the aggregate revenue of the state in 1888 when the Morung was not within Sikkim, amounted to only Rs. 8,444 and the revenue for the same area in 1850 could not possibly be higher.[7] So in 1850 the aggregate revenue of Sikkim, including that of the Morung, was less than Rs. 23,000 + Rs. 8,444 = Rs. 31,444, i.e. round about Rs. 30,000.

After the annexation of the Sikkim Morung there was no more any trace of "land revenue" and the entire revenue system of Sikkim now looked liked the Tibetan system. As Edgar says:

> *"The land is not assessed, and pays no revenue. The assessment is on the revenue-payer personally, and I think that in theory he is supposed to be allowed the use of the*

Rajah's land in order that he may live and be able to render to the Rajah the services which he is bound to do as the Rajah's live chattel; and possibly if the system were carried to theoretical perfection, he would be bound to give over to the Rajah all the produce of the land — that is all the fruit of his labour beyond what might be actually necessary to support himself and his family. In practice the subject is only bound to give a certain portion of his labour, or of the fruit of his labour, to the State; and when he does not give actual service, the amount of his property is roughly assessed, and his contribution to the State fixed accordingly; but such assessment is made without the slightest reference to the amount of land occupied by the subject. The value of his wives and children, slaves, cattle, furniture, etc. are all taken into account but not the extent of his fields".[8]

Edgar says that this system was typical of a number of countries adjoining Sikkim. As he continues:

"I believe this to be the revenue system in all Indo-Chinese states. It is so in Munnipore, Bhootan, Thibet, Sikkim, and, I believe in Burmah. It was so in Cachar and Assam, and indeed the Assam land revenue system bears traces of it to this day. I have been told that in Nepal Sir Jung Bahadoor is trying hard to substitute for it a system based on some sort of ownership in and ability to pay according to the land actually held."[9]

About the mode and rate of taxation during the pre- 1889 period very little is known from the contemporary writers. Campbell wrote in 1852 that "the payments are in kind ... in quantities and proportions I could not determine, nor are they fixed I believe by any specific agreement."[10]

Campbell reports that herders of Lachen paid to the Sikkim King in terms of curds, ghee and kine. They also paid to Tibet in shingles, bamboos, dye stuffs and dairy products.[11] In the same report we find that the people in the Lachung valley paid in ponies, yaks, blankets and salt.[12]

Regarding labour services Campbell says that transportation service was used in moving both people and goods. The revenue in kind from the Lachen and Lachung valleys was taken to Chongtam (modern Chungthang) and thence to the court from village to village by the unpaid people.

When the Raja was at Chumbi goods were sent there. The people of Lachen and Lachung took them to Geree in Tibet. The people of Raja's estate in Dobta went there in two days and carried the goods in six more days to the King's palace at Chumbi.

Rennie says in 1866 that the Lepchas of the Darjeeling area paid in rice and pigs.[14]

Edgar says in 1874 that the herders on the Chola range between Sikkim and the Chumbi valley in Tibet paid revenue both to the Raja of Sikkim and to the Tibetan Government in butter and cheese.[15]

In Macaulay's description of 1885 we find that during the early trip of the King to Chumbi the peasants of the crown lands were required to help in carrying the King's effects, and the other peasantry throughout Sikkim had to pay Rs. 2 per house except in cases of great poverty. In the same description we find that the people of the Lachung valley of Sikkim paid taxes to the King in terms of one seer of butter for each milch yak and a seer of salt for each house.[16] Most of these taxes in kind were later on substituted by taxes in cash when the British took over the administration of the country.

B. Revenue System Since 1889

As has already been stated, remarkable changes were introduced by the British in the budgetary system of Sikkim in the year 1889 and thereafter. John Claude White, the first Political Officer in Sikkim described the state of affairs in Sikkim when he assumed office in that year in the following terms:

"Chaos reigned everywhere, there was no revenue system, the Maharaja taking what he required ... from the people, those nearest the capital having to contribute the largest share, while those more remote had the toll taken from them by the local officials in the name of the Raja, though little found its way to him; no courts of justice; no police; no public works, no education for the younger generation. The task before me was a difficult one, but very fascinating, the country was a new one and everything was in my hands."[17]

The British introduced many important changes in the

budgetary system of Sikkim such as preparation of the modern budget showing both the receipts and expenditures sides, introduction of new items of revenue and expenditure and, above all, monetisation of the budgetary system.

As regards monetisation of the budgetary system we may mention that before the British came to power practically all revenues were in kind as we have seen in the previous section. Some later reports also testify that:

"Formerly tax used to be collected in kind (a system known as Bisa Panja) but since very many years, practically from the time the State fell under British Superintendency in 1887, all taxes are collected in cash."[18]

The above statement, however, related to the official state budget of the country. But behind the official state budget there were still some taxes paid in kind by the loyal subjects to their King. This privilege was enjoyed by the monarch and overlooked by the British.

Waddel states in 1900 that some levies, specially labour services, were due to the King whenever the people were called upon to furnish them.[19] He also says that the assessment of taxes was based on "the number of persons and cattle and not on land."[20] Waddel, however, seems to have overlooked the fact that already by 1898 the Maharaja consented to commute forced labour as much as possible into money payment and take in kind only in special cases,[21] and that already by 1889 land revenue was well-established in Sikkim.[22]

We know from the accounts of Das in 1902 that the peasants of the Sikkim King's Debta estate in Tibet paid tribute to the King at the rate of half the produce of the fields.[23] The King's influence in Tibet, however, gradually declined and White mentions in 1909 that at that time transportation service was the only tax paid by the subjects of the King in Tibet.[24]

Again, we find in the writings of Bell in 1928 that the cultivator was taxed according to his "general prosperity".[25] Gorer says in 1938 that the people still had the obligation to supply boys to act as servants in the King's palace, and others to be trained as state carpenters.[26] These writings, however, do not depict the general picture of the country because by the end of the 19th century the modern budgetary system had already been well-established and there were only a few trivial remnants of the past.

The first budget of the state prepared by Mr. White in 1889 was a very simple and small one. The actuals for that year may be noted in this connection:

Actuals of Receipts and Expenditures of the Sikkim State in 1889

Sl. No.	*Receipts*	*Amount Rs.*	*Sl. No.*	*Expenditures*	*Amount Rs.*
1.	Land Revenue	13,585	1.	Public Works	9,742
2.	Forests	2,752	2.	Allowance to Raja	4,575
3.	Excise	1,448	3.	Agriculture	64
4.	Miscellaneous	2,551	4.	Miscellaneous	588
	Total	20,336		Total	14,969

It may be noted here that Mr. White completely abolished the earlier system of ad-hoc taxation and public expenditure and replaced it by the modern budgetary system. Land, for the first time, was taken as a source of revenue and, it fact, it accounted for the major portion of the state revenue. Another natural resource, forests, was also brought within the purview of taxation. Moreover, excise taxes were introduced to enhance the resources of the state exchequer. These sources of revenue were not, however, untapped previously, but that was not regular, systematic and categorical.

After the establishment of British control we find two systems of land revenue prevalent in Sikkim — the "kuth" and "pathi" systems. The kuth system was used in the case of permanent cultivation whereas the pathi system was used in the case of shifting cultivation.

As the Nepalis introduced permanent cultivation from Nepal through terracing the hill slopes and cultivating rice year after year in the same land, they introduced the corresponding revenue system of Nepal—the kuth system—in which one-fourth of the produce of land was to be given to the landlord as rent.

In the pathi system revenue was assessed on the amount of seed sown in a particular amount and quality of land. This was an indirect way of taxing the produce of land as the produce was related to the amount of seed sown. This sort of taxation can be found in the recent history of Tibet, but we do not find any reference to it in Sikkim before the Nepali settlement and it is difficult to say whether or how it came from Tibet. The pathi system was also sometimes used in permanent cultivation.

We find the first mention of these two systems in the writings of White. He says that so far as the kuth system was concerned, both the Paharias i.e. Nepalis and the Lepcha-Bhutias paid one-fourth of the produce of all irrigated paddy lands. But in the case of the pathi system the area of land on which could be sown one pathi (four seers*) of maize was to be charged at fourteen annas per pathi for the Paharias whereas for the Lepcha-Bhutias the corresponding rent was eight annas only.[27]

The Imperial Gazetteer of India (1908) also mentions the existence of this dual land revenue system. It says that in the case of terraced rice lands about 6 pathis and in the case of maize and other "dry" lands of fair quality about 4 pathis went to the acre. Accordingly, the rates of revenue in the pathi system during the late 19th and early 20th centuries were as follows:

Pathi System of Land Revenue, 1908

Category of Tenants	*Rent Per Acre*	
	Wet Land	*Dry Land*
1. Lepcha & Bhutia	Rs. 3	Rs. 2
2. Nepali	Rs. 5. 4 as	Rs. 3. 8 as

It is stated that by the beginning of the 20th century the kuth and pathi systems were adopted throughout the greater part of Sikkim. In the kuth system new lands paid no rent for the first three years in consideration of the labour involved in constructing the terraces. In the pathi system the sum payable by each ryot was fixed by an informal committee of headmen and villagers, presided over by the landlord and his agent.[28]

The rate of rent in the kuth system was later on changed. *The Administration Report of the Sikkim State for 1912-13* mentions that the rates of assessment of terraced rice fields were fixed

* A seer is slightly less than one kilogram.

at one-fifth of the produce for the Nepalis and one-eighth for the Lepcha-Bhutias in accordance with the report of a committee appointed to enquire into the matter.

Sidkeong Namgyal, the then Maharaja of Sikkim, however, was of the opinion that those rates bore somewhat heavily on the tenants and he proposed that the assessment should be on the pathi of seed sown and not on the produce. Accordingly at a meeting of the Council held on the 26th of January, 1915 the *kuth system was abolished* and new rates of assessment in the pathi system were agreed to in accordance with the fertility of land. These new rates of rent were the following:

Pathi System of Land Revenue: 1915

Category of Tenants	*Rent Per Pathi of Seed Sown* First Class Land	Second Class Land	Third Class Land
	Rs. - as - p	Rs. - as - p	Rs. - as - p
1. Lepcha & Bhutia	1 - 8 - 0	1 - 2 - 0	0 - 12 - 0
2. Nepali	2 - 0 - 0	1 - 8 - 0	1 - 0 - 0

The classification of land was on the basis of fertility. We find in a report: "By first class land is meant land on which in average years four manas or less of seed produce one Murhi of paddy, second class land on which in average years between four and six manas of seed produce a Murhi of paddy, and third class land on which more than six manas of seed are required to produce a Murhi of paddy."[29]

The classification of terraced rice lands was completed by the end of 1915 and in all 15,581 plots were classified covering approximately 10,000 acres and giving an average yield of 80,000 maunds of rice. It was stated that the price of rice in 1916 was about seven seers for the rupee, which would give the cultivator a cash return of about Rs. 46 per acre of paddy sown. Under the new rates of assessment the Nepali paid an average rate of about Rs. 8 per acre and the Lencha-Bhutia about Rs. 6 per acre as rent.[30]

The land rent was not directly collected by the State but through intermediaries. The position towards the beginning of the 20th century is well described in a letter written in December, 1900:

> "The lower part of the State is leased on long leases to Kazis and some Nepali ticcadars. The rents in this part of Sikkim are levied by the ticcadars and Kazis on the quantity of seed sown."[31]

In the upper part of the country the revenue system was, however, quite different. As stated in the above letter:

> "The upper portion of Sikkim consists of the reserve for Lepchas and one or two Bhutia villages in the Lachung and Lachen valleys.... In these valleys there is no assessment on the land, but the people pay by a consolidated tax, fixed annually by a panchyet of the villagers themselves, according to the number of cattle, ponies, yak and mules they own, and the quantity of land they cultivate. The demand is collected by a middleman who makes little or no profit out of it."[32]

The above revenue system which was a remnant of the old Bhutia system persisted for some years afterwards. *The Imperial Gazetteer of India* depicts a good picture of the revenue system in the two valleys in 1908. According to it in the Lachen and Lachung valleys the assessment on each village was communicated each year to the village headman who collected the rent but got nothing for his trouble except exemption from the obligation of carrying loads and from the labour tax. The headman called a committee of all the adult males over fifteen years of age at the end of the year and, in consultation with them, fixed what each individual should pay, having regard to his general condition, the number of his cows, mules, ponies and yaks, and the quantity of land in his possession. There were no fixed rates; but the assessment on animals appeared to work out at about 3 annas for each cow or yak, and 4 annas for each mule or pony. In the upper part of Lachung the villagers redistributed the fields among themselves every three years by lot, the richer people relinquishing the big plots and the poorer villagers the small ones. Grazing lands were divided in the same way, but not the house and homestead.

The Imperial Gazetteer of India mentions another remnant of the Tibetan heritage whereby the monasteries and some of the Kazis still maintained the old practice of assessing each household according to its circumstances. These cases were, however, quite few.[33]

By the year 1917 more land was brought under the lease system. At that time land was leased at rates varying from one anna to eight annas per acre for periods of 15 years to the Lepcha and Bhutia landlords and for 10 years to the Nepali landlords, the rates being liable to revision at the end of each period. A few of the older Lepcha and Bhutia landlords were granted leases for 30 years but the rent was liable to revision every 10 years. The assessed rent for the whole state in 1916-17 amounted to Rs. 83,527. In addition to this a special rent of Rs. 5 per maund was charged on the produce of cardamoms, the collection of which was farmed out and yielded Rs. 30,000. The total rent of the state in that year was, therefore, Rs. 1,13,527.[34]

The lease system was further strengthened with the introduction of elakas in 1925. By the beginning of 1930's it became the only system of rent collection in Sikkim. As has been stated in some contemporary reports:

"... land revenue tax is raised from the raiyots through middlemen known as Elakhadars. Every inch of the country is parcelled into various Elakhas, both big and small, which are leased to influential people. These Elakhadars or lessees pay to the Sirkar a fixed sum calculated at a rate per acre which varies according to the conditions of the Elakha leased. They are authorised by virtue of the terms of the lease (which are identical) to realise land revenue tax from the raiyots of the Elakha on a fixed and certain assessment, the expenses of realising are incurred by the lessees themselves."[35]

The lessee system was abolished in 1948 and the people were given the privilege of paying taxes direct to the Government. In 1951 the former land-holding unit of an elaka was substituted by a local unit called "block" which comprised one large hamlet, or two or more small hamlets with one headman called "Mandal".[36]

After discussing the land revenue system it will be pertinent to discuss other major sources of revenue taken resort to during the British period. One such source was excise. In the actuals of the first budget of Mr. White it held the third position, after forests, and was about 50% of the forest revenue and 10% of the land revenue. The proportion of excise increased in later years and by 1900 it became about equal to the forest revenue and 20% of the land revenue. In subsequent years it surpassed forest revenue and secured the second position among the revenue-earning sources of the State, next only to land revenue. In some years the revenue out of excise was more than 90% of land revenue and this indicates the rising importance of excise in the budgetary system of Sikkim.

The scope of excise gradually increased with the passage of time. In 1900 each household that brewed rice beer or pachwai paid a tax of Rs. 2, and for this they could brew for sale as well as for home consumption.[37]

The Imperial Gazetteer of India said in 1908 that the excise revenue was mainly derived from the fees charged for licences to brew rice-beer for home consumption, and from the fees charged for the manufacture and sale of country spirits.[38] By that year excise revenue had risen to about 60% of the land revenue as revealed by the statistics given in the *Gazetteer.*

In subsequent years the number of excisable articles was increased to include the following:

(i) Locally manufactured liquor, extracted from "mohuwa" flower, "goor" and grains;
(ii) Fermented pachwai made from "kodo" (millet);
(iii) Ganja;
(iv) Opium; and
(v) Imported wine and beer.[39]

Excise is still a major source of revenue and in the budget of 1970-71 the total excise revenue (general and *apkari*) was estimated as Rs. 95 lakhs. In fact, it was the largest source of revenue in that budget proposing total revenues of Rs. 2,39,35,300 excluding loans and advances.[40]

Apart from land revenue and excise the other important source of revenue was forests. Forests were also one of the earliest sources of revenue and promised a lot of revenue if proper arrangements were made. The British accordingly tried hard to tap the forest resources through various means. As pointed out by Mr. Maridin, the then Commissioner of the Rajshahi Division in 1900:

"The forests seem to afford the best chance for developing the State revenues. Besides the large forests on the lower ranges, which are already worked to some extent, there are very fine fir forests above the lower temperature zone at about 8,000 feet where, in the Lachung Valley, I saw trees of 200 feet in height and 16 to 20 feet in girth. All this magnificent timber is wasted at present for want of means to get it away. I am suggesting to Mr. White whether it would not be possible to utilise the Lachung and Lachen rivers to float logs down by the Tista to Sevoke. A system of wire ropeways also seems feasible. Apart from these fir forests, however, some development may be expected from the lower forests, and as you are aware Mr. White has this year obtained a contract with the Northern Bengal State Railway of Rs. 20,000 for the supply of sleepers.... Thus, while it is possible that the revenues of the State may increase, the chief expansion to be expected is from the forest which it will require a certain outlay to open out."[41]

In another letter Mr. Maridin says: "It may therefore be anticipated, with a fair amount of certainty, that, within the next quarter of a century, a very much larger area of the Sikkim forests will have become marketable."[42]

But the British could not undertake all the proposed measures to tap forest resources and as such the increase in forest revenue was not as spectacular as had been expected. Moreover, revenues from other sources also increased at a rapid pace and forestry no longer afforded "the best chance for developing the State revenues." Still, no doubt, the revenue out of forests increased substantially in subsequent years.

By the year 1910-11 the demarcation of the forest areas, excluding the upper forests, was completed and the survey of the same was nearly finished. The area of the sal forests at that time was 20 square miles. To facilitate the work of supervision, the forests with the exception of the Gangtok Reserve which was treated as a special area, had been divided into two ranges, viz., *(i)* Eastern Range, and *(ii)* Western Range, each in charge of a Forester, with the headquarters at Gangtok and Namchi respectively.

The Government also directed the landlords to close half their forest areas to grazing for five years and the other half for the next five years, and so on. Nearly all the landlords received half the royalty on timber sold from their forests and three-fourths of the grazing fees, the State retaining only one-fourth of the latter as supervision charges.[43] This system of revenue collection persisted in later years of the British period with only a few minor modifications.

The other major sources of revenue may be mentioned now. These were: *(i)* household tax or labour tax, *(ii)* assessed tax or income tax, *(iii)* revenue from public works, and *(iv)* interest from Government loans. The household tax was nothing but the old labour tax (paid in kind) converted into a monetary tax imposed on each household. This tax was, however, abolished in 1948 by Sir Tashi Namgyal. The income tax or assessed tax was not originally incorporated in the budget by the British, but subsequently it became a major source of revenue. In 1922-23 this tax was levied at the rate of 1% on the total value of sales of all traders and 5% on the actual profit derived by them on money lent. At that time there were 142 shops in Sikkim and the revenue derived from this source was only Rs. 2,715.[44] After 10 years this head of revenue yielded Rs. 31,300 and in 1960-61 it yielded an amount of Rs. 4,70,000.[45] Public works and interest from government loans also contributed a lot in the collection of revenues.

Our discussion of the revenue system of Sikkim will remain incomplete if we do not mention two major sources of revenue introduced in recent times. One such source is the State's transport department, viz., Sikkim Nationalised Transport which has been contributing the largest share of the country's internal revenues for the last few years. In 1960-61, for example, it contributed Rs. 10.3 lakhs as against the total revenue of the State amounting to Rs. 41.3 lakhs. In the budget of 1970-71 its contribution was estimated at Rs. 77,92,000 in a budget having total revenue heads of Rs. 2,39,35,700. All this indicates the increasing importance of Sikkim Nationalised Transport as a revenue-earning source.[46]

Another major reason for the rapid growth of the Sikkimese revenues in recent years is the fact that since 1968 the Government of India has been refunding annually the excise and other duties on the goods of Indian origin imported into Sikkim that the Sikkimese people had paid when purchasing them. According to the Treaty of 1950 no duty of any kind should be imposed on the goods that pass from one country to another. Therefore, Sikkim has a claim to the Government of India to the amount of the duties already paid in importing Indian goods. Every three years there is an approximate valuation of goods that come to Sikkim and the amount of duties on those goods is thereby ascertained and paid in instalments during the next three years. As Sikkim's exports to India is quite negligible, refund is always made to her by the Government of India. The annual refund to Sikkim by the end of 1970-71 was more than Rs. 1 crore.[47]

In the absence of rigid checkposts, strict administrative machinery and accounting of exports and imports the more natural procedure of exempting the traders from the payment of any duty on goods that are exported to Sikkim or vice versa is not followed. Perhaps the paraphernalia for the maintenance of the above procedure are too costly.

C. Public Expenditures in Sikkim

To examine the growth of public expenditures in a country like Sikkim is very difficult due to the paucity of appropriate data, particularly for the earlier periods. Some information is available regarding the process of revenue collection during the Bhutia period but practically nothing is obtainable as regards the expenditure processes during that time. This is quite natural because in a country where law and order prevails due to the existence of a strong monarchy, there must be some rules and regulations for the collection of revenues but the monarch does not generally think it necessary to control his own expenditures by any such rule or regulation. Moreover, the bulk of the revenues in such a situation is spent for the maintenance of the King and his establishment, often without any recording.

We see that even in 1888, a year before the taking over of administration by the Political Officer, the major portion of revenues collected was used for the maintenance of the King and his family. In that year the aggregate revenues of the state were Rs. 8,444 out of which an amount of Rs. 6,000 was paid to the Maharaja of Sikkim as his allowance.[48] Obviously, the remaining scanty amount of Rs. 2,444 was appropriated to meet the expenses of administration and nothing was left for any developmental work.

Apart from this allowance to the King out of internal revenues the Sikkim King also received an allowance from the British Government. Initially, since 1841 the British paid Rs. 3,000 to the King which was later increased to Rs. 6,000 and ultimately to Rs. 12,000 annually.[49] This payment was in the nature of a gesture of goodwill to the Sikkim King who in 1835 had made over the hill of Darjeeling to the East India Company for the purpose of enabling the servants of the British Government, suffering from sickness, to avail themselves of the advantages of the hill.[50] In the early budgets this amount was not shown but in later budgets it was shown as "Treaty Payment" on the revenue side.

After the conclusion of the 1950 treaty between Sikkim and India this allowance was abolished but the Government of India agreed to pay the Government of Sikkim a sum of rupees three lakhs every year out of friendship and goodwill. Article X of the Treaty says that this payment is made "having in mind the friendly relations already existing between India and Sikkim and now further strengthened by this Treaty, and being desirous of assisting in the development and good administration of Sikkim."[51]

The new payment is made in the month of August every year and is shown in the revenue side of the budget as "Government of India Grants" or "Treaty Payment". Though not mentioned as such this payment may be regarded as the continuation of the old practice of paying allowance to the King but the King has now forfeited his formal claim to it.

The King's expenses, however, have never been restricted to his allowance—the latter generally being only a small fraction of the former. The brunt of the burden of royal expenses was, thus, borne by the people through taxes. On the expenditure side of the budget royal expenses appeared under the head of Allowance to Raja, Domestic Charges or Civil List. Some heads of expenditures such as palace establishment, police or administration were also in the nature of royal expenditures, partly or wholly, but they were shown separately in the budget. In recent times a para-military force known as "Sikkim Guard" has been created for the protection of the King and his palace, and a substantial amount is spent on that account.

Another important head of expenditure in the Sikkimese

budget is public works. Since the establishment of British control over Sikkim this has been a major cause of public expenditures. In fact, public works accounted for the largest share of expenditures in all the budgets of the select years, except 1890, as shown in the Appendix. As the British were very much keen to develop Indo-Tibetan trade through the opening of a good transportation system in the trans-Himalayan region they incurred a huge amount of expenditures and this was provided for in the Sikkimese budget. Moreover, for the smooth running of the economic life also public works were indispensable. As has been pointed out:

"The provision of public works and public buildings consumes the bulk of the revenues. In a hilly country where rainfall is so heavy (about one hundred and forty inches on the average annually) it is indeed no small task to keep pathways open to traffic in all weathers and seasons."[52]

Coming to recent years we find some changes in the pattern of public expenditure in Sikkim. The budget of 1970-71 may be refered to in this connection.[53] There the largest allocation was made for Sikkim Nationalised Transport as it contributed also the largest share of state revenues. Civil List was no longer in the second position as in most of the earlier years. The budget provision for Palace Establishment was for the first time higher than that for civil list.

Though Civil List was no longer in the second position the overall monarchical paraphernalia still accounted for the second largest allocation of expenditure. Thus we see in the 1970-71 budget provisions of Rs. 9,65,000 for Civil List, Rs. 18,44,900 for Palace Establishment and Rs. 15,08,500 for Sikkim Guard — in all Rs. 43,18,400. Next came public works with the allocation of Rs. 25,73,500. The reason why the position of public works was lowered in the 1970-71 budget is perhaps the heavy investment in Sikkim Nationalised Transport. This speaks of the increasing commercial-mindedness on the part of the Government of Sikkim. But at the same time the huge expenditure on monarchical paraphernalia indicates a different attitude.

So far we have discussed the most important heads of expenditure in the Sikkimese budget. Next to these comes a host of other expenditures that are usual for the normal functioning of the state and its economy. These are general administration, police, medical and sanitation, education and the like. The classification of these heads of expenditure has not always been uniform, neither has their order of magnitude been the same over the period under study.

But the overall allocation on these heads was quite substantial because of the fact that no private enterprise was forthcoming in those fields. These expenditures were essential from the point of view of social welfare. Thus the *Administration Report of the Sikkim State for 1932-33 & 1933-34* says: "Besides public works, education, medical relief, law and order are allotted a fair share of the public funds."[54] This statement was true for the subsequent years as well.

* * *

The growth of public revenues and expenditures in Sikkim during the period may be illustrated with some select figures of actuals at the beginning of each decade since 1890. These are given in the Appendix. The figures for 1900-01 are in greater detail but those for other years relate only to the major heads. So far as 1940-41 and 1950-51 are concerned, only the figures of total revenues and expenditures could be collected from the Finance Department of the Government of Sikkim and no further detail was available. Again, only the budgetary figures for 1970-71 were available.

What impresses one who probes into the growth of public revenues and expenditures in Sikkim during the last 80 years is the tremendous increase in both public revenues and expenditures. Public revenues in 1970-71 (budget) were more than 1,000 times and public expenditures more than 1,500 times the corresponding figures in 1890 as is evident from the following table:

Growth of Public Revenues and Expenditures in Sikkim

Year	*Total Receipts (Rs)*	*Per Cent of Rise*	*Total Expenditures (Rs.)*	*Per Cent of Rise*
1890	24,686	-	16,652	-
1900-01	61,899	151	1,07,049	543
1910-11	1,91,497	209	1,96,445	84
1920-21	5,15,980	169	4,84,528	147

1930-31	6,26,067	21	6,30,481	30
1940-41	6,34,800	1	6,53,800	4
1950-51	23,41,100	269	20,78,000	218
1960-61	41,30,000	76	41,10,00	98
1970-71	2,66,10,800 (Budget)	544	2,66,63,000 (Budget)	549

Source: Appendix to Ch. 3.

From the above table we find that the revenues of Sikkim rose very rapidly during. the late 19th century and the first part of the 20th century. The receipts of the state more than doubled in the 10 years between 1890 and 1900-01, more than trebled between 1900-01 and 1910-11, and again more than doubled during the next decade, i.e. between 1910-11 and 1920-21. The receipts of the state, however, did not increase so rapidly in the following two decades. The increase between 1920-21 and 1930-31 was only 21 per cent and that between 1930-31 and 1940-41 was only 1 per cent. One reason for such a low increase in revenues at that time was perhaps the impact of the worldwide depression in the thirties.

In the next 10 years again there was a spurt in the expansion of revenue receipts — in 1950-51 the total receipts more than trebled over the 1940-41 figures. The next 10 years witnessed a moderate increase of 76 per cent but in the last decade under study there was a record jump in revenue receipts.

Coming to the expenditure side we see that here the increases were *pari passu* with those in the revenues. Both the revenues and the expenditures moved in the same direction. There was, of course, some discrepancy between the rate of increase in revenues and that in expenditures. This was due to the fact that sometimes the entire amount of current receipts could not be spent due to some unavoidable circumstances which led to a surplus opening balance in the subsequent year when expenditures naturally tended to exceed current revenues. If, however, we relate expenditures not to current revenues but to gross revenues including opening balance then it would appear that expenditures generally tended to equal gross revenues over a long period of time. The excessive increase in expenditures in 1900-01, for example, was due to the fact that in the preceding year there was a surplus of revenues over expenditures to the extent of nearly Rs. 34,700 and this amount was spent in 1900-01.[55]

As revealed in the above table, the growth of public revenues and expenditures in Sikkim has not been steady all through the period. We find that during the early decades from 1890 to 1920-21 there was a spurt in the rise of public revenues and expenditures but in the subsequent decades (except 1940-41 to 1950-51) the rise was quite dampened. In the last decade again we find a spurt — in fact, the largest one in the recorded period.

While no satisfactory answer is available to this type of fluctuations in the rise of public revenues and expenditures in Sikkim the early spurt was perhaps associated with the British initiative in the modernisation of the economy. The British opened the country to the outside world by means of providing communication and other facilities which in turn activated the economic system and increased public revenues and expenditures. They also did a great deal to tap various natural resources like forestry which were hitherto untapped or partially tapped. Simultaneously, new sources of revenue like excise were introduced. But during the later years the British became disinterested in Indo-Tibetan trade which also resulted in their lack of interest in the development of this tiny protectorate. At the same time the scope of further increasing the budgetary resources became more and more limited. The sharp rise in public revenues and expenditures during the last decade may be explained by the fact that planned economic development of the country during the period created new sources of revenue and new outlets for expenditures.

APPENDIX TO CHAPTER III.

A. Receipts of the Sikkim State.

I. Actuals of Receipts of the Sikkim State in 1890.

Major Head	*Amount (Rs.)*
1. Land Revenue	14,122
2. Forests	5,281
3. Excise	3,331
4. Miscellaneous	1,952
Total	24,686

Source: Letter No. 146 p. - D. from C. W. Bolton, Esq., Officiating Chief Secretary to the Government of Bengal, bo the Secretary to the Government of India, Foreign Department, Darjeeling, Sept. 4, 1896.

II. Actuals of Receipts of the Sikkim State in 1900-01.

Major Head	*Amount (Rs.-as.-p.)*
A. Land Revenue	
1. Land	45,115 -11 -6
2. Labour	5,605 -8-0
B. Excise	
1. Opium	10 -0 -0
2. Spirits and Marwa	9,283 -0 -0
C. Forests	
1. Sale of Sal Sleepers	8,548 -1 -0
2. Sale of tea box planking including royalty on timber	2,590 -15 -3
D. Agriculture	
1. Cardamom	5,129 -3 -6
2. Sheep	323 -0 -0
3. Fruit Gardens	102 -0 -0
E. Recovery of Debts	
1. Principal	2,590 -11 -6
2. Interests	119 -8 -0
F. Law and Justice	
1. Fines	320 -10 -3
2. Fees	271 -11 -0
G. Miscellaneous Receipts	
1. Dak bungalow fees	12 -0 -0
2. Ferries	91 -4 -0
3. Gun licenses	471 -0 -0
4. Sale of ammunition	369 -13 -3
5. House rents	420 -0 -0
6. Bazar	1,245 -0 -0
7. Grazing	597 -3 -0
8. Interest on bank deposits and Govt. securities,	63 -0 -1

9. Sale of rubber	1,095 -14 -6
10. Miscellaneous advances	1,201 -3 -0
11. Deposits	2,092 -2 -10
12. Miscellaneous	84 -8 -2
Total	61,898 -9 -7

Source: Govt. of Bengal, Proceedings of the Hon'ble The Lieutenant-Governor of Bengal during April, 1902. Political Department, (Calcutta, Bengal Secretariat Press), p. 210.

III. Actuals of Receipts of the Sikkim State in 1910-11

Major Head	*Amount (Rs.-as.-p.)*
1. Land Revenue	65,858-15-9
2. Excise Revenue	43,551-7-6
3. Forests	4,519-11-3
4. Agriculture	17,529-15-9
5. Law and Justice	6,588-10-3
6. Public Works	5,221-8-2
7. Miscellaneous	25,294-3-9
8. Debts	22,832-1-9
Total	91,496-10-2

Source: *Ad. Report for 1910-11,* pp. 19-21.

IV. Actuals of Receipts of the Slkklm State in 1920-21

Major Head	*Amount (Rs.)*
1. Land Revenue	1,13,452
2. Household Tax	24,009
3. Excise Revenue	95,084
4. Stamps	2,096
5. Assessed Taxes	191
6. Forest Revenue	28,189
7. Treaty Payment	12,000
8. Law and Justice	4,309
9. Police	785
10. Jail	251
11. Public Works	13,059
12. Medical and Sanitation	311
13. Printing and Stationary	939
14. Agriculture and Industries	8,478

15. Interest	29,059
16. Miscellaneous	1,596
17. Loans and Advances	1,81,272
Total:	5,15,930

Source: *Ad. Report for 1922-23*, p. 58.

V. Actuals of Receipts of the Sikkim State in 1930-31

Major Head	*Amount (Rs.)*
1. Land Revenue	1,72,222
2. Household Tax	55,552
3. Excise Revenue	1,09,921
4. Mines and Minerals	72
5. Stamps	9,162
6. Assessed Taxes	4,610
7. Forest Revenue	34,989
8. Treaty Payment	12,000
9. Law and Justice	7,551
10. Education	803
11. Police	1,054
12. Jail	553
13. Public works	31,435
14. Medical and Sanitation	506
15. Printing and Stationary	2,090
16. Agriculture and Industries	2,016
17. Interest	52,565
18. Miscellaneous	5,272
19. Loans and Advances	1,23,694
Total:	6,26,067

Source: *Ad. Report for 1932-33 & 1933-34*, pp. 9, 92.

VI. Actuals of Receipts of the Sikkim State In 1940-41.

Total ... ... Rs. 6,34,800

Source: Finance Department, Govt, of Sikkim, Details not available.

VII. Actuals of Receipts of the Sikkim State in 1950-51.

Total ... ... Rs. 23,41,100

Source: *Ibid.*

VIII. Actuals of Receipts of the Sikkim State in 1960-61

	Major Head	*Amount (Rs. in lakh)*
1.	Land Revenue	6.7
2.	Local Rate	0.1
3.	Excise	4.1
4.	Stamp	0.4
5.	Assessed Taxes	4.7
6.	Bazar Revenue	1.4
7.	Law and Justice	0.2
8.	Education	0.1
9.	Police	0.2
10.	Motor Vehicles	0.5
11.	Printing and Stationary	0.3
12.	Forest Revenue	3.3
13.	Public Works	0.9
14.	Medical and Sanitation	0.1
15.	Veterinary Receipts	0.5
16.	Agriculture and Industries	1.2
17.	Miscellaneous	2.9
18.	Sikkim Nationalised Transport	10.3
19.	Govt. of India Grants	3.0
20.	Interest	0.3
	Totals	41.3

Source: Govt. of India, Second Five Year Plan of Sikkim Report of the Technical Team (New Delhi: Planning Commission, 1961), p. 25.

IX. Budget Estimates of Receipts of the Sikkim State in 1970-71

	Major Head	*Amount (Rs.)*
1.	Land Revenue	6,91,900
2.	Local Rate	20,200
3.	(a) Palace Establishment	26,000
	(b) Sikkim Guard	--
4.	Mines & Minerals	500
5.	Stamps	1,01,500
6.	Assessed Taxes	17,65,000
7.	Treaty Payment	3,00,000
8.	Law & Justice	51,800
9.	Police	17,900
10.	Jail	500
11.	General Excise	75,00,000
12.	Food Supply	25,000

13.	Trade, Commerce & Industry	—
14.	P. T. Institute	2,10,000
15.	Interest & Dividend	3,71,600
16.	Miscellaneous	25,200
17.	S. N. T.	77,92,000
18.	Government Transport	3,60,000
19.	Excise (*Apkari*)	20,00,000
20.	Education	31,500
21.	Motor Vehicle	1,60,000
22.	Animal Husbandry	2,03,000
23.	Electricity	4,25,000
24.	P. W. D.	1,31,200
25.	Medical & Sanitation	8,500
26.	Printing & Stationary	2,25,000
27.	Agriculture	87,300
28.	Publicity	10,000
29.	Bazar	6,53,000
30.	Forest Revenue	7,41,700
	Total Revenue Heads	2,39,35,300
	Loans & Advances	26,75,500
	Total Receipts	2,66,10,800
	Opening Balance (+)	2,29,900
	Grand Total	2,68,40,700

Source: Finance Department, Govt. of Sikkim.

B. Expanditures of the Sikkim State

I. Actuals of Expenditures of the Sikkim State in 1890

	Major Head	*Amount (Rs.)*
1.	Public Works	1,974
2.	Survey	1,409
3.	Allowance to Raja	7,375
4.	Agriculture	774
5.	Miscellaneous	5,120
	Total:	16,652

Source: Letter No. 146. p. D. from C. W. Bolton, Esq., Officiating Chief Secretary to the Govt, of West Bengal, to the Secretary to the Govt. of India. Foreign Department. Darjeeling. Sept. 4, 1896.

II. Actuals of Expenditures of the Sikkim State in 1900-01

	Major Head	*Amount (Rs.-as.-p.)*
A.	Kazi's Commission	
1.	Fees to Kazis	7,875 - 0 - 0
2.	Subsidy to monasteries	1,530 - 0 - 0
B.	Administrative charges	
1.	Office Establishment	
	(a) Salaries	8,082 - 1 - 9
	(b) Travelling Allowance	318 - 4 - 0
	(c) Contingencies	1,005 - 4 -10
2.	Police	
	(a) Establishment	1,921 - 2 - 0
	(b) Contingencies	468 -14 - 0
C.	Agriculture	
1.	Sheep	339 - 4 - 9
2.	Mule and poultry breeding including cattle	767 - 6 - 6
3.	Lachung fruit garden	324 - 6 - 3
4.	Singtam fruit garden	360 -10 - 0
5.	Gangtok vegetable garden	434 - 7 - 0
6.	Rubber and other trees, nurseries	68 - 2 - 9
D.	Loans (Principal)	5,344 -14 - 6
E.	Forests	
1.	Cutting timber	16,697 - 6 - 9
2.	Supervision	77 - 11 - 0
3.	Royalty on timber	114 - 7 - 0
F.	Public Instruction (Gangtok Boarding School)	2,199 - 3 - 0
G.	Survey	607 - 4 - 0
E.	Medical	
1.	Dispensaries	552 - 0 - 0
2.	Vaccination	392 - 2 - 0
3.	Contingencies	87 - 4 - 0
I.	Domestic	
1.	Maharaja's Allowance	12,000 - 0 - 0
2.	Allowance to Maharaja's Family	2,250 - 0 - 0
3.	Tuition of Second Son	2,177 - 3 - 6
4.	Contingencies	1,909 - 13 - 0
J.	Public Works	
1.	Roads, original works	6,210 - 3 - 7
2.	Do., repairs	5,062 - 2 - 8
3.	Buildings, original works	12,762 - 10 - 10
4.	Buildings, repairs	1,265 - 9 - 11
5.	Miscellaneous public improvement	744 - 15 - 6
6.	Pioneers	35 - 2 - 0

7.	Permanent Works Establishment	1,239 - 5 - 6
8.	Stock	16 - 0 - 0
K.	Dak bungalows	
1.	Pay of chaukidars	504 - 0 - 0
2.	Furniture and Crockery	101 - 11 - 6
L.	Miscellaneous	
1.	Post Office at Pakhyong	219 - 0 - 0
2.	Spinning looms	115 - 4 - 0
3.	Bazars	653 - 0 - 0
4.	Purchase of ammunition	166 - 12 - 0
5.	Census	139 - 9 - 3
6.	Deposits	774 - 12 - 3
7.	Miscellaneous	713 - 6 - 10
M.	Passed to Reserve Fund	700 - 0 - 0
N.	Indian tours of Kumar	7,720 - 12 - 0
	Total	1,07,048 - 10 - 9

Sources: Govt. of Bengal, Proceedings of the Hon'ble The Lieutenant, Governor of Bengal during April. 1902, Political Department (Calcutta: Bengal Secretariat Press), p. 210.

III. Actuals of Expenditures of the Sikkim State in 1910-11

	Major Head	*Amount (Rs.-as.-p.)*
1.	Kazi's Commission	5,915 - 0 - 0
2.	Subsidy to Monasteries and Supervising Establishment	5,870 - 0 - 0
3.	Administration	28,442 - 9 - 2
4.	Agriculture	1,371 - 3 - 9
5.	Forests	7,353 - 3 - 0
6.	Public Instruction	7,618 - 4 -10
7.	Survey	668 - 8 - 0
8.	Medical	8,655 - 9 - 0
9.	Domestic Charges	39,406 -15 - 7
10.	Judicial	2,184 - 0 - 0
11.	Public Works	40,910 -10 - 5
12.	Miscellaneous	17,880 - 1 - 1
13.	Debts	26,171 - 2 - 1
	Total:	1,96,445 - 2 - 11

Source: *Ad. Report for 1910-11*, pp. 19-22.

IV. Actuals of Expenditures of the Sikkim State in 1920-21

	Major Head	*Amount (Rs.)*
1.	Revenue Refund	13,170
2.	Civil List	37,743
3.	Palace Establishment	12,480
4.	Revenue & General	17,076
5.	Forest	13,626
6.	Excise	2,020
7.	Police	11,641
8.	Law and Justice	6,665
9.	Jail	2,624
10.	Monasteries	5,409
11.	Printing & Stationery	1,992
12.	Education	7,432
13.	Medical & Sanitation	16,726
14.	Public Works	74,909
15.	Agriculture & Industries	16,108
16.	Accounts	9,046
17.	Miscellaneous	4,210
18.	Loans & Advances	2,31,651
	Total:	4,84,528

Source: *Ad. Report for 1922-23*, p. 59.

V. Actuals of Expenditures of the Sikkim State in 1930-31

	Major Head	*Amount (Rs.)*
1.	Revenue Refund	14,776
2.	Civil List	67,700
3.	Palace Establishment	11,333
4.	Revenue & General	27,122
5.	Forest	14,149
6.	Excise	2,110
7.	Police	24,048
8.	Law and Justice	17,538
9.	Jail	6,691
10.	Monasteries	5,285
11.	Printing & Stationary	4,720
12.	Education	27,733
13.	Medical & Sanitation	28,232
14.	Public Works	1,94,613
15.	Electric Charges	6,342

16.	Agriculture & Industries	1,945
17.	Accounts	12,122
18.	Miscellaneous	11,093
19.	Loans & Advance	1,52,922
	Total:	6,30,4,81

Source: *Ad. Report for 1933-34*, p. 93.

VI. Actuals of Expenditures of the Sikkim State in 1940-41

Totals Rs. 6,53,800

Source: Finance Deptt., Govt, of Sikkim, Details not available.

VII. Actuals of Expenditures of the Sikkim State in 1950-51

Totals Rs. 20,78,000

Source: *Ibid*.

VIII. Actuals of Expenditures of the Sikkim State in 1960-61

	Major Head	*Amount (Rs. in lakh)*
1.	Revenue Refund	0.5
2.	Civil List	4.6
3.	Palace Establishment	2.1
4.	General Administration	2.5
5.	Revenue General	1.2
6.	Excise	0.4
7.	Police	4.2
8.	Motor Vehicle	0.3
9.	Law & Justice	0.3
10.	Jail	0.2
11.	Monastery	0.3
12.	Printing & Stationary	0.8
13.	Bazar	0.5
14.	Account & Audit	0.6
15.	Assessed Taxes (I.T. & S.T.)	0.1
16.	Miscellaneous	2.0
17.	Establishment	0.6
18.	Forest	1.8
19.	Education	2.8
20.	Medical & Sanitation	3.1
21.	Veterinary	0.1
22.	Public Works	10.9
23.	Agriculture	0.3

24. Electricity	0.7
25. Development	0.2
Total	41.1

Source: Govt. of India, Second Five Year Plan of Sikkim, Report of the Technical Team (New Delhi: Planning Commission, 1961), p. 26.

IX. Budget Estimates of Expenditures of the Sikkim State in 1970-71

	Major Head	*Amount (Rs.)*
1.	Revenue Refund	30,000
2.	Civil List	9,65,000
3.	(a) Palace Establishment	18,44,900
	(b) Sikkim Guard	15,08,500
4.	Land Revenue	2,64,200
5.	General Excise	47,300
6.	Assessed Taxes	55,500
7.	Police	9,91,000
8.	Law & Justice	80,400
9.	Jail	80,400
10.	Ecclesiastical	2,49,000
11.	Culture	50,000
12.	Food Supply	79,400
13.	Trade, Commerce & Industry	50,500
14.	S. N. T.	59,54,800
15.	Govt. Transport	2,65,100
16.	Accounts & Audit	1,93,300
17.	General Administration	9,00,300
18.	Miscellaneous	4,82,000
19.	P. T. Institute	1,79,800
20.	Establishment	1,57,200
21.	Panchayats	78,700
22.	Election	1,00,000
23.	Electricity	6,66,900
24.	Animal Husbandry	1,91,800
25.	Bazar	1,81,900
26.	Medical & Sanitation	8,60,900
27.	Publicity	1,40,400
28.	Forest	5,29,600
29.	P. W. D.	25,73,500
30.	Agriculture	2,36,800
31.	Excise (*Apkari*)	2,20,000
32.	Education	15,67,200
33.	Motor Vehicles	37,500

34. Printing & Stationary	2,54,900
Total Expenditure Heads	2,20,58,000
Loans & Advances	46,05,000
Total Expenditure	2,66,63,000
Closing Balance (+)	1,77,700
Grand Total	2,68,40,700

Source: Finance Department, Govt. of Sikkim.

REFERENCES

1. P. Carrasco. *Land and Polity in Tibet* (Seattle: University of Washington Press, 1959, p. 211.
2. *Ibid.*
3. A. Campbell, "Journal of a Trip to Sikkim", *Journal of the Asiatic Society of Bengal*, 18, Part I (1849), 528.
4. A. Campbell, *Papers on the Sikkim Morung* Bengal Selection No. 5, (Calcutta: Military Orphan Press, 1851), p. 12.
5. Govt. of Bengal, Proceedings of the Hon'ble The Lieutenant-Governor of Bengal during April, 1863, Political Department (Calcutta: Secretariat Press), Proceeding No. 28. Hereafter referred to as *"PLGB during (Month, Year, Dept.)"*.
6. Letter No. 386 dated April 10, 1863 from the Superintendent of Darjeeling to the Secretary to the Govt. of Bengal.
7. Govt. of Bengal, *Report on the Administration of Bengal during 1889-90* (Calcutta: Bengal Secretariat Press, 1890), p. 2.
8. Edgar, Report on a Visit to Sikkim and the Tibetan Frontier in October, November and December, 1873 (Calcutta: Bengal Secretariat Press, 1874), p. 63.
9. *Ibid.*, p. 64.
10. A. Campbell, "Diary of a Journey through Sikkim to the Frontiers of Thibet," *Journal of the Asiatic Society of Bengal*, 21, p. 572.
11. *Ibid.*, p. 479.
12. *Ibid.*, p. 572.
13. *Ibid.*
14. D. F. Rennie, *Bhotan and the Story of the Door War* (London: J. Murray), p. 369.
15. Edgar, p. 4.
16. C. Macaulay, *Report of a Mission to Sikkim and the Tibetan Frontier with a Memorandum of Our Relations with Tibet* (Calcutta: 1885), p. 28.
17. Quoted in V. H. Coelho, *Sikkim and Bhutan* (New Delhi: Vikas Publications, 1971), pp. 23-24.

18. Govt. of Sikkim, *Administration Report of the Sikkim State for 1931-32, 1932-33 & 1933-34* (Calcutta: Bengal Govt. Press). Hereafter referred to as *"Ad. Report for (Year)"*.
19. L.A. Waddel, *Among the Himalayas* (Westminister: Archibald Constable & Co., 1899), p. 108.
20. *Ibid.*, p. 106.
21. See Ch. 2.
22. See below Budget Actuals for the Year.
23. S.C. Das, *Journey to Lhasa and Central Tibet* (London: J. Murray, 1902), p. 211.
24. J. C. White, *Sikkim and Bhutan: Twenty Years on the North-East Frontier, 1887-1908* (London: Edward Arnold, 1909), p. 111.
25. C. Bell, *The People of Tibet* (Oxford: Clarendon Press, 1928), p. 301.
26. G. Gorer, *Himalayan Village: An Account of the Lepchas of Sikkim* (London: Michael Joseph, 1938) pp. 120-21, 132.
37. *PLGB during July, 1898*, Judicial Dept., Proceeding No. 28.
28. *Imperial Gazetteer of India*, New Edition, Vol. 22 (London: Oxford University Press, 1908), p. 373.
29. *Ad. Report for 1914-15*, pp. 2-3.
30. *Ad. Report for 1915-16*, p. 2.
31. *PLGB during January, 1901*, Political Dept., Proceeding No. 27.
32. *Ibid.*
33. *Imperial Gazetteer of India*, pp. 371-72.
34. *Ad. Report for 1916-17*, p. 7.
35. *Ad. Report for 1931-32, 1932-33 & 1933-34*.
36. See Ch. 2.
37. *PLGB during January, 1901*, Political Dept., Proceeding No. 27.
38. *Imperial Gazetteer of India*, p. 372.
39. *Ad. Report for 1918-19*, p. 22. See also, *Ad. Report for 1922-23*, p. 22.
40. See Appendix.
41. *PLGB during January, 1901*, Political Dept., Proceeding No. 27.
42. *PLGB during October, 1902*, Political Dept., Proceeding No. 9.
43. *Ad. Report for 1910-11*, pp. 3-4.
44. *Ad. Report for 1922-23*, p. 23.
45. See Appendix.
46. See Appendix.

PART II: ECONOMIC DEVELOPMENT OF SIKKIM

(First Three Plans, 1954-71)

4

An Overview of the Plans

PLANS IN SIKKIM: AN INTRODUCTORY SURVEY

Attempts for the preparation of schemes for the development of Sikkim had been made as early as in 1946 and a Planning Commission was also later on set up under the chairmanship of the then Maharajkumar Palden Thondup Namgyal. No substantial progress could, however, be made owing chiefly to the lack of finances from the internal resources of the country. As a result, the Planning Commission became defunct and there was practically no hope for the introduction of planning in Sikkim.

Sikkim, however, was destined to have planning and events took place towards that direction. In April, 1952 the Sikkim Durbar and the people of Sikkim had the privilege of welcoming Sri Jawaharlal Nehru, the Prime Minister of India, who was greatly pleased with the rich and varied scenic beauty of the country nestled in the northeastern Himalayas. It was Mr. Nehru who at that time encouraged the Durbar to explore the possibilities of framing fresh schemes for the development of Sikkim, with the sole objective of developing the land and introducing the amenities of a modern welfare state, without affecting the essential fabric of the Sikkimese life and the traditional cultural pattern of the children of the soil.[1]

In 1953 a Planning Officer was deputed by the Government of India to assist the Durbar in the framing of the plan and in 1954 the Maharaja of Sikkim took the first positive steps for the all-round economic development of the State by introducing the First Seven-Year Development Plan of Sikkim (1954-61).

In this chapter we shall be dealing with the first three plans of SIkkim covering a total period of 17 years from 1954 to 1971. While the First Plan was of a seven-year duration the other two plans were each of a five-year duration. It may be pointed out in this connection that while India was forced to have a plan holiday for three years in between her Third and Fourth Five-Year Plans Sikkim has been rather fortunate in having no such plan holiday. Sikkim's experience in planning is, therefore, no less than India's although the latter initiated planning three years earlier i.e. in 1951.

A. The Planning Process in Protectorate Sikkim

The planning process in Sikkim was quite different from that in many other countries, and the difference was primarily due to the special relationship existing between Sikkim and India. *The entire plan expenditure in Sikkim was financed by the Government of India* — generally in the form of grants and only occasionally in the form of loans. Sikkim, therefore, did not yet experience the strains of revenue collection for the purpose of economic growth which is an unavoidable concomitant of the plans in other countries. *Plans in Sikkim were entirely outside the revenue-expenditure process of the state budget.*[1]

There was no Planning Commission or any other type of planning body in Sikkim. There was only one department—the Planning and Development Department headed by the Development Commissioner — which was responsible for the overall co-ordination of the departmental plans prepared by the different departments and their supervision while in execution. The roles of the Chief Secretary, the Sidlon (in 1949 the Govt. of India deputed an officer to act as the prime minister of Sikkim. He was known as the *Dewan* and later on as the principal administrative officer or its Tibetan synonym, *Sidlon)* and finally the Chogyal in the matter of co-ordination were no less important. Initially, the departmental plans were prepared by the respective heads of departments and then they sat together along with the Development Commissioner, the Finance Secretary, the Financial Adviser deputed by the Government of India, the Chief Secretary and the Sidlon. In this meeting the departmental plans were consolidated into a State Plan and then it was sent to the Chogyal for his approval.

After the sanction of the Chogyal the State Plan was sent to the Indian Planning Commission in New Delhi which then deputed a team of experts to investigate on the spot the needs and prospects of planned expenditure in Sikkim in the light of the State Plan. The team, after touring Sikkim and meeting different personalities and bodies, suggested some modifications, if any, of the Plan in consultation with the Government of Sikkim in which the dignitaries referred to above participated and expressed their opinion. This modified version then became the final draft of the Plan and the Government of India as a rule undertook to finance it. Sometimes, even after this final formulation changes were made to cope with unforeseen incidents and situations but that too was done through negotiations between the Government of Sikkim and the Indian Planning Commission.

There was no long-term or perspective plan in Sikkim. The plans were medium-term: the First Plan was of a seven-year duration from 1954 to 1961 but the subsequent plans have been of five-year duration. *During the First Seven-Year Plan there was no attempt to break up the Plan into annual plans* the need of which was increasingly being felt in the execution of the Plan. The First Technical Team which was deputed by the Government of India at the end of the Plan pointed out this drawback and emphasised that "in the Second Plan it will be essential to formulate the Plan of the year carefully."[2]

Accordingly, initiative was taken by the State's Planning and Development Department which was being strengthened for that purpose at the beginning of the Second Plan. It was decided that the other technical departments as well as the district administrative set-ups would also be associated with the formulation of the annual plan and once formulated, the provisions of the plan should be intimated to the respective departmental heads for their implementation. It was further decided that the annual plan would be prepared along with the budget of the State and since 1962-63 there has been regular publication of the annual plan.

In this connection a description of *the process of preparation of the State budget* may be pertinent because that *was also the process of preparation of the annual plan.* Unlike the process of budget determination in India it was quite simple in Sikkim. Each year in the month of September all the departmental heads submitted their respective budgets of anticipated receipts and expenditures during the next financial year from April to March. These departmental budgets were then scrutinised and co-ordinated by the Finance Secretary and his department, and in the month of December all the heads of departments and the Finance Secretary sat together for the finalisation of the budget. Then in the month of February next this budget was placed before the Sikkim State Council for its approval or modification. After being passed by the Sikkim State Council the budget was sent to the Chogyal for the final sanction. When the Chogyal approved, it was accepted as the final budget for the next financial year.

This budget, of course, underwent a change when the revenue and expenditure position of the different departments changed in course of the year. A revised estimate of the budget was, therefore, prepared towards the end of the financial year. Generally in the month of October the different heads of departments submitted, their respective revised estimates and in the month of December all of them, along with the Finance Secretary, sat together for the modification and co-ordination of the revised estimates of all the departments. Afterwards, in the month of January the consolidated revised estimates were presented to the Sikkim State Council and after being passed they were again sent to the Chogyal for his final approval.

The preparations of the *revised estimates* for the current year and of the *budget estimates* for the next year were made almost simultaneously. The preparation of the annual plans was similar to that of the State budget, but while the former was done under the auspices of the Planning and Development Department the latter was done under the auspices of the Finance Department.

The Planning and Development Department has also been preparing and publishing tables showing the analysis of the plan outlays and yearly *actual expenditures* since the beginning of the Second Five-Year Plan. In the tables for the Second Plan period expenditures were divided into recurring expenditure, expenditure on buildings and other non-recurring expenditure. Since the Third Plan the last category has been sub-divided into non-recurring expenditure and other capital investment. These classifications are indicative of the nature of plan expenditure in Sikkim, but unfortunately no such classification was done for the final year of the Second and Third Plans and as such the analyais remains incomplete.

As the entire finance was provided by the Government of India there was no problem of shortage of funds for the implementation of the plans. But still, the timely release of funds remained an important question. After the finalisation of a plan the Government of India did not release the entire funds, but the release was made in periodic instalments.

Previously during the First Plan period the procedure for the release of funds was that the Government of Sikkim was to furnish a two-monthly statement of expenditure to the Government of India which, on the basis of that statement, would release funds to be spent during the next two months. This entailed a lapse of time between the furnishing of the statement of expenditure and the release of funds and often the lapse was quite great.

It may be noted that while the total plan expenditure during the First Seven-Year Plan was Rs. 323.7 lakhs, the amount released in that period by the Government of India was only Rs. 317.65 lakhs. As revealed from the report of the First Technical Team the Sikkim Durbar had an outstanding ways and means advance to the tune of Rs. 6 lakhs from a Calcutta bank on account of this excess expenditure incurred on the First Plan schemes in 1960-61.[3]

This was certainly a strain on the Government of Sikkim and with a view to improving the situation, a procedure was suggested by the Government of India in October, 1962 and it was accepted by the Sikkim Government, but no final decision was taken by the Government of India till the Second Technical Team came to Sikkim in April-May, 1964. In the mid-term appraisal of the Second Five-Year Plan the Second Technical Team says: "Releases of funds for the current Plan have so far been made on an ad-hoc basis, which necessarily entail delays and consequently lead to over-drafts."[4]

To the Second Technical Team the Government of Sikkim put forward the following suggestions for consideration:

"*(i)* On the basis of annual allocation accepted for the financial year funds for the first nine months of that year be released in quarterly instalments in the first week of April, July and October promptly without directly relating such releases to actual expenditure for the period;

(ii) the statement of expenditure to be furnished by the Sikkim Durbar be quarterly (against two-monthly now) and be due by the end of the month following the quarter to which it relates; and

(iii) instalment for the last quarter may be released in February on the basis of actuals for April-December and anticipated expenditure for January-March."[5]

The Team accepted these suggestions and urged the Government of India to take an early decision in that matter. The Government of India accordinly revised the procedure towards the end of the Second Plan and since then the revised procedure was followed.

The implementation of a plan requires an efficient and coordinated administrative set-up. In Sikkim not only the initial formulation of the plans but also their execution was made by different governmental departments, and as such the role of administration in Sikkimese planning is quite important. It was particularly so in rural areas where practically all developmental works were executed through the local administrative machinery.

To put a plan's various development programmes into operation and to administer them effectively is a job of immense proportions. The main task is, however, to build up the administrative set-up in such a way that it becomes capable of performing that job. Further, the administration has to be decentralised in order to effectively and speedily implement the plan projects with higher efficiency and economy. Considering the difficult terrain, scattered population, public convenience, and effective execution of the projects the administrative set-up in Sikkim required a great deal of decentralisation and it was decentralised accordingly.

Sikkim had and still has four districts: East, West, North and South— each under a District Officer whose rank was equivalent to that of a District Magistrate or Deputy Commissioner in India. The District Officer was the administrative head of the district. There was also one Deputy Development Officer in each district for the supervision and co-ordination of district-level developmental works. He was under the Development Commissioner of Sikkim. In each district there was also one Extension Officer who was under the Director of Agriculture and supervised most of the agricultural works of the district.

Each district was subdivided into a number of blocks each of which comprised one or more villages according to the number of population. At the end of the Third Plan there were 213 blocks in all in the country. Under the Extension Officer of the district there were a number of Supervisors who supervise individually a group of blocks. Under the Supervisors there were the Village Level Workers who were the lowest agricultural extension workers. Each Village Level Worker was responsible for the supervision of all agricultural works including demonstration of superior agricultural methods in the village or villages under his jurisdiction. Generally one big or several small villages were under the supervision of a Village Level Worker.

In the execution of developmental plans the place of people's participation was no less important and in Sikkim it was channelised through the panchayat system. Each block elected a panchayat every three years and this panchayat in co-operation with the Village Level Worker, the Supervisor and other officials implemented all sorts of development work within the block.

The greatest handicap in the execution of the plans was, however, in the field of trained personnel both for administrative and technical posts. Despite the grant of scholarships on a most liberal scale for general education in arts and science as well as for technical studies like Medical and Civil Engineering the Government of Sikkim had to depend on trained personnel from outside, even though this involved a heavy drain of financial resources. In order to create progressively a cadre of trained local personnel, persons already in service were also selected and deputed outside for training.

B. The First Three Plans of Sikkim (1954-71)

The First Plan, finalised after full discussions between the Governments of Sikkim and India, stipulated originally an outlay of Rs. 225 lakhs which was covered entirely by financial grants from India. However, from the experience gained in course of the implementation of the Plan projects during the first three years, a larger outlay on various important schemes than initially provided for was found essential and the Plan outlay was finally settled at Rs. 307.21 lakhs. The actual expenditure during the Plan period was still higher at Rs. 323.69 lakhs.

Although the Plan had been timed to take effect from 1954, the first year had to be devoted mainly to the recruitment of personnel and re-organisation of the government departments to cope with the new strains and problems that were to be generated by the implementation of the various projects under the Plan. The Government of India generously deputed experts in every field at the disposal of the Sikkim Durbar. At the early stage it was also necessary to train local people so that Sikkim itself might be in a position effectively to take over the various services and carry the full weight of the subsequent plans. As a result of all these the actual execution of the Plan started a year after the scheduled time, i.e. in 1955.[6]

Towards the end of the First Plan the Sikkim Durbar made certain proposals to the Government of Indira for the formulation of the Second Plan which was to be of a five-year duration and in their Draft Second Five-Year Plan (1961-66) the Durbar envisaged a total outlay of Rs. 1190.70 lakhs. These proposals along with the Draft Plan and comments of the concerned ministries of the Government of Sikkim were considered at a meeting of the Planning Commission of India on 27th January, 1961. This meeting was attended by the then Maharaja of Sikkim and the Maharajkumar who later became the last Ghogyal of Sikkim. The Maharajkumar then expressed the view that the Durbar would appreciate if a team of experts from India visited Sikkim early in April, 1961 and examined the Draft Plan.

Accordingly, the Planning Commission appointed a team in consultation with the Ministry of External Affairs and other Ministries. This team reached Gangtok in early April, held discussions with the Maharajkumar, the Dewan, the Executive Councillors, the various departmental heads and the Indian Political Officer in Sikkim and also heard representatives of local political parties as arranged by the Durbar. A number of representations, both written and oral, from individuals as well as organised bodies, about the problems of the different areas were also received. After these discussions and consultations the team prepared the Second Five-Year Plan of Sikkim with a total outlay of Rs. 820.70 lakhs.

This Plan was, however, revised later on. When the Draft Plan had been discussed in the Planning Commission, a suggestion was made that the provision for buildings should be carefully examined by the team of experts. The above outlay was estimated without any such examination. As such a communication was issued to the Dewan of Sikkim requesting for a precise estimate of the provision for buildings having regard to their specification, cost and justification. This information was compiled and made available to the team by the different departments. After a preliminary discussion the team visited different parts of the country and observed carefully the standards which were being maintained.

Sikkim is a high-rainfall area and the cost of transportation of building materials was very high. The Sikkim Public Works Department had to keep these two factors in view while preparing the estimates of the cost of buildings required by the various departments.

It was felt, however, that as the building programmes would henceforth have to be on a much larger scale, the Sikkim Durbar might review the current specification and adopt a specification which might be more economic. For example, with the availability of power in different regions it might be possible to establish saw mills near the forest areas and the centres which required bulk of the building programmes so that processed wood at a cheaper rate could be utilised as building materials which would lower the cost of construction of buildings.

After discussion with the team of experts the Maharajkumar and the Dewan of Sikkim accepted this approach and consequently, instead of Rs. 820.70 lakhs as recommended by by the team previously, the final total outlay for the Second Plan was estimated at Rs. 813.30 lakhs with a 5% cut in the previous buildings outlays under different heads of development.[7]

It may be pointed out in this connection that in both the revisions made by the team no alteration was done in the original priorities set forth by the Government of Sikkim. As has been said in the team's report:

"While proposing revisions in the Second Plan outlay, priorities of the Second Plan are strictly left intact. The very few new schemes that are now proposed are intended for achievement of these priorities. Hence, the revisions are mostly adjustments within the schemes and among the schemes under a head of development. In many cases where revisions in schemewise outlays were necessitated they increased the cost of buildings. However, an attempt has been made not to include any new items of buildings."[8]

After three years from the commencement of the Second Five-Year Plan India's Ministry of External Affairs requested the Planning Commission of India to make an assessment of the progress of the Second Five-Year Plan of Sikkim. Accordingly, the Planning Commission in consultation with the concerned central ministries appointed a team of technical experts which visited Sikkim from April 27 to May, 1964.

The terms of reference of the team were:

(a) to make a mid-term appraisal of the Second Five-Year Plan of Sikkim,

(b) to identify the main factors which were holding up the progress in some sectors of development, and

(c) to suggest changes in emphasis or method to be adopted and fresh measures to be taken for speedy implementation of the various programmes and reorientation of the Plan for meeting the emergency.

Consequently the Sikkim Durbar was requested in February, 1964 to furnish information on the following to be placed before the visiting team:

(i) progress made, both in financial and physical terms, of individual schemes under different heads of development,

(ii) proposals for any adjustment to be considered by the technical team, and

(iii) the bottlenecks in plan implementation, e.g., shortage of materials and personnel.

Accordingly, the Planning and Development Department of the Government of Sikkim prepared a document of comprehensive progress report for 1961-64 with critical reviews and proposals and it was placed before the team for discussion. The proposals for revision of the Second Five-Year Plan indicated by the Sikkim Durbar were discussed by the team of experts with different heads of departments. The original plan outlay was more or less retained in the revised Plan—the new outlay was Rs. 813.00 lakh, against the original outlay of 813.30 lakhs. However, some adjustment were made particularly with regard to the heads of development like: Agriculture, Power, Industry and Mining. These changes were made because of various factors that were experienced during the past years like: *(a)* availability of key materials and technical personnel, *(b)* public participation and association in the implementation of the Plan, and so on.[9] The actual expenditure during the Plan period was, however, much lower than the final outlay, viz. Rs. 636.37 lakhs only.

The Third Five-Year Plan began in 1866. Originally, the Government of Sikkim proposed an outlay of Rs. 1247.79 lakhs for the Third Five-Year Plan of Sikkim and this proposal was sent to the Planning Commission of India for approval. A team of experts was subsequently sent on behalf of the Government of India to Gangtok for an on-the-spot appraisal of the needs and problems of planned development programmes in Sikkim as well as for the finalisation of the Plan. After the discussions that were held in Gangtok during March, 1966 between the Government of India and the Government of Sikkim it was agreed that the outlay for Sikkim's Third Five-Year Plan would be Rs. 900 lakhs. There was a further agreement that the Government of India will finance the entire Plan by a grant of Rs. 750.00 lakhs and the rest by loan amounting to Rs. 150 lakhs.

The schemes that were to be financed by the above loan were the following:

Sl. No.	Name of Schemes	Rs. (in lakhs)
1.	Medium-Scale Industrial Loans	75.00
2.	Small-Scale Industrial Loans	25.00
3.	Sikkim Nationalised Transport	40.00
4.	Bacon Factory	6.00
5.	Forest utilisation	4.00
	Total	150.00

The Government of India also thought that the tea garden scheme which had an outlay of Rs. 60 lakhs should be financed by a loan. However, the Government of Sikkim did not agree to this proposal because it held that the scheme was part of the rehabilitation, scheme for Tibetan refugees which should be financed by grants from the Government of India as the latter undertook the responsibility of rehabilitating Tibetan refugees. The controversy arose because it had been decided that Tibetan refugees would be employed in the proposed tea garden as labourers.[10]

After three years' execution it was felt that the outlays in the Third Five-Year Plan needed a revision and consequently a revised Plan outlay was formulated. Two considerations were behind such a revision of the outlays:

(i) First, increases were unavoidable in the outlays under Co-operation, Soil Conservation, Power, Roads, Health, Press and Rural Development,

(ii) Secondly, in order to meet the requirements of higher expenses in the above heads of development *(a)* provisions were reduced where the physical and financial achievements had been poor during the first three years of the Third Five-Year Plan, and *(b)* greater reductions were made in those cases where it was felt that the scheme could be more effectively implemented in the Fourth Five-Year Plan period.

However, the savings out of these reductions were insufficient to cover the increased expenditures in other heads of development; and the Government of Sikkim approached the Government of India for releasing additional funds, especially, for restoration and consolidation works. It may be pointed out in this connection that the devastating flood of 1968 caused substantial damages to the economy and various provisions, particularly roads, were urgently required for the restoration and sustainance of transport and communication which was the lifeline of the economy. The revised Plan outlay was Rs. 1040.40 lakhs, but the actual expenditure for the entire Plan period was Rs. 971.83 lakhs only.[11]

C. An Analysis of Plan Expenditures in Sikkim

In analysing the plan expenditures in Sikkim it may be mentioned that they have been rising at a very high rate — Rs. 323.69 lakhs in the First Plan, Rs. 636.37 lakhs in the Second Plan and Rs. 971.83 lakhs in the Third Plan. In percentage terms while the increase in plan expenditures during the Second Plan was 97% over the First Plan expenditures, that during the Third Plan was 53% over the Second Plan expenditures. It indicates that the spurt in economic activities in Sikkim was increasing at a diminishing rate. This is shown in the following figure:

Figure I: Growth of Plan Expenditures in Sikkim

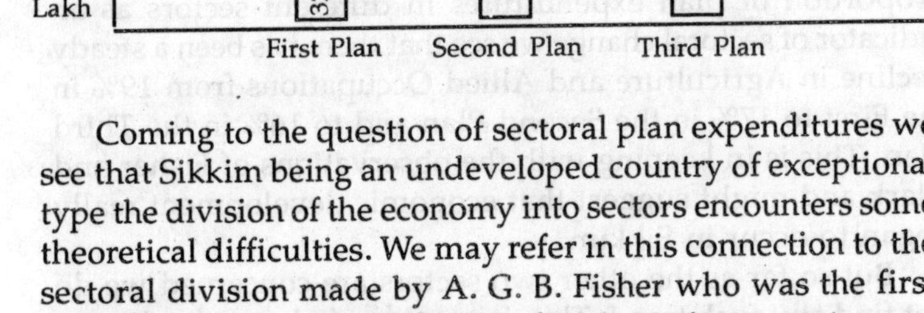

Coming to the question of sectoral plan expenditures we see that Sikkim being an undeveloped country of exceptional type the division of the economy into sectors encounters some theoretical difficulties. We may refer in this connection to the sectoral division made by A. G. B. Fisher who was the first to introduce the concept.[12] In his division primary sector was defined to include agriculture and allied occupations, secondary sector included manufacturing, generally mining and construction, and the tertiary sector comprised transport and communication, trade, government, personal and domestic services etc.

In the case of Sikkim, however, we think that transport and communication should be included within the secondary sector. The hilly region of Sikkim requires easy transport and communication as a basic pre-requisite for the growth of the economy, which is not the case for other countries, and as such it cannot be given tertiary importance. This will be evident from the fact that the percentage share of plan expenditures on roads and road transport did not change over the plan periods — it remained constant at the high level of *48% of the total expenditures in all the three plans.*

From the works of A. G. B. Fisher and Colin Clark,[13] it appears that the proportion of the labour force in agriculture and allied occupations declines, as a country advances, from about 80 per cent for the least developed to about 12 per cent for the most developed. The proportions of labour force engaged in secondary and tertiary sectors increase with growth. The secondary sector increases rapidly at first but gradually the rate of increase diminishes until the proportion of labour force engaged in this sector reaches a level between 40 and 50 per cent. The tertiary sector, on the other hand, increases slowly at first but gradually the rate of increase increases. The proportion of labour force engaged in the tertiary sector ultimately becomes in-between 38% and 48% when the economy is fully developed.

In the case of Sikkim the data on the proportion of labour force engaged in different sectors is lacking, but taking the proportion of plan expenditures in different sectors as an indicator of sectoral change we see that there has been a steady decline in Agriculture and Allied Occupations from 19% in the First to 17% in the Second Plan and to 16% in the Third Plan. This is in keeping with the observations of Fisher and Clark and might suggest that economic development really began to occur in Sikkim.

But so far as the other two sectors are concerned we do not find any such trend. The proportion of plan expenditures in the secondary sector decreased during the Second Plan and again rose during the Third Plan, but was still below the First Plan level — it was 63% in the First Plan, 59% in the Second Plan and 62% in the Third Plan. The proportion of plan expenditures in the tertiary sector was 18% in the First Plan, 24% in the Second Plan and 22% in the Third Plan. The proportion of plan expenditures in different sectors during the three plans may be shown in the following figure:

Figure II: Percentage Share of Different Sectors in Plan Expenditures

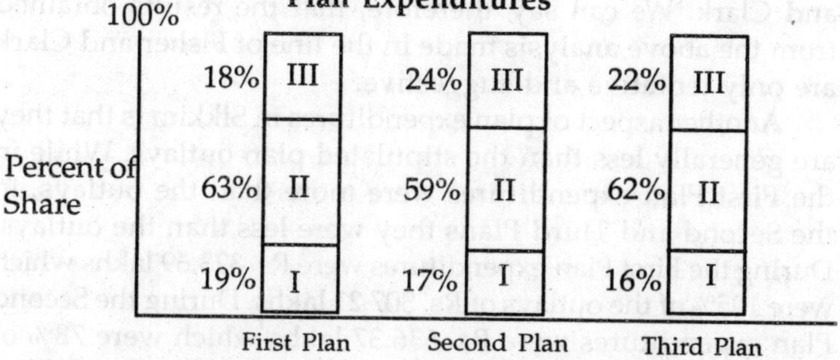

The relative decline in agriculture and allied occupations during three plans is an indicator of economic growth in Sikkim. The fact that so far as the secondary and teriary sectors are concerned there is no such definite trend suggests that in Sikkim, which is being developed from a very low level, both the sectors are equally important. The services sector may account for larger share of plan expenditures in the future when economic development reaches a substantially high level and peoples marginal propensity to consume services provided by the tertiary sector becomes higher than that for goods and services provided by the secondary sector.

A note of caution is, however, necessary in this connection regarding the propriety of such an analysis for Sikkim. First of all, the heavy expenditure on transport and communication accounting for about 48% of the overall plan expenditures during seventeen years of planning is unprecedented in the history of planned economic development and is not in keeping with the general framework of Fisher and Clark. As a contrast we can point out that the plan provision for transport and communication during the First, Second and Third Five-Year Plans in India were only 24%, 29% and 20% respectively.[14]

Whether we include transport and communication in the secondary or tertiary sector, its inclusion makes the proportion of plan expenditures in that sector higher than that in any developed country. This indicates that Sikkim is an underdeveloped region of a special type. Moreover, we have not taken into account in our analysis the non-plan expenditures in Sikkim. The use of the proportion of expenditure in the sectors instead of the proportion of labour force engaged within them is yet another deviation from the path of Fisher and Clark. We can say, therefore, that the results obtained from the above analysis made in the line of Fisher and Clark are only tentative and suggestive.

Another aspect of plan expenditures in Sikkim is that they are generally less than the stipulated plan outlays. While in the First Plan expenditures were more than the outlays, in the Second and Third Plans they were less than the outlays. During the First Plan expenditures were Rs. 323.69 lakhs which were 105% of the outlays of Rs. 307.21 lakhs. During the Second Plan expenditures were Rs. 636.37 lakhs which were 78% of the outlays of Rs. 813.00 lakhs. During the Third Plan expenditures were Rs. 971.83 lakhs which were 92% of the outlays of Rs. 1060.39 lakhs. This indicates that while the First Plan was cautious, the other two plans, particularly the Second, were over-ambitious — they did not take into account the capacity of the economy to carry out the envisaged level of plan activities. The Second Plan's over-ambitiousness might have been the result of the over-fulfilment of the First Plan; and when disillusionment came, the planners became more conscious about their capacity and as a result the Third Plan was more realistic and only marginally underfulfilled.

The over-ambitious nature of Sikkimese planning is more evident in the annual plans which are prepared by different departments of the Government of Sikkim. One reason for their over-ambitiousness might be the fact that they are not prepared by the experts of the Planning Commission of India.

Each department wants to spend as much as possible before the expiry of the year after which money allotted for that year cannot be obtained unless the spill-over is included in the next annual plan. This urge for excessive spending is specially more evident during the last years of a plan, particularly the last year, when there are brisk activities to fulfil the targets before the expiry of the plan after which money allotted for the plan cannot be disbursed at all. But inspite of all brisk activities it becomes impossible to spend the entire fund effectively.

The figures for all available years indicate that plan expenditures in all annual plans. Here less than the budget proposals. The revised estimates for the years were also generally (excepting 1969-70 and 1970-71) less than the budget proposals which suggests that the makers of the annual plans subsequently took into account the bottlenecks and limitations that were encountered in course of the implementation of the plan. But yet the revised estimates were not realistic — excepting 1968-69. They were always greater than the actual plan expenditures which indicates that the planners were still more ambitious than realistic.[15]

The exceptional cases of the years 1968-69, 1969-70 and 1970-71 as mentioned above were all the result of the devastating flood of October, 1968. The severity of the flood was unprecedented in the recent history of Sikkim. The damages done to the economy, particularly in the field of roads and bridges, were so extensive that full repairs of them were not possible until the end of the first year of the Fourth Five-Year Plan.

The planners were so depressed by the flood of 1968 that they slashed down the budget proposals of Rs. 234.98 lakhs for 1968-69 to the revised estimates of Rs. 174.70 lakhs only. Since it was not possible to carry on works on many schemes due to flood the revised estimates were lowered so that the year's financial targets might be achieved. Actually, many planned projects could not be undertaken or finished, but the repair works necessitated by the flood towards the end of the year led the expenditure figure to a higher level — Rs. 193.98 lakhs.

So far as the years 1969-70 and 1970-71 were concerned we may say that the increased revised estimates were the result of the necessity and desire on the part of the planners to expedite the works of repair and consolidation. The actual expenditures in these two years were, however, less than the revised estimates as the implementation of the programmes was faced with various bottlenecks. The revised estimates for 1969-70 were Rs. 283.50 lakhs whereas the actual expenditures were Rs. 201.76 lakhs and the revised estimates for 1970-71 were Rs. 349.98 lakhs whereas the actual expenditures were Rs. 290.21 lakhs.

Excepting these three years, actual plan expenditures were always less than revised estimates and revised estimates were always less than budget proposals. All this indicates that in spite of best efforts on the part of the Government plan activities in Sikkim were generally less than desired. What were the reasons for this lagging of plan activities?

First of all may be mentioned the lack of technical personnel essential for the execution of the plans. As has been pointed out regarding the annual plan of 1962-63:

> "In spite of best efforts it was not possible to obtain officers on deputation for most of the posts set apart for them under the Plan. Neither have the attempts to recruitment from open markets for other jobs, e.g. engineers, doctors, compounders etc. met with any measure of success. The programme of sending out candidates for training at various institutions in India also could not be carried out according to schedule as the finalisation of arrangements with the institutions has been taking more time than expected."[16]

Secondly, communicational difficulties also pose serious problems in the implementation of the plans. As has been said about the annual plan of 1962-63:

> "Again for implementing most of the Plan schemes it is necessary to construct a large number of buildings both residential and non-residential. To undertake the building programme it is essential to provide in the first instance proper road communications for transporting materials to the sites. Breaches on the existing roads because of heavy rains have also contributed to the delay in the construction programmes"[17]

Thirdly, sometimes legal problems such as the acquisition of sites for plan purposes pose difficulties. Referring again to the annual plan of 1962-63 it has been said: "Further, the acquisition of sites for construction of buildings at places where suitable Government lands are not available has presented certain difficulties."[18]

Fourthly, sometimes the difficulty in the procurement of key materials and other equipments proves to be a major bottleneck. This was particularly true for Sikkim which imports most of the key materials and equipments from outside, mainly India.[19]

Fifthly, heavy rains and floods also sometimes cause the deferment of the execution of plan programmes as occurred in 1968 to which we have already referred.

Sixthly, administrative delays which are characteristic of all underdeveloped countries were also a major cause of non-execution or partial execution of the plan projects in Sikkim. In 1969-70, for example, administrative delays accounted for a very poor performance in respect of dairy development and marketing centres; and to some extent the agricultural and animal husbandry programmes had also suffered on this account.[20]

Due to all these reasons we find that the actual expenditures of the annual plans in Sikkim are always less than the budget proposals and in most cases also less than the revised estimates.

We may now refer in this connection to another special feature of the annual plan expenditures in Sikkim: it is that expenditures during the second half of the year were generally greater than those during the first half. The reason for this might be sought in the fact that most of the difficulties and bottlenecks referred to above in the execution of annual plans were generally eased out towards the end of the year and as such expenditures during the second half of the year became larger than those during the first half.

A perennial problem for Sikkim which is particularly important in this connection is the prolonged rainy season which practically covers the entire first half of the financial year during which due to disruptions in communications and other difficulties plan activities: naturally decrease. In Sikkim there are practically two seasons: the rainy season from April to September and the winter from October to March. As the financial year starts from April, much work, particularly of the Public Works Department, cannot be undertaken during the first six months. Consequently, there is slackness in developmental activities during the first half of the year and higher tempo during the second half.

The inconveniences of the rainy season were the main cause of delayed starting of the projects like land development, road building and plantation. Sometimes this delay coupled with other contingencies and emergencies leads to the non-implementation of the scheme within the year.

A study can be made of some selected schemes for the year 1969-69 as below:

(Rs. in lakhs)

Sl. No.	*Scheme*	*Expenditure*	
		April to September	*October to March*
1.	Tea Garden	1.60	8.50
2.	Water Supply	3.06	14.38
3.	Nationalisation & Dieselisation	-	4.20
4.	Development of Land	-	1.19

It has been said that the implementation of various projects under the Tea Garden Scheme could only be undertaken during the working season which accounted for heavy expenditure during October, 1968—March, 1969. Again, the procurement of pipes for the Gangtok Water Supply Scheme was possible only in the second half of the year and this alone accounted for more than Rs. 9 lakhs of expenditure. Similarly, under Nationalisation and Dieselisation Scheme vehicles could be obtained only in the second half of the year. In the case of Development of Land the proposal from the District Officer had to be checked and scrutinised before they could be put up for sanction. All this led the scheme to be undertaken in the second half of the year.[21]

So far as the overall plan expenditures are concerned, they were also in general more in the second half of the year than in the first. In 1968-69, for example, plan expenditures during the first half of the year were Rs. 80.26 lakhs as against Rs. 49.40 lakhs during the first half. This was also true for the earlier two years of the Third Plan.[22] Again, the overall plan expenditures during the first six months of 1970-71 were only Rs. 84.82 lakhs whereas in the second half of the year they were Rs. 205.40 lakhs.[23] The reason for this higher level of over-all plan expenditures during the second half of the year was that most of the schemes of the annual plans were either not undertaken at all or only partially undertaken during the first half of the year the causes being the same as explained earlier.

Now let us consider another aspect of the annual plans in Sikkim: the question of relative share of recurring and non-recurring expenditures. This aspect is indicative of the extent of capital formation or capital - intensity in the economy as well as in the different sectors. We shall try to analyse this aspect using the available data of annual plan expenditures with their sub-divisions into recurring, building and other non-recurring expenditures.[24] Actually, building expenditures and other non-recurring expenditures should together be regarded as capital expenditures. But a distinction has been made by the Sikkimese planners to indicate the difference between the two types of capital expenditure—for buildings and for machinery etc.

We, however, lack the data for the First Plan period as well as for the last years of the Second and Third Five-Year Plans. Still, we resort to the analysis expecting that the results obtained would be applicable, more or less, to the entire period of the three Plans and they would be representative of the nature of planning in Sikkim, particularly of the extent of growth of capital.

So far as recurring expenditures are concerned, they were Rs. 170.59 lakhs or about 15% of the total expenditures of Rs. 1150.08 lakhs for all available years. This indicates that on the whole capital formation is going on at a high rate in Sikkim, capital expenditures being 85% of the total. Again, we see that recurring expenditures were highest in the Tertiary Sector with Rs. 90.89 lakhs or about 53% of the total of recurring expenditures for all years. Next was the Primary Sector with Rs. 66.48 lakhs or 39% of the total and the least amount of recurring expenditures occured in the Secondary Sector with only Rs.13.22 lakhs or about 8% of the total.[25]

The provision for social services such as education and health is recurring in nature and as such we find highest recurring expenditures in the Tertiary Sector. Development of agriculture etc. also requires recurring expenditures in the form of supply of manures, pesticides, seed etc. and this accounts for the substantial amount of recurring expenditures in the Primary Sector. This is not the case for Power, Transport and Industry. A power house once built, a road or bridge once constructed or an industry once established requires comparatively less recurring expenditures for its maintenance.

Of all non-recurring expenditures those for the construction of buildings are of a special type and as such they have been separately classified. Building expenditures are, however, only Rs. 122.22 lakhs or about 11% of the total expenditures for all years; yet they are not very much less in importance for the percentage is quite close to that of recurring expenditures.

Building expenditures are again the highest in the Social Services and Miscellaneous Sector, with Rs. 72.21 lakhs or about 59% of the total building expenditures for all years. Next come the Primary and Secondary Sectors with Rs. 26.78 lakhs or 22% of the total and Rs. 23.23 lakhs or 19% of the total respectively. The construction of hospitals, health centres, school-buildings and other premises of public welfare account for the very high percentage of building expenditures in the Tertiary Sector. In the other two sectors those expenditures are mainly for the construction of office-buildings and staff quarters and as the requirements of the two sectors are not very dissimilar we find a close proximity of the percentage in the two sectors.[26]

Coming to the other non-recurring expenditures we see that they constitute the highest percentage of the total plan expenditures. These expenditures were Rs. 857.27 lakhs or about 74% of the total plan expenditures for all years. This indicates that the Sikkimese Plans are emphasising more on capital formation than on current consumption.

So far as the different sectors are concerned we see that these expenditures were the highest in the Power, Transport and Industry Sector with Rs. 685.23 lakhs or about 80% of the total of other non-recurring expenditures for all years. This sector is basically capital - intensive which is the reason behind such a high percentage. So far as the other two sectors are concerned, they fare more or less equally with Rs. 85.58 lakhs and Rs. 86.45 lakhs — both about 10% of the total. This indicates that while capital formation was very high in the

Secondary Sector, it was equally low in the other two sectors, excluding, of course, building expenditures.

D. Some Features of Sikkimese Planning

It may be worthwhile to point out here some salient features of Sikkimese planning. First of all, Sikkimese planning can be called democratic planning. Any plan in Sikkim was to pass through the Sikkim State Council which was composed mainly of representatives, of the people. Though some members of the Council were nominated by the Chogyal and though the Chogyal was the final sanctioning authority, a good deal of people's participation is evinced in the deliberations of the elected members whose say is no less important in the preparation or execution of the plans.

Secondly, Sikkimese planning was centralised planning, Sikkim being a very small country it became convenient for the Government to plan its economic activities centrally. Any plan for the development and management of the economy as a whole cannot be separated from central decision-making on fundamental questions. The obvious precondition for this centralised decision-making is the concentration of all material and financial resources of the economy at the hands of the state. In Czechoslovakia the way was opened by the nationalisation of the basic branches of industry, transport, banks and trade.[28]

In the case of Sikkim, however, no need for nationalisation arose because there were few industiral enterprises by private initiative before the launching of the plans. On the other hand, the massive financial and technical aid from India has enhanced the powers of the planning mechanism. Even after integration with India in 1975, we see the entire economy being dominated by Government undertakings.

In Sikkim the plan targets and means were determined at the apex of administration with little scope for regional decision-making. This does not mean that the plans were unrelated to the regional endowment of natural resources or that the plan targets were unrelated to social demands. But yet, so far as plan decision was concerned it was from above and not from below. Perhaps that is due to the backwardness of the different regions in Sikkim. In this respect it resembled Indian planning and, in fact, it is the Indian experts who assisted in the drawing up of the Sikkimese plans.

Thirdly, Sikkimese planning was not comprehensive. It was not comprehensive in the sense in which Soviet planning was. The plans in Sikkim did not dealt with every sector of the economy in detail rather they deal with only a cross-section of the economy taking the most important economic programmes of the country. Side by side with the public sector there was the private sector and as such Sikkimese planning was non-comprehensive being operative in a mixed economy.

In fact, in all these respects Sikkimese planning was a proto-type of Indian planning. This was not only because of political affinity, and geographical proximity with India but also because of India's participation in the preparation and execution of the plans. India was the only source of financial resources as well as guidance for the implementation of the plans. Even the timing of the Sikkimese plans was determined according to that of the Indian plans. When the First Five-Year Plan of India was in its fourth year, the First Plan of Sikkim was launched, purposely with a duration of seven years, so that the Second Five-Year Plan of Sikkim could coincide with the Third Five-Year Plan of India.

The role of people's participation was also highlighted in Sikkimese planning. A plan that is capable of ensuring fast and effective economic development depends heavily for its realisation on the active participation of the broad mass of people. The message of His Highness, Sir Tashi Namgyal on the occasion of the launching of the First Plan is worth citing in this connection:

> "It gives me great pleasure to introduce the Sikkim Development Plan to the people of my State... Its effective implementation will depend, primarily, on the support and co-operation of every single person in the State. This support and co-operation will, I know, be forthcoming, unstintingly, from all my people."[12]

Plan measures will not be effective in any country unless they have the consent and support of the public in general. Indeed, the success of planning in developing countries is closely linked with the readiness with which the people respond to the demands of economic progress. This response may come spontaneously if the people think that the plans fully conform to their needs. But if this conformity is not so obvious to the people a deliberate policy should be adopted to arouse social consciousness. The situation in Sikkim in this respect is worth noticing:

> "The response of the people in the form of free land and labour, cash donations etc. was forthcoming [during the First Plan] in respect of construction of schools, dispensaries, village roads, health campaigns etc. Publicity work is, however, lagging behind. It is felt that if suitable steps are taken for adequate publicity of the Plan, it may be possible to elicit more of public participation and association in the implementation of the Second Plan."[13]

It may be pointed out in this connection that just as public co-operation is essential for the success of a plan, the latter is also necessary for kindling interests in the plan and co-operative motives among the people. The Draft Second Plan says:

> "As a result of the various welfare activities undertaken during the First Plan period, the people have become conscious of their self needs and as such there is a great demand for intensification of the development programmes."[14]

It is to be remembered that the people's will to pursue effectively the policies for economic development is far more important than the technical competence displayed by the planners in the formulation of plans. Inadequate data and lack of technical experience in drawing up the plans may increase the margin of error; but both the quality of data and technical competence tend to improve in the planning process. But whatever may be the excellence of technical competence, it alone cannot lead to the success of the plan — people's participation is a *sine qua non* for planned economic growth.

Another important feature in Sikkimese planning is the problem of cultural change. The attempt to raise per capita income or other economic objective should not minimise the significance of social and cultural change which is a corollary to any such process of economic change. In a country like

Sikkim where traditional values and customs are deep-rooted, the problem assumes still greater importance. Any adverse change in the cultural fabric of the society should, therefore, be weighed against the gains from economic development of the country.

The more backward the people, the faster must be the rate of development and the more intense will be the social and cultural disturbances and shocks. But the refusal to take steps to improve communications, provide education and bring about improvement in the standard of living on the ground that these will render cultural shocks would be quite wrong. No doubt, some sort of shock is unavoidable in the process of economic expansion but it is the duty of the administration to see that the people, because of their education and adaptability, are gradually conditioned to absorb the shocks. Along with this there should be a deliberate policy to bring about development in such a way that social and cultural shocks will be at a minimum. It will be relevant here to quote Professor Gunnar Myrdal:

> *"Advice not to hurry economic change has, therefore, to be rejected. The anthropologists are right, however, in saying that the cultural and social effects of economic change may be disastrous—and that further, these effects may also soon frustrate economic development. They are then assuming, however, that these effects are left to take care of themselves. If the political necessity of rapid economic development is assumed, the obvious conclusion is the opposite—that the cultural and social changes have to be planned and controlled; to a certain extent they have even to be induced."*[15]

Moreover, the fear of cultural shock is not so real as is generally thought to be. It has been observed that as a country develops with more communication facilities, monetisation of the economy and the like, not only a higher level of economic prosperity is noticed but one also finds a desire for change and willingness to adjust to the changing socio-economic conditions on the part of the people.[16] This voluntary and spontaneous adjustment on the part of the people should also be augmented by a deliberate policy of rousing public interests in plan activities as has been pointed out earlier. This would definitely reduce cultural shock and tension, if any.

So far as Sikkim is concerned, the people accepted the plans and realised the necessity of adjustments in their mode of thinking and way of life. The ustinated offer of public co-operation towards plan measures strengthens that contention. The problem of cultural shock seems to have been resolved in Sikkim—what remains is the problem of economic development.

APPENDIX

Table I: Outlays and Expenditures under the First Seven—Year Plan of Sikkim

(Rs. in lakh)

Head of Development	*Initial Outlay*	*Revised Outlay*	*Actual Expenditure.*
I. Agriculture and Allied Occupations:			
1. Agriculture	16.00	16.00	13.00
2. Animal Husbandry	6.00	5.94	2.92
3. Dairy Development	4.00	5.36	5.52
4. Minor Irrigation	6.00	3.25	1.55
5. Co-operation	8.25	7.02	5.42
6. Forests	9.00	25.48	22.58
7. Horticulture	11.00	9.26	11.21
Total	60.25	72.31	62.20
II. Power, Transport and Industry:			
1. Power	11.00	26.63	29.83
2. P. W. D. (Roads & Bridges)	78.00	131.63	139.01
3. Road Transport	8.50	13.46	16.70
4. Post & Telegraph	—	0.05	0.01
5. Aerial Ropeway	22.00	—	—
6. Cottage Industry	7.00	5.50	3.87
7. Other Indusries	10.00	7.90	14.40
Total	136.50	185.17	203.82
III. Social Services and Miscellaneous:			
1. Education	18.00	19.95	23.22
2. Health	10.25	15.12	22.73
3. Housing	—	12.96	10.26
4. Publicity & Cultural Activity	—	1.70	1.46
Total	28.25	49.73	57.67
Grand Total	255.00	307.21	323.69

Source: 1. Govt. of Sikkim, *Sikkim Development Plan* (Gangtok: Sikkim Durbar Press, 1955), p. 39.

2. Govt. of Sikkim, *Seven Years of Progress, 1954-61* (Gangtok: Sikkim Durbar Press, 1962), p. 32.
3. Govt. of India, *Second Five-Year Plan of Sikkim: Report of the Technical Team.* (New Delhi: Planning Commission, 1961), p. 17.

Table II: Initial Outlays Under the Second Five-Year Plan of Sikkim

(Rs. in lakh)

Head of Development	*Outlay Proposed by the Govt. of Sikkim.*	*Outlay Recommended by the Technical Team.*	*Outlay after 5% Cut on Buildings.*
I. Agriculture and Allied Occupations:			
1. Agriculture	88.50	46.20	45.56
2. Animal Husbandry	59.61	24.90	24.00
3. Dairy Development	5.31	2.00	2.00
4. Minor Irrigation	5.44	5.30	5.28
5. Co-operation	30.03	9.30	9.14
6. Forests	81.90	70.10	69.38
7. Soil Conservation	11.90	5.00	5.00
8. Fisheries	1.53	0.40	0.40
Total	284.22	163.20	160.76
II. Power, Transport and Industry			
1. Power	165.00	50.00	50.00
2. Roads	372.00	300.00	299.85
3. Road Transport	51.91	47.50	46.66
4. Tourism	10.00	7.50	7.13
5. Cottage Industry	18.73	11.50	11.25
6. Other Industries	9.92	30.00	30.00
Total	672.56	446.50	444.89
III. Social Services and Miscellaneous:			
1. Education	208.20	98.00	95.80
2. Health	11.60	72.00	71.40
3. Housing	17.50	7.00	7.00
4. Press	5.63	6.00	5.97
5. Publicity	5.69	4.50	4.46
6. Marketing Centre	5.25	2.00	1.90
7. Secretariat Extension	8.50	5.00	4.75
8. Community Centre	5.50	3.50	3.35
9. Planning Department	9.30	11.50	11.52
10. Cultural Activity	1.75	1.50	1.50
Total	278.92	211.00	207.65
Grand Total	1190.70	820.70	813.30

Sources: 1. Govt. of India, *Second Five-Year Plan of Sikkim: Report of the Technical Team* (New Delhi: Planning Commission, 1961), p. 20.
2. Govt. of Sikkim, *Second Five-Year Plan: 1961-66* (Gangtok Planning and Development Department, 1962), Statement I.

Table III: Revised Outlays and Expenditures Under the Second Five-Year Plan of Sikkim

(Rs. in lakh)

Head of Development	*Revised Outlay Proposed by the Govt. of Sikkim.*	*Final Revised Outlay*	*Actual Expenditure*
I. Agriculture and Allied Occupations:			
1. Agriculture	42.75	46.2	28.92
2. Animal Husbandry	21.09	28.02	11.79
3. Dairy Development	4.10	4.20	2.09
4. Minor Irrigation	3.41	3.41	1.45
5. Co-operation	6.28	6.28	3.15
6. Forests	65.94	69.48	53.79
7. Soil Conservation	5.00	5.00	4.56
8. Fisheries	0.40	0.40	0.26
Total	148.97	163.04	106.01
II. Power, Transport and Industry:			
1. Power	59.50	69.00	53.05
2. Roads	300.49	300.34	260.84
3. Road Transport	45.60	48.07	44.00
4. Tourism	7.50	7.50	5.24
5. Cottage Industry	11.00	10.23	9.35
6. Other Industries	27.00	20.00	2.41
Total	451.09	455.14	374.89
III. Social Services and Miscellaneous:			
1. Education	96.91	94.11	76.82
2. Health	70.42	60.74	42.67
3. Housing	7.00	7.00	6.32
4. Press	5.97	5.97	4.40
5. Publicity	2.03	2.03	1.40
6. Marketing Centre	2.15	2.15	1.74
7. Secretariat Extension	5.25	5.25	5.25

8. Community Centre	3.50	3.50	3.06
9. Planning Department	11.52	12.52	12.42
10.Cultural Activity	1.30	1.55	1.39
Total	205.75	194.82	155.47
Grand Total	805.81	813.00	636.37

Sources: 1. Govt. of Sikkim, *Second Five-Year Plan of Sikkim: Progress Report 1961-61: Review of Plan,* Proposals for Revision of Plan (Gangtok: Planning and Development Department, 1964), Key Statement.

2. Govt. of India, *Mid-Term Appraisal of Second Five-Year Plan of Sikkim: Report of the Technical Team* (New Delhi: Planning Commission, 1964), p. 13.

3. Govt. of India, *Progress Through Parnership* (Gangtok: Office of the Political Officer in Sikkim), p. 24.

Table IV: Outlays and Expenditures Under the Third Five-Year Plan of Sikkim

(Rs. in lakh)

Head of Development	*Outlay proposed by the Govt. of Sikkim.*	*Initial Outlay*	*Revised Outlay*	*Actual Expenditure.*
I. Agriculture and Allied Occupations:				
1. Agriculture	64.00	61.41	56.66	48.11
2. Animal Husbandry	36.12	35.71	18.43	16.82
3. Dairy Development	4.16	3.00	1.60	0.15
4. Minor Irigation	11.20	11.20	8.00	9.09
5. Co-operation	8.50	6.50	9.00	17.00
6. Forests	68.35	58.00	48.95	49.76
7. Soil Conservation	7.00	6.88	7.88	13.25
Total	199.33	182.70	150.52	154.28
II. Power, Transport and Industry:				
1. Power	125.00	28.00	71.99	71.47
2. Roads	338.00	236.75	506.38	421.92
3. Road Transport	47.00	40.00	35.00	39.92
4. Tourism	4.50	1.00	1.00	3.82
5. Cottage Industry	7.00	7.77	6.57	4.22
6. Other Industries	260.00	160.00	80.00	64.92
Total	781.50	473.52	700.94	606.27

III. Social Services and Miscellaneous:				
1. Education	110.32	108.42	71.00	77.25
2. Health	113.74	96.13	101.53	90.73
3. Housing	5.00	—	—	—
4. Press	4.80	2.20	3.00	2.83
5. Publicity	5.75	2.00	1.30	1.78
6. Marketing Centre	6.00	1.75	1.50	0.79
7. Rural Development	10.00	10.00	13.00	17.06
8. Planning Department	11.35	12.60	12.60	16.07
9. Training		10.68	5.00	4.77
Total	266.96	243.78	208.93	211.28
Grand Total	1247.79	900.00	1060.39	971.83

Sources: 1. Govt. of Sikkim, *The Third Five-Year Plan: Draft Proposals, 1966-71*, Vol. I (Gangtok: Planning and Development Department, 1965), Statement II.

2. Govt. of Sikkim, *The Third Five-Year Plan 1966-71: Final Draft*, Vol. I (Gangtok: Planning and Development Dept., 1966) Inroduction.

3. Govt. of Sikkim, *The Third Five-Year Plan of Sikkim: Mid-Term Proposals and Revised Outlays 1966-71*. (Gangtok: Planning and Development Dept., 1969).

4. Figures of actual expenditures for the entire Plan were not available. The figures in the above table were prepared by addir up the figures of plan expenditures for individual years. Vide Table X as well as the Sources mentioned thereafter.

Table V: Yearly Budget Proposals During the Second Five-Year Plan of Sikkim

(Rs. in lakh)

Head of Development	*1962-63*	*1963-64*	*1964-65*	*1965-66*
I. Agriculture and Allied Occupations:				
1. Agriculture	16.93	16.25	14.71	19.37
2. Animal Husbandry	9.82	9.64	9.10	14.33
3. Dairy Development	1.00	0.84	0.27	1.63
4. Minor Irrigation	1.83	1.62	1.13	1.35
5. Co-operation	4.35	3.87	1.91	1.74
6. Forests	18.53	18.25	14.54	20.71
7. Soil Conservation	0.80	1.25	1.00	1.40
8. Fisheries	0.10	0.19	0.01	0.12
Total	53.36	51.91	42.67	60.65

II. Power, Transport and Industry:				
1. Power	16.65	4.70	4.50	12.00
2. Roads	86.34	94.03	82.25	94.07
3. Road Transport	25.87	18.06	16.36	6.71
4. Tourism	3.85	1.00	0.50	1.50
5. Cottage Industry	6.03	6.62	3.60	2.60
6. Other Industries	5.00	5.00	5.00	12.62
Total	143.74	129.41	112.21	129.50
III. Social Services and Miscellaneous:				
1. Education	30.75	32.90	27.93	34.50
2. Health	18.99	19.57	16.75	23.45
3. Housing	2.75	3.50	4.66	4.40
4. Press	3.43	4.41	0.73	1.32
5. Publicity	1.30	0.99	0.50	0.81
6. Marketing Centre	0.75	0.91	1.00	0.72
7. Secretariat Extension	3.80	2.47	1.12	0.15
8. Community Centre	1.00	2.80	2.15	0.95
9. Planning Department	3.87	4.83	2.54	2.40
10. Cultural Activity	0.35	0.30	0.30	0.40
Total	66.99	72.68	57.68	69.10
Grand Total	264.09	254.00	212.56	259.25

Note: Figures for 1961-62 were not published.

Source: 1. Govt. of Sikkim, *Second Five-Year Plan of Sikkim: Budget Proposals for Annual Plan 1962-63 and Revised Estimates 1961-62*, (Gangtok: Planning and Development Dept.), Summary Statement. Hereafter referred to as "BP (Year) and RE (Year)" or "RE (Year)" in the case of the final year of the Plan.

2. *BP (1963-64) and RE (1962-63)*, Summary Statement.
3. *BP (1964-65) and RE (1963-64)*, Summary Statement.
4. *BP (1965-66) and RE (1964-65)*, Summary Statement.

Table VI: Yearly Revised Estimates During the Second Five-Year Plan of Sikkim

(Rs. in lakh)

Head of Development	*1962-63*	*1963-64*	*1964-65*	*1965-66*
I. Agriculture and Allied Occupations:				
1. Agriculture	9.30	7.92	14.70	12.90
2. Animal Husbandry	4.78	3.62	8.27	8.90
3. Dairy Development	0.80	1.15	1.27	1.15

4. Minor Irrigation	0.90	0.17	0.62	0.96
5. Co-operation	2.47	1.78	1.50	2.60
6. Forests	16.45	13.88	14.45	15.79
7. Soil Conservation	0.80	0.80	1.10	1.40
8. Fisheries	0.10	0.19	0.10	0.12
Total	35.60	29.51	42.01	43.82
II. Power, Transport and Industry:				
1. Power	13.25	11.37	5.29	6.49
2. Roads	66.61	74.89	76.34	58.34
3. Road Transport	17.27	12.92	17.52	12.93
4. Tourism	4.20	1.46	0.50	0.11
5. Cottage Industry	1.51	2.78	3.91	4.02
6. Other Industries	—	—	1.38	2.72
Total	102.84	103.42	104.94	84.61
III. Social Services and Miscellaneous:				
1. Education	22.48	19.73	21.70	32.31
2. Health	11.98	10.47	13.79	20.23
3. Housing	1.50	1.14	1.75	5.00
4. Press	0.55	3.21	2.04	0.68
5. Publicity	0.71	0.17	0.38	0.48
6. Marketing Centre	0.72	0.50	0.51	1.22
7. Secretariat Extension	2.20	3.00	2.40	0.39
8. Community Centre	0.50	1.00	2.55	1.79
9. Planning Department	2.98	3.68	4.26	3.81
10. Cultural Activity	0.30	0.25	0.25	0.40
Total	43.92	43.15	49.63	66.31
Grand Total	182.36	176.08	196.58	194.74

Note: Figures for 1961-62 were not published.

Sources: As for Table V excepting No. 1; and RS (1965-66), Summary Statement.

Table VII: Yearly Plan Expenditures During the Second Five-Year Plan of Sikkim

(Rs. in lakh)

Head of Development	*1961-62*	*1962-63*	*1963-64*	*1964-65*	*1965-66*
I. Agriculture and Allied Occupations:					
1. Agriculture	1.66	1.89	3.68	11.09	10.60
2. Animal Husbandry	1.45	1.21	0.38	2.99	6.76
3. Dairy Development	0.05	0.29	0.41	0.73	0.61
4. Minor Irrigation	0.16	0.24	0.08	0.11	0.86

5. Co-operation	0.37	0.22	0.01	0.73	2.82
6. Forests	6.38	11.97	11.25	10.47	13.72
7. Soil Conservation	0.57	0.52	1.21	0.87	1.39
8. Fisheries	—	0.09	0.09	0.08	—
Total	9.64	15.99	18.01	25.61	36.76
II. Power, Transport and Industry:					
1. Power	18.84	18.99	6.49	5.02	3.71
2. Roads	22.88	56.25	48.90	77.59	55.22
3. Road Transport	6.31	9.12	6.96	10.72	10.89
4. Tourism	0.80	3.49	0.72	0.18	0.05
5. Cottage Industry	1.21	1.25	1.09	2.33	3.47
6. Other Industries	—	—	—	0.60	1.81
Total	50.04	89.10	64.16	96.44	75.15
III. Social Services and Miscellaneous:					
1. Education	7.99	13.71	11.78	16.31	27.03
2. Health	5.62	7.68	6.26	7.49	15.62
3. Housing	—	0.20	0.11	1.35	4.66
4. Press	0.02	1.47	0.63	1.84	0.44
5. Publicity	0.38	0.30	0.06	0.14	0.52
6. Marketing Centre	0.37	0.23	0.07	—	1.07
7. Secretariat Extension	0.33	0.76	1.61	2.16	0.39
8. Community Centre	—	—	—	1.46	1.60
9. Planning Department	0.85	2.62	1.75	2.93	4.27
10. Cultural Activity	0.25	0.25	0.25	0.25	0.39
Total	15.81	27.22	22.52	33.93	55.99
Grand Total	75.49	132.31	104.69	155.98	167.90

Note: Separate figures of plan expenditures for 1965-66 were not available. These figures were to be incorporated in the *Budget Proposals for Annual Plan 1967-68 and Revised Estimates 1966-67,* but as these years were in the Third Plan period the document did not include the 1965-66 figures. In the above table the figures for 1965-66 have been calculated from the total figures for the entire Plan published in Govt. of India, *Progress Through Partnership* minus the sum of the figures for the earlier four years.

Source: As for Table VI; and Govt. of India, *Progress Through Partnership* (Gangtok: Office of the Political Officer in Sikkim), p. 24.

Table VIII: Yearly Budget Proposals During the Third Five-Year Plan of Sikkim

(Rs. in lakh)

Head of Development	*1966-67*	*1967-68*	*1968-69*	*1969-70*	*1970-71*
I. Agriculture and Allied Occupations:					
1. Agriculture	13.36	13.47	13.59	13.37	11.44
2. Animal Husbandry	10.07	10.73	10.05	8.17	4.70
3. Dairy Development	1.31	1.23	1.23	1.10	1.15
4. Minor Irrigation	2.20	2.25	1.23	3.40	4.43
5. Co-operation	1.50	1.60	1.35	2.25	2.40
6. Forests	7.19	14.08	14.36	15.30	14.41
7. Soil Conservation	0.85	1.16	1.15	2.15	5.84
Total	36.48	44.52	42.96	45.74	45.37
II. Power, Transport and Industry:					
1. Power	10.00	10.00	8.95	5.00	23.47
2. Roads	55.60	75.18	71.84	53.14	129.42
3. Road Transport	5.50	7.74	9.05	14.28	7.29
4. Tourism	0.25	0.25	0.25	0.40	0.40
5. Cottage Industry	1.64	1.99	3.46	1.12	1.08
6. Other Industries	13.52	17.45	21.00	22.00	30.00
Total	86.51	112.61	114.55	95.94	191.66
III. Social Services and Miscellaneous:					
1. Education	23.62	32.43	36.85	36.94	22.92
2. Health	25.00	30.25	32.04	22.85	27.28
3. Housing	—	—	—	—	—
4. Press	0.15	1.65	—	—	—
5. Publicity	0.43	0.49	0.43	0.74	0.68
6. Marketing Centre	0.78	1.25	1.00	0.50	0.50
7. Rural Development	2.60	3.15	2.95	3.38	3.80
8. Planning Department	2.45	2.84	2.75	2.82	4.08
9. Training	2.11	1.88	1.45	1.06	0.56
Total	57.14	73.94	77.47	68.29	60.02
Grand Total	180.13	231.07	234.98	209.97	297.05

Sources: 1. For Budget Proposals for Annual Plan 1966-67 see Govt. of Sikkim, *Third Five-Year Plan: 1966-71 Final Draft*, Vol. 1 (Gangtok: Planning and Development Dept., 1966).

2. BP (1967-68) and RE (1966-67), Summary Statement.

3. BP (1968-69) and RE (1967-68), Summary Statement.
4. BP (1969-70) and RE (1968-69), Summary Statement.
5. BP (1970-71) and RE (1969-70), Summary Statement.

Table IX: Yearly Revised Estimates During the Third Five-Year Plan of Sikkim

(Rs. in lakh)

Head of Development	*1966-67*	*1967-68*	*1968-69*	*1969-70*	*1970-71*
I. Agriculture and Allied Occupations:					
1. Agriculture	14.93	11.26	13.26	10.57	15.81
2. Animal Husbandry	5.73	5.27	5.62	4.56	4.59
3. Dairy Development	0.87		0.25	0.35	1.70
4. Minor Irrigation	0.51	0.32	1.30	4.74	2.11
5. Co-operation	2.10	1.35	1.50	1.31	4.85
6. Forests	7.77	9.36	8.85	13.21	21.57
7. Soil Conservation	0.35	1.66	1.03	3.15	5.84
Total	32.76	29.22	31.81	37.89	56.47
II. Power, Transport and Industry:					
1. Power	6.00	13.00	9.85	13.82	26.75
2. Roads	65.06	93.02	50.57	144.88	150.55
3. Road Transport	4.27	4.25	10.00	15.42	9.22
4. Tourism	0.25	--	0.40	0.41	0.47
5. Cottage Industry	1.64	1.40	1.99	1.67	1.11
6. Other Industries	12.50	11.28	15.75	20.14	35.81
Total	39.72	12.95	88.56	196.34	223.91
III. Social Services and Miscellaneous:					
1. Education	19.92	18.34	20.41	20.71	28.09
2. Health	27.20	26.12	27.74	21.58	28.21
3. Press	0.15	2.50	0.01	0.14	0.30
4. Publicity	0.20	0.27	0.37	0.39	1.00
5. Marketing Centre	0.50	0.50	0.50	0.28	0.52
6. Rural Development	2.90	2.65	3.17	2.53	5.05
7. Planning Department	2.51	2.56	2.27	3.01	5.66
8. Training	1.80	1.37	0.86	0.63	0.87
Total	55.18	54.31	55.33	49.27	69.60
Grand Total	177.66	206.48	175.70	283.50	349.98

Sources: As for Table VIII excepting No. 1; and *RE (1970-71)*, Summary Statement.

Table X: Yearly Plan Expenditures During the Third Five-Year Plan of Sikkim

(Rs. in lakh)

Head of Development	*1966-67*	*1967-68*	*1968-69*	*1969-70*	*1970-71*
I. Agriculture and Allied Occupations:					
1. Agriculture	9.77	7.74	16.48	5.39	8.73
2. Animal Husbandry	3.46	2.73	3.35	3.65	3.63
3. Dairy Development	—	—	—	—	0.15
4. Minor Irrigation	0.13	0.22	0.48	6.76	1.50
5. Co-operation	3.12	1.98	2.19	0.30	10.11
6. Forests	5.23	7.75	8.35	12.24	16.19
7. Soil Conservation	0.77	1.85	1.14	3.13	6.36
Total	22.48	22.27	31.99	30.87	46.67
II. Power, Transport and Industry:					
1. Power	2.81	18.04	13.86	14.93	21.83
2. Roads	51.76	71.90	78.90	94.16	126.06
3. Road Transport	1.83	3.89	11.57	13.53	9.10
4. Tourism	—	—	0.19	0.34	3.29
5. Cottage Industry	1.20	2.47	0.58	0.72(-)	0.75
6. Other Industries	3.92	11.43	14.51	12.25	22.81
Total	61.52	106.87	119.61	135.93	182.34
III. Social Services and Miscellaneous:					
1. Education	8.64	12.49	13.34	14.32	28.46
2. Health	16.78	18.59	22.87	13.92	18.57
3. Press	—	2.40	0.01	0.07	0.35
4. Publicity	0.02	0.15	0.31	0.13	1.17
5. Marketing Centre	0.06	0.26	—	—	0.47
6. Rural Development	2.77	3.38	3.02	3.47	4.42
7. Planning Department	2.16	2.32	2.03	2.49	7.07
8. Training	1.52	1.19	0.80	0.56	0.70
Total	31.95	40.78	42.38	34.96	61.21
Grand Total	115.95	169.92	193.98	201.76	290.22

Sources: As for Table IX; and the figures for 1970-71 were collected from Planning and Development Dept., Govt. of Sikkim.

Also see, Govt. of Sikkim, *The Third Five-Year Plan: Progress Report April, 1969-March, 1970* (Gangtok: Planning and Development Dept.), pp. viii-ix.

Table XI: Yearly Budget Proposals, Revised Estimates and Plan Expenditures During the Second and Third Five-Year Plans of Sikkim

Grand Totals *(Rs. in lakh)*

Year	*Budget Proposals*	*Revised Estimates*	*Plan Expenditures*
1962-62	...	...	75.49
1962-63	264.09	182.36	132.31
1963-64	254.00	176.08	104.69
1964-65	212.56	196.58	155.98
1965-66	259.25	194.74	167.90
1966-67	180.13	177.66	115.95
1967-68	231.07	206.48	169.92
1968-69	234.98	175.70	193.98
1969-70	209.97	283.50	201.76
1970-71	297.05	249.98	290.21

Source: loc. cit.

Table XII: Yearly Budget Expenditure in Sikkimese Plans

(Rs. in lakh)

Year	*Agriculture and Allied Occupations*	*Power, Transport and Industry*	*Social Services and Miscellaneous*	*Total*
1961-62	2.96	1.72	9.40	14.08
1962-63	3.28	1.88	11.26	16.42
1963-64	6.53	1.97	11.27	19.77
1964-65	9.83	2.26	14.81	26.90
1966-67	7.07	1.20	8.03	16.30
1967-68	9.95	1.21	10.42	21.58
1968-69	12.33	1.32	11.16	24.81
1969-70	14.53	1.66	14.54	30.73
All Years	66.48	13.22	90.89	170.59

Note: Figures for 1965-66 and 1970-71 not available.

Sources: 1. RE (1965-66), Statements II to V for the years 1961-62, 1962-63, 1963-64 and 1964-65.

2. RE (1970-71), Annexures II to V for the years 1966-67, 1967-68, 1968-69, and 1969-70.

Table XIII: Yearly Building Expenditures in Sikkimese Plans

(*Rs. in lakh*)

Year	*Agriculture and Allied Occupations*	*Power, Transport and Industry*	*Social Services and Miscellaneous*	*Total*
1961-62	0.34	1.31	4.46	6.11
1962-63	3.84	5.29	12.72	21.85
1963-64	5.39	6.65	8.92	20.96
1964-65	6.84	6.76	11.84	25.44
1966-67	2.24	0.33	7.20	8.77
1967-68	3.09	0.99	11.13	15.21
1968-69	2.21	1.04	8.46	11.71
1969-70	2.83	23.23	72.21	122.22
All years	85.58 (10%)	685.23 (80%)	86.46 (10%)	857.27 (100%)

Note: Figures for 1965-66 and 1970-71 not available.
Sources: Loc. cit.

Table XIV: Yearly Other Non-Recurring Expenditures in Sikkimese Plans

(*Rs. in lakh*)

Year	*Agriculture and Allied Occupations*	*Power, Transport and Industry*	*Social Services and Miscellaneous*	*Total*
1961-62	6.34	47.01	1.95	55.30
1962-63	8.87	81.93	3.24	94.04
1963-64	6.09	55.54	2.33	63.96
1964-65	8.94	87.42	7.28	103.64
1966-67	13.17	59.99	16.72	89.88
1967-68	9.23	104.67	19.23	133.13
1968-69	17.45	117.25	22.76	157.46
1969-70	13.49	133.42	12.95	159.86
All Years	85.88 (10%)	685.23 (80%)	86.46 (10%)	857.27 (100%)

Note: Figures for 1965-66 and 1970-71 not available.
Sources: Loc. cit.

Table XV: Composition of Yearly Plan Expenditures into Recurring, Building and Other Non-Recurring Expenditures

(Rs. in lakh)

	Type of Expenditure			
Year	*Recurring*	*Building*	*Non-Recurring*	*Total*
1961-62	14.08	6.11	55.30	75.49
1962-63	16.42	21.85	94.04	132.31
1963-64	19.77	20.96	63.96	104.69
1964-65	26.90	25.44	103.64	155.98
1966-67	16.30	9.77	89.88	115.95
1967-68	21.58	15.21	133.13	169.92
1968-69	24.81	11.71	157.46	193.98
1969-70	30.73	11.17	159.86	201.76
All Years	170.59	122.22	857.27	1150.08
	(15%)	(11%)	(74%)	(100%)

Note: Figures for 1965-66 and 1970-71 not available. Sources: loc. cit.

REFERENCES

1. Govt. of Sikkim, *Second Development Plan* (A Five-Year Plan 1961-62—1965-66), Unpublished Draft, Part I, 1960. Introduction. Hereafter, referred to as "Second Plan (Unpublished)".
2. Govt. of India, *Second Five-Year Plan of Sikkim: Report of the Technical Team* (New Delhi : Planning Commission, 1961), p. 15. Hereafter referred to as "First Team's Report."
3. *Ibid.*, p. 5.
4. Govt. of India, *Mid-Term Appraisal of the Second Five-Year Plan of Sikkim: Report of the Technical Team* (New Delhi: Planning Commission 1964), p. 11. Hereafter referred to as "Second Team's Report."
5. *Ibid.*
6. Govt. of Sikkim, *Second Five-Year Plan: 1961-66* (Gangtok: Public Relations Officer), p. 1.
7. First Team's Report, pp. 9-11.
8. *Ibid.*, Preface.
9. Second Team's Report, p. 6.
10. Govt., of Sikkim, *The-Third Five-Year Plan of Sikkim: Mid-Term Proposals and Revised Outlays 1966-71* (Gangtok: Planning and Development Dept., 1969), p. 1.

11. See Appendix, Table X.
12. A.G.B. Fisher, "Primary, Secondary and Tertiary Production", *Economic Record,* June, 1939, pp. 24-38.
13. C. Clark, *The Conditions of Economic Progress,* 3rd ed. (New York: St. Martin's, 1957), ch. 7.
14. A. Ghosh, *Indian Economy: Its Nature and Problems,* 7th ed., rev. and enlarged (Calcutta: The World Press Private Ltd., 1963), pp. 132-35.
15. See Appendix, Table XI.
16. Govt. of Sikkim, *Second Five-Year Plan of Sikkim: Budget Proposals 1963-64 and Revised Estimates 1962-63* (Gangtok: Planning and Development Dept.), pp. 2-3. Hereafter referred to as "BP (Year) ana RE (Year)" or "RE(Year)" in the case of the final year of a plan.
17. *Ibid.*
18. *Ibid.*
19. BP 1969-70 and RE 1968-69, Explanatory Memorandum. Also see *RE 1970-71,* pp. iii-iv.
20. Govt. of Sikkim. *The Third Five-Year Plan: Progress Report April 1969 — March, 1970* (Gangtok: Planning and Development Dept., 1970) Forward. Hereafter referred to as *"Progress Report (Month Year) -' (Month, Year)."*
21. Progress Report October, 1968 — March, 1969, Introduction.
22. *Ibid.,* Statement I.
23. RE 1970-71, p. iv.
24. See Appendix, Table XV.
25. See Appendix, Table XII.
26. See Appendix, Table XIII.
27. See Appendix, Table XIV.
28. United Nations, *Planning for Economic Development* (New York: Dept. of Economic and Social Affairs, 1963), p. 5.
29. Govt. of Sikkim, *Sikkim Development Plan* (Gangtok: Sikkim Durbar Press, 1955), Introduction.
30. Second Team's Report.
31. Second Plan (Unpublished), p. 3.
32. G. Myrdal, *International Economy: Problems and Prospects* (London: Routledge & Kegan Paul, Ltd., 1959), p. 79.
33. National Council of Applied Economic Research, *Socio-Economic Conditions of Primitive Tribes in Madhya Pradesh* (New Delhi: 1963), p. xii.

5

Forestry and Agriculture

In the last chapter we made an introductory survey of the first three plans of Sikkim. In this and the subsequent chapters we shall try to have a critical appraisal of the achievements of the plans in different sectors of the economy. First, we shall take up "Forestry and Agriculture" which may be regarded as representative of the Primary Sector. Secondly, we shall take up "Power, Transport and Industries" which, in our schema, constitute the Secondary Sector; and lastly, we shall consider developments under planning in the fields of "Health Services and Education" which may be regarded as the core of the Tertiary Sector.

A. Development of Forestry during the Plans

Although Sikkim falls practically in the north temperate zone, because of wide latitudinal range of altitudes the climate exhibits a great variety of conditions. As one goes northward, one can see climatic conditions varying from almost tropical in the south to Alpine in the north. Moreover, with the increase in altitude rainfall also increases, though it is not strictly the case throughout Sikkim. The latitudinal range, altitude and variations in rainfall account for the great profusion of flora and fauna—of orchids, rhododendrons and butterflies, to name only the three remarkable gifts of nature to the country.

From the point of view of the botanist, Sikkim is a herbarium containing in its whole extent types of every flora from the tropics to the poles, and probably no other country of equal size on earth can present so many features of interest to a naturalist.

Generally speaking, three distinct types of forests are seen in Sikkim: *(i)* the sal forests which occupy an area of 8,500 acres extending from an altitude of 700 feet to about 3,000 feet in the Tista, Rangit and Rishi valleys; *(ii)* the broad-leaved forests comprising the middle and upper hill forests; and *(iii)* lastly, the coniferous forests which extend over 45,000 acres along the valleys of Lachen, Lachung and Dombang. While in the eastern and western Sikkim deciduous and ever-green forests are more commonly found, northern Sikkim is predominated by coniferous forests.

Mr. M. M. Rasaily, the Conservator of Forests in Sikkim, has, however, divided the forests into five zones as follows:

(i)	Lower-Hill Forests Between	700′ - 3,000′
(ii)	Middle-Hill Forests Between	3,500′-5,500′
(iii)	Upper-Hill Forests Between	7,000′- 9,500′
(iv)	Conifer Forests Between	8,000′-10,000′
(v)	Rhododendron Forests Between	9,000′- 11,500′

Source: M. M. Rasaily, *Sikkim: Its Flora and Fauna*, Part I, *Sikkim Herald*, May, 29, 1970.

There was also a legal classification of the forests in Sikkim which was operative during the period under review. The classifications as well as their respective areas may be mentioned as below:

(i)	Reserve Forests	572.68 Square Miles
(ii)	Private Estate Forests	125.00 Square Miles
(iii)	Khasmahal Forests	39.62 Square Miles
(iv)	Gorucharan Forests	10.70 Square Miles
(v)	Slip Reserve & Road Reserve Forests	N.A.

In Sikkim there was a forest manual which had been serving as a statute book since 1909 when it was first compiled. Since then it has been supplemented from time to time. According to that manual no rights and concessions to the people existed as far as Reserve Forests were concerned. So far as Private Estate Forests were concerned, all rights, of course, devolved upon the owner landlords and their tenants. In the case of Khasmahal Forests people had the right of free supply of timber and fire-wood but this could be availed of only after obtaining formal permission from the Forest Department. In Gorucharan

Forests the local people had the right of free grazing and collection of deadwood and fodder. Slip Reserve and Road Reserve Forests were maintained by the state for the prevention of soil erosion and the protection of roads and no rights were allowed in those forests.[1]

When the Second Plan was launched in Sikkim out of the total surface area of 2,828 square miles in Sikkim, the forests occupied 748 square miles excluding Slip Reserve and Road Reserve Forests for which figures are not available. This means that more than one-fourth of the total surface area of the country was covered by forests. Forests occupied nearly 310 square miles in the northern zone, while in the intensely cultivated eastern and western zones forests covered only 203 and 235 square miles respectively.

In western Sikkim heavy damages were done to the forests as the Nepali immigrants settled there just before the beginning of the 20th century. Forest administration at that time was solely in the hands of land-lessees who were responsible for construction of forest roads, demarcation of boundaries and apprehension of offenders but actually little care was taken in those respects.

Sikkim turned to Government-sponsored forestry at the beginning of 20th century when a Department of Forests came into existence under the Chogyal Sidkeong Tulku, who was responsible for having the forest reserves demarcated for the first time. The major role played by the forest personnel was, however, the policing and protecting of natural resources of the country, and little attention was paid to the development of those resources in a planned and scientific manner.[2] Administration of forests was still in the hands of the land-lessees and that was surely a stumbling block to the development of scientific forestry in the country.

Forest administration was taken over directly by the state in 1950 and the next year a working plan was prepared by Mr. K. C. Ray Choudhury, the then Deputy Conservator of Forests. The plan, however, did not cover the coniferous forests of north Sikkim. But it was the first systematic and conscious effort towards development of forestry in Sikkim.

A much more comprehensive plan for forest development was initiated during the era of development planning. The salient features of development of forestry during the First Plan period may be mentioned under the following heads: *(i)* re-organization of the Forest Department, *(ii)* soil conservation and afforestation programmes, *(iii)* opening up of the forest areas, particularly in the north, for exploitation, through the programme of floatation of timber, and *(iv)* the cultivation of some medicinal herbs. A total amount of Rs. 22.58 lakhs was spent during the Plan for all these programmes.

Before the First Plan the Forest Department was under a Forest Manager. In order to meet the needs arising out of the Government's desire to exploit forest wealth as a source of income, the Forest Department was re-organised during the Plan period. A Conservator of Forests was appointed and three forest divisions were created. The headquarters for western Sikkim was at Temi while those for eastern and northern Sikkim were established at Gangtok. These forest divisions were placed in charge of Divisional Forest Officers.

Sikkim is the catchment area of the Tista and Rangit rivers which flow through the country into West Bengal. Sikkim, therefore, receives heavy rainfall during the monsoon. These rains often cause floods and lead to excessive soil erosion and land-slides. During the Plan one Soil Conservation Range was started with headquarters at Gangtok to take up soil conservation work throughout the state. The purpose of this Range was to prevent landslips, land-slides and soil erosion which are common in Sikkim and which, apart from damaging highways and bridges, are a positive hindrance to the agricultural development of the country.

Three thousand acres were covered during the Plan by the soil conservation and afforestation programmes which were taken up along the main highways and certain areas in the interior. Soil Conservation Nurseries were established at Gangtok, Rhenock, Temi, Shyampani and Soreng. About 55 lakh seedlings were produced in these nurseries. Moreover, sal and other valuable species were planted at Song and Melli on 80 acres of land. Demarcation of forest boundaries in order to guard against encroachment was extended to 28 miles of forests in western Sikkim and 38 miles in eastern Sikkim.[3]

During the First Seven-Year Plan of Sikkim the Forest Department constructed several miles of roads and forest paths, range officers quarters, godowns and inspection huts. It also sent 24 trainees to India —two of them to the Superior Forest Service Course in Dehra Dun and the rest to the Forest Rangers' Course in Dehra Dun and Kurseong.

Under the major scheme of "floatation of timber" (initiated in 1951) the expected results could not be achieved. Once, in 1955, because of flood some 26,000 out of 36,000 floated timber scantlings had been washed away and the loss to the Indian contractor was enormous. This resulted in a lull in further operations. In 1959 and early 1960 a total of 110,000 cubic feet of timber was sawn departmentally in north Sikkim and sold to a Sikkimese contractor.[4]

This time also the results were discouraging. Out of the total of 1,10,000 cubic feet of timber floated in two consignments, 86,000 cubic feet were lost in floods and only 24,000 cubic feet of timber could be salvaged. The saw mill which was set up under the Plan at Rangpo could not be fully utilised because of the failure of the timber floating operation. This mill had been run by the Forest Department and had been used primarily for supplying packing-cane wood to the fruit preservation factory and distillery near Rangpo. Due to a shortage of timber arising out of the failure of the floatation programme the mill could not meet the requirements of the above-mentioned factories, and it had to close down ultimately.[5]

All this suggests that a critical scrutiny of the entire programme of floatation of timber should be made and improvements in the technique and manner of floatation initiated to make it a success. If it were possible to make the programme a success, it would be a boon to Sikkim, because it would then enable the Government, practically without any cost, to exploit the vast untapped forest resources of Sikkim, particularly in the north. It is to be noted that in the coniferous forests of north Sikkim alone an estimated 18 lakhs cubic feet of fir timber is available for felling every year.[6] The total amount of salvaged timber out of the floatation programme during the entire seven-year period of the Plan was, however, only about 1.5 per cent of that potential.

Prima facie the failure of the floatation programme appeared to the Second Technical Team to be due to the ill-timing of the launching of timber. It was, therefore, suggested by the Team that flood-peaks in the Tista river along with the average dates of the break of monsoon should be closely studied and thereby the most suitable time of launching arrived at. It might be, according to the Team, somewhere between mid-October and early March. The Team also suggested that the operation of floating might be done in two stages: from the launching site to Naga and from Naga to Sevoke in West Bengal. This might reduce the loss of timber during floatation.[7]

Apart from the extraction of timber there is a great potentiality in Sikkim for the cultivation of medicinal herbs which can be an important source of revenue to the Government. Certain experimental schemes were undertaken during the First Plan period, particularly for raising Ipecac, Rauwoulfia Serpentina and Lycopodium. In Sikkim these grow in natural state and attempts were made to collect them in natural state as well as to introduce improved varieties.

Under the Second Five-Year Plan the programmes that were started in the First Plan were further continued and intensified with special emphasis on afforestation, soil conservation, floating of timber and development of medicinal herbs, particularly Ipecac. The aim of the Second Plan was to collect a total forest revenue to the tune of Rs. 49 lakhs as against the actual revenue of Rs. 17 lakhs earned during the First Plan from forestry.

For the prevention of deforestation and the development of forest resources various programmes were undertaken during the Plan. An important programme related to plantations. Here, against the Plan target of 8100 acres, it was possible to plant up to 6094 acres only in areas extending from the sal belt in the valley to the high-altitude coniferous belt at 10,000 feet height. Of these, 4428 acres were planted up by 609 Taungyadar families and the remaining 1666 acres were planted up departmentally.

In the progress report of the Second Five-Year Plan three reasons have been shown for the non-fulfilment of the Plan target of 8100 acres of plantation. First of all, a good number of Taungyadar families were unable to plant up 4 acres of land per year as planned—in practice, the average family could plant up only two acres of land per year. This indicates defects in Plan estimates.

Secondly, a lot of Taungyadars left their homesteads because of the comparatively higher wages offered to them by road building and other construction agencies. Here also the planning authorities should have estimated the future level of wages in different sectors and tried to eliminate wage-differentials.

Lastly, it was often found during plantations that the stereotyped methods of plantation were ineffective in the areas that had been lying barren and exposed to grazing for more than a decade.[8] The experience indicates that any plan for afforestation should be made on a long term basis after careful examination of soil conditions and environmental pre-requisites.

During the Plan period 10 field nurseries covering approximately 30 acres were established. These met the need for quality saplings for field plantations. In addition, ornamental trees and trees of economic value were planted along 180 miles of roads and highways throughout the State.

For soil conservation approximately 25,00,000 seedlings of soil-binding species were raised at 12 different nurseries and these seedlings were planted on an area covering 3,070 acres scattered over many places where soil erosion was rampant. In addition, other measures like gully-plugging, check-damming, seed broadcasting and fencing off of vulnerable areas were also carried out.[9]

During the Second Plan period various effective measures were taken for the exploitation of forest resources. One such measure was the construction of forest paths, roads and bridges connecting the interior regions of forests with the existing links of communication. The Plan provided for the construction of 280 miles of such paths and roads but it was possible to construct only 205 miles, because the remaining 75 miles fell within the 'prohibited zones'. Four bridges with a span of over 75 feet were also constructed during the Plan period.

Apart from the construction of roads and bridges, the Second Plan also laid emphasis on the already undertaken scheme of floatation of timber which was so far a failure. An important feature of this scheme in this period was that the Indian Railways showed interest in purchasing sleepers, specially of silver fir timber, and negotiations were under way in that matter. Consequently, during the Plan 3,34,000 cubic feet of timber was converted into sleepers at the Lachung-Dombang Reserve Forest in north Sikkim and then these sleepers were floated in the river. This time also a large number of sleepers were lost in the process of floatation.

The main factor behind the set-back of the scheme was the nature of the river between Dombang and Chungthang. It was on this 12 miles stretch of the river that the greatest loss of sleepers occurred. This loss could have been avoided if the transportation of sleepers from Dombang to Chungthang was by road and then floatation was resorted to. There was also the problem of loss of sleepers at the boom site because of sudden and unexpected floods.[10]

Medicinal herbs are an important resource of the Sikkimese forests and effective measures should, therefore, be taken for their exploitation. During the Second Five-Year Plan the construction of 530 sheds for the growing of Ipecac was undertaken and it was possible to harvest 850 kilograms of Ipecac roots with a high alkaloid content.

The Second Plan also undertook various other measures for the overall development of forestry such as expansion of the Forest Department by recruiting officers and subrodinate staff, construction of official and residential buildings, training of staff and survey-scum-demarcation of forests.

During the Third Five-Year Plan period attention was paid mainly to the consolidation and extension of what had already been achieved in forestry during the previous two plans. Two of the continuing projects then given priority comprised (i) expansion of the existing plantations and nurseries, and (ii) extending the cultivation of Ipecac and other medicinal herbs. At the end of the Third Plan there were 9,000 acres under plantations and nurseries of valuable species and they were being added to at the rate of 1,200 acres per annum.[11]

During the Plan period measures were taken on a national scale to counter the erosion of soil. Strict closures were adopted in forest slip areas where dragging and felling of trees was strictly prohibited. An extensive afforestation programme was also launched and engineering measures such as gully-plugs, check-dams and contour-terraces were adopted in all slip areas. There was also an expansion of nurseries specialising in fast-growing and soil-binding saplings required for soil conservation. To check encroachment and maintain proper control over the forest reserves, expensive demarcation had been carried out and approximately 400 miles of boundary lines had been surveyed during the Plan period.[12]

As part of the programme to protect the country's natural resources, the Forest Department was engaged in the preservation of wild life and in a publicity drive creating public awareness to this problem. The preservation of wild life is, however, a long-term scheme and only a start was made during the Plan period with the seasonal feeding of animals, to be followed later on with the setting up of sanctuaries and reserve parks.

Apart from these programmes the Forest Department created a Utilisation Division to cater to the public need for fuel, charcoal and timber. The timber was shaped and treated at the Department's saw mill and seasoning kiln located at the banks of the Tista five miles above Rangpo. The Division was serviced by a fleet of trucks, and gravity ropeways were used to extract raw forest produce from areas inaccessible to vehicles.

The 17 years of planning, as we have seen, have brought about remarkable development in the field of Sikkimese forestry. But the scope for further development still remains. Forests, particularly the northern coniferous ones, are the biggest single natural resource of the country, and as such a much bigger plan than hitherto undertaken is required for tapping this vast resource. Moreover, forests form an expanding source of revenue to the Government and an early development of this source in a planned and scientific manner would greatly facilitate the financing of the State's development plans.

In this connection the question of optimal use of forest resources naturally crops up. It is to be seen whether the simple export of timber and other forest products is better than their export after some industrial processing. In this regard the Second Technical Team recommended the setting up of some forest-based industries in Sikkim; but this recommendation still awaits to be translated into action.

At the same time the Team was also of the opinion that in a hilly country like Sikkim at least 60 per cent of the total land surface should be under forests. At present forests occupy only 30 per cent of the total land surface.[13] It is incumbent, therefore, on the part of the planners to bear this point in mind while formulating the plans.

B. Development of Agriculture During the Plans

Just like any other underdeveloped country the basic occupation in Sikkim is agriculture. Nearly 95 per cent of the people in Sikkim depend mainly on agriculture for their livelihood.[14] Agriculture here is more a "way of life" than a mode of business. It is followed as part of the traditional pattern of life and as the simplest method of obtaining food for the family. The working unit in agriculture is very often the household itself and the family income is divided among the members not according to productivity but according to needs. The needs are generally unfulfilled, particularly in the case of foodgrains, and imports are then the only alternative.

Though there is deficiency in the production of cereals, a sizeable amount of cash crops, principally cardamom, oranges, potatoes and apples are produced and exported to India. Just before the introduction of developmental plans the estimated value of annual exports was about Rs. 45 lakhs of which cardamom was responsible for Rs. 30 lakhs, oranges Rs. 10 lakhs, potatoes Rs. 4 lakhs and apples Rs. 1 lakh. A certain amount of vegetables and pulses were also exported, mostly to the neighbouring Darjeeling district in West Bengal.[15]

Along with agriculture some subsidiary occupations are undertaken like diary and poultry farming. Their products are important sources of protein. But production in these lines is small and prices are high. As such the quality of the average Sikkimese diet is not up to the mark.

Surprisingly, the Sikkimese planners are not aware of this and even before the commencement of the Second Plan when there was little development in dairy, poultry and fisheries they claimed that "from the nutritional point of view the diet of the Sikkimese people is quite satisfactory."[16] Obviously, the planners were over-eulogistic about their performance.

While fish is a rare commodity in the hills and can hardly be bred commercially, the production of milk, meat and eggs can be augmented to a great extent through appropriate planning. If that is done it could relieve the pressure on agriculture appreciably.

The proportion of contribution of agriculture including animal husbandry and forestry to the net domestic product of Sikkim is about 30 per cent.[17] In 1965-66 while the net domestic product of Sikkim was Rs 894.58 lakhs the contribution of the agricultural sector including animal husbandry and forestry was Rs. 721.16 lakhs.[18] It is clear, therefore, that the agricultural sector plays a very important role in the economy of Sikkim.

The cultivated area in Sikkim is 2,50,000 acres* of which the area under irrigation is 28,000 acres.[19] The main characteristic of agriculture in Sikkim is that it is adapted to the area where it is practised. Since it is practised at all levels between 700 feet and 13,000 feet and in relatively dry (60" rainfall) to relatively wet (200" rainfall) areas and in level ground as well as steep hill sides, the variations are extremely marked. In general, cultivation is either wet (paddy) or dry (other crops). Wet cultivation is terraced and sometimes irrigated whereas dry cultivation is more often not. "Jhuming" or shifting cultivation is practised in some places, particularly Zongu, but it is gradually being replaced by permanent cultivation.[20]

Agriculture in Sikkim is necessarily influenced by the nature of the terrain, soil and climatic conditions. The terrain is hilly, but the soil is generally good. Plentiful rainfall and varying altitudes and climate provide opportunities for raising a large variety of food and cash crops. However, the average yield is generally low and the country is deficient in foodgrains.

The most important cereal crops are *maize* and *paddy*. *Cardamom*, potatoes, oranges, apples and vegetables are the major cash crops and they are exported in sizeable quantities. The area under cultivation in Sikkim can be broken up (for different crops) as follows:

* According to another source the total cultivated area is 2,02,690 acres. Vide Govt. of Sikkim, *Sikkim Through Figures*, p. 7.

Area under Cultivation in Sikkim

Crops	*Acres*
1. Maize	135.000
2. Paddy	30,000
3. Cardamom	15,000
4. Millet	12,000
5. Wheat & Barley	11,000
6. Oranges	5,000
7. Potatoes	4,000
8. Apples	2,000
9. Buck Wheat	2,000
10. Other crops	34,000
Total (All Crops)	250,000

Source: Govt. of Sikkim, *Sikkim - The Land and the People*, p. 5.

Maize is the most important staple crop of the State occupying an area of 135,000 acres. At present the average yield of maize is very low and is only about 4 quintals per acre. The yield can be substantially increased by growing hybrid maize as well as by the application of fertilizers, adoption of plant protection measures and imporved agricultural practices.[21] In fact, the yield has increased in many places through the adoption of these measures during the years of developmental planning.

After maize, paddy is the next important staple crop of the State, occupying an area of 30,000 acres. The yield of rice per acre is about 4.5 quintals[22] and it is necessary that this acreage be increased. The Second Technical Team was of the opinion that the varieties of paddy which respond to high dozes of fertilizers should be introduced in the State because they found that it was very difficult to increase the yield of the local varieties through the application of fertilizers.[23]

Sikkim is one of the world's largest suppliers of cardamom. Cardamom is also Sikkim's major cash crop. It grows almost like a weed on shaded mountain-sides around Gangtok. It is only due to cardamom that the Sikkimese cultivators are often more prosperous than their counterparts in India, Nepal or Bhutan. Indeed, in the words of an Indian trader it is Sikkim's Fairy

Godmother, Godfather and Salvation — all in one.[24] The average yield of cardamom is about 2 quintals per acre and the high price of the crop makes it more profitable than most other crops.[25]

Mandarin orange is already growing in the State on lower elevations and covers nearly 5,000 acres. Practically all these trees have been raised from seed and as such are growing on their own roots. It has been observed that under proper management the trees can remain healthy and vigorous for many years. There are certain trees which are more than 100 years old.

However, at present there is no suitable variety of mandarin orange available in the country which can be taken up for preservation in the fruit preservation factory situated at Singtam. It was suggested by the Second Technical Team that some plants of Unshiu Mikan variety of seedless mandarin orange from Japan might be grown on some Government farms for adaptive trials.[26] However, the trial has not yet been initiated and it remains to be proved whether this variety can survive at all in the climatic conditions of Sikkim.

Potato is also an important cash crop of Sikkim. There is a huge demand for seed potatoes in West Bengal and Bihar and it is estimated that, if proper care is taken, Sikkim can meet all the requirements of seed potatoes of both these areas.[27] The average yield of potatoes per acre is about 4.5 quintals and it is very low compared to the average yield in India which is about 30 quintals.[28] However, the quality of Sikkimese potatoes is generally excellent and for this reason it has a high demand for seed purposes in the neighbouring states. One reason why the yield is so low is that the cultivators often do not harvest their crop in proper time but leave it on the fields during the entire rainy season as they have no place to store the produce. This results in heavy wastage in the fields and in order to avoid this loss, it is essential to arrange for cold storage.[29]

Apples form one of the main sources of cash income. Large quantities of apple are taken to the various markets in India. Previously, when there was free trade with Tibet, apples were exported to the Tibetan markets of Shigatse and Yatung in return for *tsampa* (parched barley flour), *chhurpi* (hard cheese), butter and dry meat.

As the average fainfall in the State is pretty high, the area does not seem to be quite suitable for a large-scale cultivation of apples. The apples grown in Sikkim are of poor quality and in short supply. These are mostly grown in the western and northern districts of Sikkim where average rainfall varies from 60 to 80 inches. The Second Technical Team suggested that the area under apple cultivation should be extended. Moreover, it also suggested that if the fruit failed to develop proper colour due to high rainfall and cloudiness, it could be utilised for preparing apple juice and other products in the fruit preservation factory at Singtam.[31] However, up till now no development has taken place in this respect.

Millet, wheat, barley and buck-wheat are cultivated extensively in Sikkim. But their yield is very low and they are consumed mostly by the poorer sections of the people in the lean season when the usual crops like maize and paddy are short in supply.

Apart from these principal crops a host of other crops are raised in Sikkim and it is necessary to pay adequate attention to their proper development. The Second Technical Team suggested a much greater diversification of the agricultural sector, particularly in the field of horticulture which is the main source of export earnings. The Team suggested that along with the mandarin orange, pineaple can also be grown in the same area. The general practice in Sikkim is, however, to grow maize in the mandarin orchards. But it would be more paying to grow pineapples instead of maize in such cases and the people should be encouraged to take the initiative.[32] In the opinion of the Team there is also scope for growing lichi on lower elevations and the possibility of extending the area under this fruit should be explored.[33]

There are many wild pear trees growing in the state. These trees can be top-worked to commercial varieties of pear as is being done in Himachal Pradesh, particularly in the Mandi district. The Second Technical Team suggested that some workers should be sent to Mandi to see and learn the top-working of pear trees and they should be employed to take up the same type of work in Sikkim when they come back.[34] The suggestion, however, has not yet been implemented and the development in this field is quite negligible.

Development of agriculture is essential for industrialisation as well as for the overall growth of an economy. As such it should be given high priority in any developmental plan.

B. Development of Agriculture During the Plans

The development of agriculture in Sikkim faced with various types of difficulties. These difficulties arise mainly from the hilly nature of the terrain, lack of irrigation facilities, limited extent of arable land and the out-dated mode of production. Any agricultural plan for the country should specially consider these aspects and chalk out a programme accordingly. In Sikkim, while natural factors can hardly be changed, human factors can be moulded to play a great role in the development of agriculture.

It was in the light of these considerations that the objectives of the agricultural programmes in the First Seven-Year Plan were formulated. The main objectives of agricultural development under the Plan were: "to develop agriculture on scientific lines, increase the per acre yields of important crops and make the State self-sufficient in some of the food-grains which were being imported from outside."[35]

If we analyse the above objectives we shall see that the objective of developing agriculture on scientific lines was of primary importance for a country like Sikkim where traditional, and sometimes primitive, modes of production prevailed and where agriculture was much more difficult to reorganise than in the plains due to reasons already referred to. In fact, a scientific mode of production is the *sine qua non* for agricultural development in such a situation. The achievements of Japan and Israel in the field of agriculture can be mentioned in this connection as examples of how countries with natural barriers can develop their agriculture through the use of better techniques.

The other two objectives, viz., increase in the per acre yields of important crops and making the State self-sufficient in some of the food-grains which were being imported from outside, were corollary to the first objective — they could be achieved only through the development of agriculture on scientific line. The objective of self-sufficiency, however, ultimately proved to be unrealistic as the importation of food-grains continued as usual even after the First Plan. There was a belated realisation that Sikkim had much scope for agricultural development but there was a limit.

A conscious effort to advance agriculture was initiated with the commencement of the First Seven-Year Plan (1954-61). A sum of Rs. 13.00 lakhs was spent during the Plan period for agriculture and rural development and Rs. 11.21 lakhs for horticulture.[36] It was during these years that public consciousness was aroused for the first time to adopt modern scientific means of cultivation and a separate department was set up for the purpose. There was no Department of Agriculture before the First Plan. A nucleus organisation was started in 1955 with the appointment of a Director of Agriculture assisted by some sub-ordinate staff.

In the first phase of development the Department introduced and placed under trial improved varieties of crops from India and arranged for supply of seeds of superior performance. The use of fertilizars as a direct aid in stepping up crop yields and adoption of plant protection measures to save the crops were taken up.

In terms of physical targets, 88,000 cardamom seedlings, 56,351 sub-tropical and 31,548 temperate fruit plants were distributed. During the plan 271 maunds of potato seed, 38 maunds of wheat seed and 68 maunds of hybrid maize seed were supplied to the growers. Moreover 50 tonnes of fertilizers, 2,600 lbs, of insecticidal dusts and 80 gallons of concentrates were distributed. A crop area of 5,510 acres and 26,100 individual fruit trees were protected against diseases and pests.[37]

During the First Plan steps were taken to establish experimental centres at Tadong and Lachung, a potato farm at Temi, two cardamom nurseries at Gangtok and Rongli, a nursery nine miles from Gangtok for sub-tropical fruits in the lower elevation, an apple orchard at Lachung, and a temperate fruit nursery at Lagyap.

A fruit preservation factory was set up at Singtam mainly for the benefit of the orange-growers. Loans for agriculral purposes amounted to Rs. 61,000 during the Plan. During this period 28 Sikkimese were trained in different courses relating to agriculture and animal husbandry.

Another important feature of the Plan was to develop agriculture by disseminating knowledge of improved agricultural methods through extension workers. During the First Plan period a National Extension Service was introduced and it collaborated with the Agriculture Department in various matters.

With the same purpose of disseminating agricultural knowledge 4 agricultural exhibitions were held at Gangtok, Geyzing, Jorathang and Rangrang where a variety of agricultural produce was exhibited, demonstrations were given in improved methods of cultivation and improved varieties of seeds were put on show. These exhibitions provided the cultivators with an opportunity of witnessing the various methods that the Government had adopted to improve agricultural production in the State as well as to exhibit their own produce.[38]

The main task under the Second Plan was the consolidation of the gains already achieved and to carry further the process as well as to make the economy of the country self-reliant and self-generating. Self-reliance was still retained as an objective but only in vague terms. In the field of agriculture further development was envisaged retaining mainly the line of approach of the First Plan. The First Technical Team which visited Sikkim prior to the launching of the Second Five-Year Plan took into consideration the special features of the Sikkimese economy and clearly indicated that agricultural development in Sikkim should proceed along four considerations: local conditions, live-stocks, needs of the people and export value. As the Team observed regarding agricultural objectives of the Second Plan:

"Crop improvement should be based on a more realistic approach to local conditions and the needs of the people and livestock be taken into account. It should also keep prominently in view the promotion of crops which have an exoprt value".[39]

Taking these observations into account it was proposed in the Draft Second Plan to lay emphasis on the following:

(i) development of horticulture by encouraging people to plant orchards;

(ii) development of cash crops like seed potatoes, cardamom, oranges and other fruits;

(iii) intensification of plant protection measures and stabilization of cash crops;
(iv) organisation of the Agriculture Department; and
(v) training of local personnel.

It was also decided that in order to achieve these objectives, the existing activities would be continued and expanded and emphasis would also be laid on agricultural research and education.[40]

With a viev to achieving the objectives as laid down in the report of the First Technical Team as well as in the Draft Second Plan, the Second Technical Team which visited Sikkim in the middle of the Second Plan observed that there was need for re-orientation of the Plan with particular emphasis on agriculture and animal husbandry which form the base of economic development in a country like Sikkim. It also proposed that a "crash" programme should be undertaken in the field of agriculture on the lines of Intensive Agricultural District Programmes being implemented in India. This should embody agricultural production, irrigation and development of cattle, poultry and piggery. Besides, more attention should be given, the Team said, to horticulture and vegetable growing particularly with a view to meeting the demands of the Indian army stationed within Sikkim. Most of the other requirements of the army were, however, met by the Government of India through supply from India.

During the Second Five-Year Plan Sikkim's agricultural policy, apart from the extension of services already initiated during the First Plan period, concentrated on co-ordinating the three inter-related areas of operation demanded by modern agriculture — training technical staff, continuing research and the extension services of providing practical education to the farmers through field demonstrations. The experienced Sikkimese farmers were soon found to be adapting to the improved methods of cultivation recommended by the Government; and in taking the calculated risks involved they were rewarded with greater yields and considerably larger monetary gains.[41]

During the Second Plan period a sum of Rs. 28.92 lakhs was spent for the development of agriculture, Rs. 1.45 lakhs for minor irrigation and 4.56 lakhs for soil conservation. The largest portion of the expenditure of Rs. 28.92 lakhs for the development of agriculture was used for the strengthening of the Agriculture Department which had a crucial role in the implementation of the programmes.

Coming to the specific achievements of the Second Five-Year Plan in agricultural development we may mention, first of all, the establishment of the Government Seed Farm at Geyzing. After prolonged preparatory work for about two and half years an area of 200 acres was acquired in 1963-64 for that purpose. During 1964-65 works relating to seed production, land reclamation, plantation and vegetable production were initiated. By the beginning of 1965-66 the farm was brought into full activity. During the Plan period one farm manager and two research assistants joined and the construction of buildings, excepting office premises, was complete by the end of the Plan.[42]

During the Plan a few schemes under the auspices of the Indian Council of Agricultural Research (ICAR) were initiated for the introduction of improved agricultural techniques in Sikkim. The ICAR co-ordinated maize trials were conducted in the Government farms at Tadong and Geyzing. The Addey variety of paddy as well as two other varieties was selected, multiplied and released to the progressive farmers for further multiplication. Works of selection and multiplication of vegetables were also continued. One orchid sanctuary was started in an area of 35 acres at Deorali in 1961. At the end of the Plan it possessed more than 300 species of valuable orchids of Sikkim.

During the Plan a potato farm was established at Ribdi. A beginning was made with only five acres of land which was obtained from the Forest Department. But at the end of the Plan 100 acres of land in total had been put under cultivation and improved varieties of potato were being planted for further multiplication and distribution among the farmers.[43]

Intensive agricultural programme was another important aspect of development during the Plan. This programme launched in May, 1964 was intended to bring about the impact of improved agricultural practices in concentrated pockets. It envisaged the combination of all known suitable agricultural practices such as improved seeds, fertilizers and plant protection measures. These items were made available to the farmers at a 50 per cent subsidy.

During the first year of the programme 1292 families, and during the second year 1400 families were benefited by this programme. The following table will show the achievements of this programme in different fields such as the distribution of seed, plant etc. during the two years when it was operative:

Sl. No.	*Name of Items*	*Unit*	*1964-65*	*1965-66*
1.	Orange Seelings	Nos.	19,635	20,685
2.	Pine Apple Suckers	Nos.	7,000	3,000
3.	Temperate Fruit Plant	Nos.	6,219	5,876
4.	Rabi Vegetable Seeds	Acres	56	50
5.	Kharif Vegetable Seeds	Acres	50	50
6.	Potato Seed	Maunds	1,062	1,270
7.	Ade Cuba Maize	Maunds	5	55
8.	Paddy (Addey)	Maunds	-	69½
9.	Hybrid Maize	Kilograms	2,958	2,012
10.	Wheat	Kilograms	-	1,300

Source: Progress Report: April, 1961-February, 1966, p. 37.

In addition to the above, 181 tonnes of mixed and straight fertilizers in 1964-65 and 67 tonnes in 1965-66 were supplied to the farmers in the "intensive" areas at a 50 per cent subsidy. The programme became very popular and a large number of farmers resorted to vegetable, potato, hybrid maize and fruit cultivation.[44]

Systematic plant protection measures were started and carried out effectively by the end of the year 1964-65. In the last year of the Plan there was a bumper crop of oranges and apples mainly due to the success of plant protection measures. In addition to these, over 2500 acres of standing maize, paddy, cardamom and vegetables were sprayed against pests and diseases. For the first time field rat control campaign was organised from 16th October, 1965 and the success achieved was encouraging.

During the Second Plan some progress was made in the field of land development. The intention of this scheme was to subsidise the terracing of land, in areas where shifting cultivation was practised, at the rate of Rs. 250 per acre. Due to various reasons it was not possible, however, to fully implement this scheme with the result that only 100 acres of land were terraced during the last year of the Plan involving an expenditure of Rs. 25,000 only compared to the plan outlay of Rs. 3.75 lakhs.

During the Plan a sum of Rs. 4,60,535 was advanced as loans to 1253 needy farmers for the purpose of improvement of land, extension of fruit orchards, purchase of seeds and seedlings, bullocks and fertilizers etc. In addition to this a sum of Rs. 31,500 was advanced for the purpose of purchase of milch cattle. This scheme was more or less fully successful, because out of a Plan outlay of Rs. 6.00 lakhs nearly Rs. 5.00 lakhs were disbursed as advances.[45]

Along with the Agriculture Department there was also the strengthening of the National Extension Service for carrying out different developmental programmes. For the purpose of extension work in Sikkim the whole country was divided into 24 sectors, each sector being under the charge of a village level worker (V.L.W.). Each such worker had a number of blocks under his jurisdiction. For the supervision of the work of the V.L.W.s two Extension Officers were appointed in 1964 — one posted at Namchi to look after the western and southern districts and the other posted at Gangtok to look after the eastern and northern districts.

The extension work covered the dissemination of knowledge of improved agricultural practices, supply of improved seeds, fruit plants, fertilizers, pesticides and the like. The V.L.W.s contacted the villagers, aroused their interests, provided them the know-how of improved agricultural practices and led them to adopt those practices. Intensive propaganda regarding green manuring, rural compost and the use of fertilizers was carried out. Improved seeds of food crops and vegetables were also supplied to the farmers.[46]

During the Third Plan a more realistic approach was adopted for the development of agriculture. The limitations of the scope of planned development in the field of agriculture were for the first time realised by the planners and in the final draft of the Third Plan it was categorically said:

"In view of the limitations imposed by the mountainous terrain, terrace cultivation, lack of assured irrigation facilities and the increasing population, it is not possible to attain self-sufficiency

in food-grains but all efforts should be made towards substantially increasing the per acre yields of cereals and cash crops and thereby raise per capita income and the standard of living of the people."[26]

This realisation also induced the planners to reduce expenditures in those fields where productivity was not commensurate with costs. As has been said:

"Also in the Third Plan attempts have been made to keep to a minimum the outlay on additional staff and buildings which are not directly productive."[48]

Thus the basic objectives of Sikkim's agricultural plan were simply defined as the following:

(i) to achieve an appreciable increase in agricultural production; and

(ii) to increase per capita incomes by diversified crop pattern and development of horticulture, cash crops and mixed farming.[49]

Even though the limitations of agricultural development were recognised the importance of agriculture was not denied in the Third Plan. During the Third Plan period a total amount of Rs. 48.11 lakhs was spent for the development of agriculture while Rs. 9.09 lakhs and Rs. 13.25 lakhs were spent for minor irrigation and soil conservation respectively. These expenditures were nearly double the corresponding expenditures during the Second Plan. This indicates that agricultural development was given high priority in the Third Plan.

Between 1966-71 a realistic approach was made towards what is generally known as the Green Revolution. Urged by the competitive drive and the prospects of reaping greater harvests, the farmers' participation in agricultural development was now assured, which was reflected in the fact that Sikkim's expenditure on agricultural inputs for a single year in the Third Plan period almost equalled the total expenditure on similar inputs during the period of the First and Second Plans. To keep abreast of this development the Agriculture Department was proportionately expanded by the strengthening of the technical staff and more seed farms were established to serve the requirements demanded by varying climatic conditions in Sikkim.[50]

Sikkim's two main crops are maize and paddy, and the Department of Agriculture carried on invaluable research in maize and paddy development programmes during the Third Plan period. To improve upon the existing standard of Sikkim's maize crops, the Department implemented a project demonstrating the advantages of using improved varieties of seed, fertilizers and the latest scientific know-how for the benefit of the farmers. According to the Agriculture Department's statistics, the majority of the farmers living in east, west and south Sikkim showed marked trends in using better seeds, fertilizers and the advice provided by the Department, and naturally their crops also showed marked improvement.

An important break-through in the field of paddy cultivation was the introduction of the Taichung variety during the Plan and it is expected to revolutionise the cultivation of paddy in Sikkim. This variety is most suitable where natural fertility of the soil is very high and the farmer is prepared to implement agricultural programme with better seeds, fertilizers and plant protection measures. The advantages of Taichung are early maturing, wide adaptability and resistance to lodging due to its dwarf and strong plants.

The greatest advantage of Taichung is, however, its ready response to fertilizers. Since there is no chance of increasing paddy field acreage in Sikkim, the only alternative is to grow such high-yielding varieties. With proper management of irrigation channels, there is every possibility of growing this variety alone in lower and mid-zone paddy areas, which incidentally represent about four-fifths of the total paddy acreage in Sikkim. The suitability and higher yield of the Taichung paddy were also amply proved. In 1968 eight farmers tried this variety and could easily double the produce per acre. In 1970 it was reported that a farmer in Tadong could increase the yield three-fold which indicates that the Taichung variety is on the way to revolutionise Sikkimese agriculture.[51]

Achievements in some specific fields at the end of the Plan may be mentioned as follows: Steps were under way for the trial of paddy varieties with still higher yield than Taichung and these were being obtained from the International Research Institute in the Philippines and well-known research centres in India. A co-ordinated programme to demonstrate the suitability of imported potato seeds resistant to the "wart" disease was successfully carried out among a number of selected farmers around the Government farms at Hilley. A programme of effective demonstration of scientific methods to halt the decline in the output of orange was started. At the same time the sub-tropical fruit garden at the 9th Mile concentrated on the production of select orange seedling. The Geyzing farm continued to serve as a centre for trials and maintenance of imported verieties of maize, paddy, millet, citrus fruits etc.

In spite of all these achievements in the agricultural sector Sikkim remained deficient in food supply. All essential food articles like rice, sugar etc. had to be imported from India during the Third Plan period and even afterwards; and it seemed there was little prospect for Sikkim being self-sufficient in those commodities in the near future.[52]

The magnitude of the import of food articles for some select years during the Third Plan period may be shown as follows:

Food Articles Imported into Sikkim
(Amount in Quintals)

S.No.	*Articles*	*1966*	*1967*	*1968*
1.	Rice	66,048	66,048	66,048
2.	Wheat	11,820	17,820	17,820
3.	Sugar	7,800	7,800	7,800
4.	Maida	4,500	5,700	8,100
5.	Atta	3,500	3,156	3,156
6.	Suji	--	180	54

Source: Govt. of Sikkim, *Sikkim Through Figures*, 1969, p. 14.

The Government of India generally had a prior commitment to supply a specified amount of food articles for a particular year and the Government of Sikkim distributed those articles through rationing. But there were also a few other food articles and necessities like salt, vegetable oil and kerosene which were often in short supply, specially in rural areas. This was particularly so during the monsoon when communications were disrupted and people living in remote corners of the country were cut off from the outside world.

As Sikkim is likely to remain deficient in food supply in

the foreseeable future, a package programme of production, importation and rationing seems to be the most suitable policy. Apart from this the main purpose of agriculture should be to produce and export cash crops to the greatest possible extent, as this would appear to be the simplest answer to the problem of low earning capacity of the Sikkimese farmer.

REFERENCES

1. Govt. of Sikkim, *Second Five-Year Plan, 1961-66* (Gangtok: Public Relations Officer), p. 3. Hereafter referred to as "Second Plan (Non-Detailed)".
2. "The Process of Planned Development: Forests", *Sikkim Herald*, May, 1972, p. 1.
3. Govt. of Sikkim, *Seven Years of Progress: 1954-61* (Gangtok: Sikkim Durbar Press, 1962), p. 10. Hereafter referred to as "Progress Report: First Plan".
4. *The Statesman* (Calcutta), June 2, 1960, "Sikkim: A Statesman Supplement," p. III.
5. *Ibid.*
6. Govt. of Sikkim, *Sikkim Development Plan* (Gangtok: Sikkim Durbar Press, 1955), p. 11. Hereafter referred to as "First Plan".
7. Govt. of India, *Mid-Term Appraisal of the Second Five-Year Plan of Sikkim: Report of the Technical Team* (New Delhi: Planning Commission, 1964), p. 46. Hereafter referred to as "Second Team's Report".
3. Govt. of Sikkim, *The Second Five-Year Plan of Sikkim: Progress Report for the Period April 1961-February 1966*, Part I (Gangtok: Planning and Development Dept.), p. 11. Hereafter referred to as "Progress Reports April, 1961 - February 1966".
9. *Ibid.*, p. 14.
10. *Ibid.*, pp. 11-12.
11. *Sikkim Herald*, May 18, 1972, pp. 1-2.
12. *Ibid.*
13. Second Team's Report, p. 48.
14. Progress Report: First Plan, p. 1.
15. First Plan, p. 2.
16. Second Plan (Non-Detailed), p. 5.
17. Govt. of Sikkim, *Sikkim Through Figures* (Gangtok: Planning and Development Dept. 1969), p. 1.
18. *Ibid.*
19. First Plan, p. 2.
20. *Ibid.*
21. Second Team's Report, p. 33.

22. Govt. of Sikkim, *Sikkim Through Figures,* p. 9.
23. Second Team's Report, p. 33.
24. *The Statesman,* p. III.
25. Govt. of Sikkim, *Sikkim Through Figures,* p. 9.
26. Second Team's Report, p. 33.
27. First Plan, p. 3.
28. Govt. of Sikkim, *Sikkim Through Figures,* p. 9.
29. First Plan, p. 3.
30. *Ibid.*
31. Second Team's Report, p. 34.
32. *Ibid.*, p. 33.
33. *Ibid.*
34. *Ibid.*, p. 34.
35. Progress Report: First Plan, p. 1.
36. *Ibid.*
37. Govt. of India, *Second Five Year Plan of Sikkim: Report of the Technical Team* (New Delhi: Planning Commission, 1961), p. 30.
38. Progress Report: First Plan, p. 4.
39. Quoted in Second Team's Report, p. 31.
40. Govt. of Sikkim, Second Development Plan. (A Five-Year Plan 1961-62 — 1965-66), Unpublished Draft, Part I, 1960, p. 15.
41. "The Process of Planned Development: Agriculture", *Sikkim Herald,* May 13, 1972.
42. Progress Report: April, 1961 - February, 1966, p. 1.
43. *Ibid.*, pp. 4-5.
44. *Ibid.*, pp. 3-4.
45. *Ibid.*, p. 6.
46. *Ibid.*, p. 2.
47. Govt. of Sikkim. *The Third Five-Year Plan 1966-71: Final Draft,* Vol. I (Gangtok: Planning and Development Dept., 1966), Section on Agricultural Production.
48. *Ibid.*
49. *Ibid.*
50. *Sikkim Herald,* May 13, 1972.
51. "Chief Secretary's Reports, January 21, 1971", *Sikkim Herald,* April 4, 1971, p. 7.
52. *Address of Mr. I.S. Chopra, Sidlon of Sikkim,* on April 4, 1972. Published by the Govt. of Sikkim, p. 7.

6

Power, Transport and Industries

Power, transport and industries constitute the Secondary Sector in our schema and their growth may be regarded as an index of development of the traditional economy of Sikkim. Whereas power and transport facilities are essential for the growth of industries, the latter are the only means of transforming an agrarian economy into an industrial one. In the following sections we shall see to what extent the economic plans of Sikkim have been successful in developing this crucial sector.

A. Development of Power during the Plans

Development of power is a *sine qua non* for the rapid industrialisation of any country. In fact, the per capita consumption of electricity is often taken as the measuring rod of industrialisation of a country. From that point of view Sikkim is quite fortunate in having a large potential for electric power. The amount of electricity generation at present is not, however, very high compared to the power potential and more attention is needed towards that direction. If simultaneously attention is paid to the utilization of the existing raw materials, manpower and technical know-how, Sikkim can certainly hope to be industrialised—at least moderately—within a very short time.

Sikkim being a hilly state and having a large number of turbulent streams has a great potentiality for hydro-electric power. This potentiality of the state's vast water-resources was appreciated by the Government of Sikkim in the early part of the 20th century. Gangtok was electrified for the first time in 1927 with the setting up of a hydro-electric turbine set. This turbine set having a capacity of 50 Kw was installed on the left bank of the river Rani Chu at the foot of Sachey Bustee below Gangtok. In 1934 the power was augmented by installing another hydro-electric turbine set of 50 Kw. The total power generating capacity of the state thereby became 100 Kw and this situation prevailed until the initiation of the First Development Plan.[1]

At the time when the First Development Plan was started, the hydel power supplied to Gangtok met only half the requirement of the town and there was no power supply to any other part of the country.[2]

Moreover, with the launching of the Plan there was more demand for power in the capital with the increasing number of buildings, development offices and the growth of town dwellers. To cater to these needs a diesel power house was constructed at Gangtok with two sets of diesel generators of 275 Kw and 100 Kw. The former was commissioned in 1958 and the latter in 1961 when the total power available in the state — both hydro and diesel— was 475 Kw.[3]

Previously, industrial use of electricity was quite negligible in the country excepting for the small Sikkim Government Press. The installation of the diesel power house during the First Plan period paved the way for an efficient and economic functioning of a number of small-scale industries in and around Gangtok. Most notable among them were the mechanised carpentry section of the Palden Thondup Institute of Cottage Industries, the Government of India Press, the enlarged Sikkim Government Press, the flour mill and the defence water-supply pumping station.

The use of domestic electric appliances also increased to a great extent during the period. Before the commencement of the First Plan there were only 350 domestic connections. At the end of the Plan an additional number of 350 domestic connections was given bringing the total to 700. Moreover, due to the installation of the new power plant, the revenue from electricity increased from Rs. 26,000 in 1954 to Rs. 1,16,000 by the end of the First Plan period.[4]

The main development in power during the Second Plan period was with respect to the Rongni Chu or Rongnek Chu Hydro-Electric Project. Already the project had been initiated in 1957 in collaboration with the Central Water and Power Commission, Government of India, but it was scheduled to be completed during the Second Plan period. The project was actually completed towards the end of the Second Plan. It may be pointed out in this connection that the Rongni Chu Hydro-Electric Project continuing from the First Plan should have been completed long ago, but due to occasional changes in designs, delays in erection and faults in construction, it took so much time for commissioning. The power house and the transmission lines had been completed as early as in 1963 but due to seepage in the forebay tank it was not possible to store water and run the turbines.[5] The project was ultimately commissioned in April, 1965.

The Rongni Chu Project had 6 turbo impulse turbines with the rated output of 350 Kw each, one of these being installed for meeting the peak-hour load of short duration as well as for maintenance and over-hauling facilities. The power house, as a consequence, had a total capacity of 2,100 Kw of which 1750 Kw was firm power and the remaining 350 Kw was utilised to meet peak load requirements. Towards the end of the Second Five Year Plan the country had, therefore, a total power generating capacity of 2575 Kw — both hydro and diesel included.[6]

The Rongni Chu Project had a great impact on the economy of Sikkim. It provided electricity to the residential areas in Singtam and Rongpo as well as to the increased demands in Gangtok. Besides, the power generated by this project was supplied to the Sikkim Mining Corporation located near Rongpo. In addition, it paved the way for the setting up of cottage and small-scale industries in and around Rongpo, Singtam and Gangtok.

The other schemes completed within the Second Plan period were the remodelling of the Gangtok distribution system and the 150 KVA diesel alternator set for Gangtok. Regarding the micro hydel schemes, however, not much progress could be achieved. The micro hydel stations proposed for Manul, Rothak, Rongli and Geyzing were deferred to the Third Plan period. The Lagyap Hydel Scheme for harnessing power from three rivers near Nathu La in eastern Sikkim was the most promising of all hydel schemes. This project, when complete, was expected to generate 6,000Kw of power.[7] The project was scheduled to be started during the Second Plan period, but by the end of the Plan the Sikkim Public Works Department had only completed the survey work on the third phase of the project.[8]

During the Third Plan not much progress could be witnessed in the field of power. The achievements were restricted to the completion of only three micro hydel projects at Manul, Rothak and Rimbi. The Manul Project was completed in 1969 with, a power-generating capacity of 50 Kw. The Rothak Project was completed in 1970 with a power-generating capacity of 200 Kw and the Rimbi Project with a similar capacity was completed in 1971.

The development of power in Sikkim upto the end of the Third Plan is summarised in the following table:

Development of Power in Sikkim

Year of Completion	*Place of Project*	*Type of Project*	*Additional Power (Kw)*	*Total Power (Kw)*
1927	Rani Chu	Hydro	50	50
1934	Rani Chu	Hydro	50	100
1958	Gangtok	Diesel	275	375
1961	Gangtok	Diesel	100	475
1965	Rongni Chu	Hydro	2,100	2,575
1969	Manul	Hydro	50	2,625
1970	Tothak	Hydro	200	2,825
1971	Rimbi	Hydro	200	3,025

Sources: Figures for the Third Plan period collected from the office of the Sikkim Public Works Departmentin May, 1972. Sources for other figures cited earlier.

One important consideration in the context of development of electricity is worth mentioning here — it is that the cost of production must not be too high. It has been calculated by the engineers of Sikkim that a scheme implemented with an over-all cost within Rs. 4,000 per Kw. of installed capacity should be rated as an economic project. But unfortunately most of the schemes completed so far do not prove to be economic by that standard. Some figures may be mentioned in this connection:

Cost of Electricity in Sikkim

S.No.	*Name of the Project*	*Installed Capacity Kw*	*Cost per Kw Rs.*
1.	Manul Micro Hydel	50	10,000
2.	Rimbi Micro Hydel	200	9,000.
3.	Rothak Micro Hydel	200	6,500
4.	Rongni Chu Hydel	2,100	6,000
5.	Lagyap Hydel	12,000	1,500 to 5,000

Source: The Process of Planned Development: Power, *Sikkim Herald,* June 22, 1972, p. 2.

It is clear from the above table that the cost of electricity per Kw. decreases with the increase in installed capacity which means that bigger projects are more economical than smaller ones. It is advisable, therefore, that Sikkim should embark on big power projects like the Lagyap Power Complex even if it requires a strain on the financial resources of the country, for ultimately it would be beneficial to the entire economy due to a lower cost structure.

We may point out in this connection that so far as the generation of electricity is concerned Sikkim certainly made a big headway during the first three plans. The increase in electricity generation during the period was quite remarkable — it increased by about 3,000 per cent at the end of the Third Plan over the pre-plan figure. Coming to particular plans we see that the increase was highest in the Second Plan in both absolute and relative terms. The lowest increase in absolute terms was during the First Plan whereas in relative terms the lowest increase was during the Third Plan. The position may be summed up in the following table:

Increase in Electricity Generation during the Plans

Plan	*Net Increase (Kw)*	*Percentage Increase*
First Plan	375	375
Second Plan	2,100	442
Third Plan	450	18
All Plans	2,925	2,925

It may be noted that during the first two plans the tempo of development was on the increase while during the Third Plan it was appreciably dampened. While the percentage increases in electricity generation during the First and Second Plans were 375 and 442 respectively, it was only 18 during the Third Plan. One major reason for this low increase during the Third Plan was the devastating flood of 1968 which hampered construction work to a great extent.

On the whole, however, the development of electricity during the plans was satisfactory. But the power potentiality of Sikkim is not yet fully tapped. The innumerable streams and rivulets of Sikkim still go unutilised. It is also estimated that the Tista river which rises at about 16,800 R.L. and drops to 4,000 R.L. in 50 miles within the Sikkim territory can alone provide about 12,000 Kw of electricity.[9] Its main tributaries, the Rangit and the Rongpo, are also potentially good for development of power. With a rough estimate it is estimated that Sikkim can produce about 30,00,000 Kw of electric power whereas at the end of the Third Plan the actual production was only 3,025 Kw. at full capacity — i.e. about one-tenth of one per cent of the total power potential.

It is clear, therefore, that if the entire power potential of Sikkim is harnessed it will really revolutionise the economy by releasing a huge amount of electricity. If electric power can be generated economically it is possible to supply not only the required amount within Sikkim but also the surplus electricity to the adjoining states of India, Nepal and Bhutan thereby greatly augmenting the financial resources of Sikkim.[10] There lies an immense possibility of the state's economic development through the utilisation of the huge power potential.

B. Development of Transport during the Plans

Transport is an indispensable part of economic life in a hilly region like Sikkim and it should, therefore, be given priority in any large-scale plan for economic development. Without a good transport system none of the development schemes can be executed: medical aid and disease control remains static, the farmer's market becomes limited, and education, if it can blossom at all, remains compartmentalised. Due to these reasons considerable stress was given on the development of transport in all the plans of Sikkim. Nearly half the outlay of the First Seven-Year Plan was allocated to the development of road transport; and in the subsequent plans similar provisions were made.

While the importance of transport in the Sikkimese economy cannot be over-emphasised, the difficulties associated with it, both operational and financial, cannot also be overlooked. In spite of the fact that roads are like arteries in the economic life of Sikkim road-building is a stupendous job there. It is really an engineering feat to construct highways across lofty mountains and torrential rivers. Moreover, during the prolonged and heavy monsoon communications are disrupted leading not only to inconveniences in construction work but also to the problem of procuring food for the labourers employed in road-building. The latter problem is much more acute because heavy road-building machines cannot be easily moved or used in hilly regions and greater reliance must be placed on manual work. Consequently, the number of workers in any road-building project in Sikkim is excessively high as compared with that in the plains, and this leads to considerably higher costs.

Of all the roads in Sikkim special mention must be made of the twisting mountain highway that runs along the course of the Tista river from Siliguri to Gangtok, the capital of the state, and pushes for nearly 80 miles into the Inner Himalaya. It is really the life-line of the state which has neither railroads nor air-fields nor any navigable water-system. Along this road comes much of the food and processed goods that Sikkim needs, the equipment that is helping her to develop her economy, the Indian military convoys for the protection of her frontier and the occasional tourists with big purses. The main exports of Sikkim such as copperware, liquor, processed fruit, handicrafts and cash crops also pass through this road to the different Indian markets. In fact, more than 90% of Sikkim's trade and commerce is conducted through this vital road.[11]

Our study of the development of transport in Sikkim will be divided into two parts: *(a)* Construction of roads and bridges, and *(b)* transport services. At present the former is conducted by the Sikkim Public Works Department while the latter is carried on by the Sikkim Nationalised Transport. But there are also other agencies. India's Central Public Works Department and Border Roads Organisation are responsible for the construction and maintenance of roads and bridges in certain strategic areas. Again, some private agencies provide transport services in some routes, but they are gradually being nationalised.

(a) Construction of Roads and Bridges

We have seen that in a hilly region like Sikkim the importance of transport can hardly be over-estimated. But surprisingly enough, until the British captured political control over Sikkim there was little development in this field. It was only due to British interests in Sikkim that the construction of roads and bridges of modern standard was undertaken. In 1879, the British had completed an unpaved road to the Jelep La so as to facilitate their travel to Lhasa in order to further the Indo-Tibetan trade. In 1881 a branch of the East Bengal Railway was extended from Siliguri, the gateway to Sikkim from the south, to Darjeeling whence there were road connections with Gangtok and other places in Sikkim.[12]

The British interest in the development of transport in Sikkim is evident from the heavy expenditure on the construction and maintenance of roads in Sikkim. The following table shows the costs on the three main roads in Sikkim from the year 1888-89 to the year 1899-1900:

Cost of Construction and Maintenance of Roads in Sikkim 1888-89 to 1899-1900

S. No.	*Name of Road*	*Construction Rs.*	*Maintenance Rs.*	*Total Rs.*
1.	Pedong-Gangtok Road	45,411	26,791	72,202
2.	Rishi-Jelep La Road	35,487	54,313	89,300
3.	Lachen Road	1,87,869	39,601	2,27,470
	All Roads	2,68,767	1,20,705	3,89,472

Source: Statement B in letter No. 1297 P from C.E. Buckland, Esq., C.I.E. Officiating Chief Secretary to the Govt. of Bengal to the Secretary to the Govt. of India, Foreign Dept. Dated Calcutta, the 18th April, 1901.

The position at the beginning of the 20th century is described by the *Imperial Gazetteer of India* (1908) as:

"Good roads, properly bridged throughout, have been opened since 1889 from Pedong in British territory to the Jelep La and to Tumlong, and in 1903-4 the State contained 376 miles of road. A cart road has recently been constructed from Rongpo to Gangtok from Imperial funds, and a mule track on a gradient of 1 in 15 has been made from Gangtok to Chumbi via the Nathula. Iron bridges have been constructed across the Tista, the Rangit and other streams".[13]

The first wheeled vehicle traversed the road from Siliguri to Gangtok in the year 1906 and since then regular vehicular traffic continued between the two towns. Unfortunately, there was little expansion in the subsequent period in the matter of construction of roads and. the position remained practically the same until 1954, the beginning of the First Seven-year Plan. In that year, the only motorable road in Sikkim was that connecting Gangtok with Siliguri and its continuation within the state capital. The Gangtok-Siliguri road was, however, maintained by the Government of India and only its continuation within Gangtok town known as Gangtok Circular Road and having a length of one and a half miles only was maintained by the State Government, The State Government also maintained 223.5 miles of bridle roads and 130 miles of village paths.[14]

During the plans substantial development occurred in the field of roads and bridges, but the expansion was done almost entirely during the first two plans and practically nothing was done during the Third Plan. In an interview on May 18, 1972 with the Chief Engineer of the Sikkim Public Works Department it was known to the author that the construction of roads and bridges during the Third Plan period was carried on only in the first two years of the Plan after which due to the devastating flood of 1968 no construction of new roads and bridges was possible and the last three years of the Plan were devoted mainly to the repair of flood damages. The repair work continued even upto the end of the first year of the Fourth Plan. We shall, therefore, confine ourselves to the study of the *development of roads and bridges during the first two plans only*.

Taking into account the importance of road transport in Sikkim, considerable stress was placed on the development of roads and bridges during the period of the first two plans. During the First Plan about 300 miles of roads, excluding village paths, had been added to the existing roads. During this time the Government spent Rs. 139.01 lakhs on construction of roads of all categories as against the allocation of Rs. 131.63 lakhs. In the Second Plan a further addition of 325 miles was envisaged while the actual addition, excluding village paths, approach roads and feeder roads, was 315 miles. The actual expenditure for that was Rs. 261 lakhs as against the allocation of Rs. 300 lakhs. It is important to note here the tremendous rise in allocation and expenditure on roads and bridges in the Second Plan signifying the prime importance of road transport in the hilly economy of Sikkim.[15]

During the First Plan period 42 miles of new motorable roads were constructed. These roads were: (i) Melli-Nayabazar-Legship Road or Namgyal Highway covering a distance of 33 miles and (ii) Singtam-Makha Road covering a distance of 9 miles. These two roads were maintained by the State Government. Already the Gangtok Circular Road covering a distance 1 and half miles was under the maintenance of the State Government, so that at the end of the First Plan 43 and half miles of motorable roads in total were maintained by the State Government. Of all the three roads the Namgyal Highway was the most important and provided the basis for development of western Sikkim.

During the Second Plan it was envisaged to increase the mileage of motorable roads maintained by the State Government from 43.5 to 92 miles — an addition of 48.5 miles. The total length of motorable road maintained by the State Government by the end of the Second Plan was, however, 99 miles — an addition of 55.5 miles. This addition was mainly for the construction of a new road — The Rongpo - Pakyong-Gangtok road.

In December, 1961 construction began on an alternative highway from Rongpo on the Indo-Sikkim border to Gangtok via Pakyong. It was intended to ensure un-interrupted heavy vehicular traffic between Rangpo and Gangtok when the old highway between Rongpo and Gangtok via Singtam becomes disrupted during the monsoon. The construction was completed within the Second Plan period. Before the construction of this road Gangtok and the major portion of Sikkim were often completely cut off from the outside world for several days, even months, due to disruption or destruction of the old highway during the monsoon.

Apart from this road two other important motorable roads were constructed during the Second Plan period out of funds outside the Plan outlay and financed entirely by the Government of India. These were: *(i)* the North Sikkim Highway, and *(ii)* the Gangtok-Nathu La Highway. During the First Plan no roads had been provided in the northern and eastern parts of the country and most of the road development had been related to the western zone. In the Second Plan period it was decided, therefore, to construct and renovate further roads in northern and eastern Sikkim as a result of which the above two roads were constructed.

The North Sikkim Highway was built in north Sikkim linking Gangtok with Chungthang via Kangan, a distance of 70 miles. From Chung-thang the road branches off in two directions, one towards Lachen and Dorikung and the other to Lachung and Yumthang. It traverses locations at an attitude of 9,000 feet and facilitates the movement of forest-produce and apples from north Sikkim to the markets in the lower region.

The Gangtok-Nathu La Highway was another strategically important motorable road linking Gangtok and Nathu La in east Sikkim. The expenditure on this road including some other roads in east Sikkim, particularly that from Rishi on the West Bengal border to Jelep La on the Tibet border, was about Rs. 9 crores. A ropeway from Gangtok to Thegu, covering a distance of 50 Kilometres on the road to Nathu La was also constructed by the Government of India out of its own non-plan grants for catering to the needs of the armed forces guarding Sikkim on the Tibet border.[17]

The two important roads, North Sikkim Highway and Gangtok-Nathu La Highway, were constructed directly by the Government of India with its own control and supervision, apart from finances. It may be pointed out in this connection that the construction work had already started in the First

Plan period though the two roads were completed only in the Second Plan period. It may also be noted that the above two highways along with Gangtok- Siliguri Highway* have been being maintained by the Government of India since their construction. At the end of the Second Plan period the Indian Border Roads Organisation and the Central Public Works Department of India had constructed and maintained 282 miles of roads while the Sikkim Public Works Department had 280 miles to their credit.[18]

Progress was also made in regard to the construction of various types of non-motorable roads. At the commencement of the First Plan there were no jeepable roads in Sikkim. During the First Plan period 75 miles of jeepable roads were constructed. In the Second Plan period it was envisaged to constructed 92 miles of new jeepable roads.[19] The total length of jeepable and fair weather jeepable roads at the end of the Second Plan was, however, 149 and 52 miles respectively. Altogether five new jeepable roads had been constructed in the Second Plan period.

Regarding bridle roads it has been said in one plan document: "At the beginning of the First Plan there were 215 miles of bridle roads or mule tracks. During 1954-61, about 50 miles of these bridle roads were upgraded into 42 miles of motorable roads and 12 miles of jeepable roads. The length of the remaining 165 miles of bridle roads was increased by 12 miles of Dikchu-Sangklang road to 177 miles".[21]

During the Second Plan, however, there was little progress in respect of bridle roads as most of the work started only in 1964-65. The Second Plan envisaged to construct 10 new bridle roads of a total length of 109 miles, but only four roads were actually constructed during this period. The total length of bridle roads including pre-plan road mileage at the end of the Second Plan was 309 miles.[22]

The importance of village paths in a hilly region like Sikkim cannot be denied. The population in Sikkim is scattered and huts are generally built in the fields. Narrow village paths are, therefore, the main line of communication. Over 200 miles

* The section between Sevoke and Gangtok being called National Highway No. 31A branching off from the Indian National Highway No. 31 at Sevoke.

of such paths existed before the First Plan and during the First Plan period 138 miles were added, of which 40 miles were in north Sikkim, 45 miles in east Sikkim and 53 miles in west Sikkim.[23]

During the Second Plan period development of village paths was taken up as a joint enterprise of the Government and the people. Traditionally, the villagers take the initiative and contribute substantially towards the maintenance, and sometimes construction, of village paths and foot bridges. But this was often inadequate and as a result the Government took up a scheme for the development of village paths. The scheme was implemented by the Planning and Development Department as part of the rural development programme. The roads were constructed by the villagers and the work was supervised by the District Development Officer and an overseer. In the construction of the roads the Government's share was Rs. 500 per mile and the rest was contributed by the villagers.

This scheme started only in 1964-65 and the public responded quite satisfactorily. A total of 58 villages had been taken up during the Plan period and 42 roads covering a length of 242 miles were completed by the end of the Second Plan.[24]

Some other new road-building schemes were also taken up in the Second Plan period. One such was the scheme of constructing approach roads to the various colonies that had come into existence in course of the Plan period. Mention may be made of the colony at Mangan where buildings of many departments had come up in an area that required to be linked up with an approach road. The same was true for the development area at Namchi and the Government area at Rabdentse. During the Plan period, however, it was possible to build only two approach roads at Mangan and Namchi.[25]

Another new scheme worth mentioning was the provision of feeder roads during the Second Plan. In Sikkim many bazars were cut off from the main roads because such roads had to follow a specified alignment that did not allow such roads to pass through the bazars.[26] These bazars were located at Makha, Kewzing, Mangan, Dikchu, Soreng and Rhenock. During the Second Plan it was possible to undertake the construction of only two feeder roads to the Kangan and Kewzing bazars.[26]

As regards bridges, very few of them were constructed during the First Plan due to the paucity of funds.[27] Only the following bridges were constructed under the First Plan:

(i) One Suspension Bridge at Dikchu: 282′ span.
(ii) One Suspension Bridge at Sanklang 275′ span.
(iii) One Cantilever Wooden Bridge: 60′ span.
(iv) Four Log Bridges ...... 30′/40′ span.

During the Second Plan the bridges at the following places were completed in all respects:

(i) Legship : 200′ span.
(ii) Rothak : 170′ span.
(iii) Pabung : 170′ span.
(iv) Hee : 170′ span.
(v) Dentam : 150′ span.
(vi) Kalej : 125′ span.
(vii) Ranikhola : 120′ span.

The Nehru Bridge at Nelli which had been completed within the Second Plan period was unfortunately severely damaged by landslides that shattered the foundations of the anchor house on the Sikkim side. The bridge was being re-built at the time the Plan ended. The same was the case with the Rashyap Bridge at Sirwani. The Sanklang Bridge had also to be re-built because of severe damages caused by the bursting of the Zemu Glacier in 1962. The Sikkim Public Works Department also undertook during the Plan period the construction of RCC bridges and fabricated steel bridges at various places.[28]

(b) Transport Services

Road transport under the aegies of the Government was introduced in Sikkim as early as in 1944 — a decade before the initiation of planned development. With an initial fleet of 10 trucks obtained from the Defence Department Disposal Agencies in India (Later that year the fleet was increased to 20 trucks) and a loan of Rs. 1.40 lakhs from the Rationing Department, the the Maharajkumar of Sikkim organised what was then known as the Truck Department of the Government of Sikkim. With garages located in the palace compound, a workshop with tools stored in two small almirahs, a small team of dedicated workers and very personal supervision, the Truck Department was entrusted with the transportation of controlled and rationed commodities.[29]

Initially the Truck Department operated on the two main routes connecting Gangtok with Kalimpong (50 miles) and with Geilikhola (42 miles), the one-time rail-head of the Darjeeling Himalayan Railway in the Tista Valley. Results were immediately encouraging. In the very first year the total tonnage lifted amounted to 600 tonnes earning for the Department a gross revenue of Rs. 49,900.

With the introduction of the Truck Department not only was there a speed-up in transportation but the effect of the new and more efficient mode of transportation was felt almost everywhere in the economy. Traders were now able to sell their merchandise in the remotest corners of the country at a cheaper rate as well as in a shorter time. That was also true for the agriculturists who could now get their agricultural produce like oranges, apples, cardamoms and vegetables to the more profitable markets.

A more important aspect of the new transport system was the revitalisation of the Indo-Sikkimese trade. While Sikkim found new outlets in India for its produce in the very first months of the introduction of state transport, it quickly discovered that many newly imported articles had also flooded the local bazars. Prior to 1944 most of these trade articles were carried on bullock carts and pack ponies and the cost factor along with the time required kept the volume low and prices proportionately high. But now the situation changed.

There was also the elimination of loss due to damages during transit. Previously, fruits which are one of Sikkim's major exports, perished in large quantities in the process of transportation to the plains. Valuable imports like cement were also ruined by days of exposure to rain. But now all these were things of the past.

The swift development of the Truck Department in the subsequent years was due, in part, to the devastating flood of 1950 when the Tista river damaged the railway line between Siliguri and Geilikhola beyond repair. The railway was abandoned and in 1951 the transport department of the country had to extend its operations to the railhead at Siliguri — a further 30 miles from Gellikhola. The Pradhannagar offices and warehouses were also established the same year at

Siliguri.[30] Also in 1951 contractual arrangements with the Northeast Frontier Railway in India and the Indian Posts and Telegraphs Department resulted in the opening of the railway out-agencies at Rangpo and Gangtok and the carriage of postal mail between Gangtok and Kalimpong. In 1952 the Department was re-designated as the Sikkim State Transport Service. In its 8 years of service the Truck Department had achieved a gross earning of Rs. 18,71,124.[31]

Between 1952 and 1954 a 10-seater passenger bus service was introduced between Gangtok and Siliguri, the first petrol pump for consumers was installed at Rangpo and the Namgyal Highway linking Jorathang with Melli was nationalised. The end of 1954 brought to a close, what is now referred to as the "pre-plan" period, and ushered in the era of planning in the development of road transport in the country. During the 10-year period 1944-54 the state transport had succeeded in earning a gross revenue of a little over 49.53 lakhs.

April 1, 1954 ushered in the era of development plans, and during the seven years of the First Plan the Department was financed with an outlay of Rs. 16 lakhs provided as aid. During the first year of the Plan diesel-driven trucks were introduced on the Gangtok-Rongpo route for the first time. Diesel-driven trucks were found so perfectly suitable to the nature and needs of transport services in Sikkim that a radical decision was adopted in 1955 to convert the entire fleet of vehicles from petrol to diesel operation. One great advantage of diesel locomotion was that its operation cost was too low compared to that of petrol engines.[32]

During the first year of the Plan certain other achievements also took place. Passenger services were extended to the Gangtok-Darjeeling route using Landrovers. There was an agreement for the counter-signature of route permits by the West Bengal authorities. This agreement enabled the vehicles of the Sikkim State Transport Service to operate on certain routes in North Bengal which were vital to the economy of Sikkim. At Rongpo the State Transport Service's offices were constructed the same year.

To cope with its rapidly increasing fleet of vehicles, exposed to unusually severe strains and stresses, the transport department had to improve its workshop facilities considerably. The central workshop at Gangtok was equipped with necessary tools and machineries for carrying out minor as well as major repairs. The local personnel who had received training in automobile engineering and motor mechanics in India were employed to man the workshop.

In the second year of the First Plan the Rongli-Rongpo road was nationalised. This year brought about another change of name — the Sikkim State Transport Service was re-designated as the Sikkim Nationalised Transport and was made a permanent department of the Government of Sikkim.

During the last three years of the Plan the North Sikkim Highway upto Mangan was nationalised, passenger and goods services were introduced on the Gangtok-Nathu La Highway and the railway out-agency at Melli was opened.

Besides providing a quick and economical means of transport for goods and passengers the Sikkim Nationalised Transport became one of the biggest revenue-earning sources of the Government. The total gross earnings of the department during the First Plan period of seven years amounted to Rs. 1,43,62,003 with a net profit of Rs. 52,17,347.[33]

Daring the Second Plan an outlay of Rs. 48.07 lakhs was made available to the Sikkim Nationalised Transport by the Planning and Development Department out of the aid received from the Government of India and it concentrated on six specific schemes comprising: (i) dieselisation, (ii) expansion, (iii) plant and machinery, (iv) training, (v) construction, and (vi) nationalisation. Under the scheme of dieselisation the petrol-driven vehicles on the Gangtok-Siliguri route were replaced by diesel-powered vehicles. Diesel-driven 35-seater buses and freight-carrying trucks were brought into service on the North Sikkim Highway, the Namgyal Highway and the Namchi-Jorathang road. Under the expansion scheme additional vehicles were added on all the routes to cope with the increase in passenger and freight traffic. Under the plan and machinery programme essential workshop machinery and equipment were procured. A training scheme was implemented to make available qualified technicians. Under the construction programme booking offices, waiting rooms, warehouses, roadside shelters for passengers and essential staff-quarters were provided at Gangtok, Mangan, Namchi, Rongpo, Singtam, Melli, Jorathang and Legship. Consumer pumps for petrol and diesel oil were installed at Jorathang and for diesel oil at Rongpo.

As regards nationalisation of new routes all the targets could not be achieved in the Second Plan period. There were various reasons for that. First of all, the non-completion of roads and bridges was an important cause for the delay in the implementation of the scheme in some routes. Secondly, difficulties were faced with regard to constructional activities such as preparation of plans and acquisition of land which impeded the implementation of the programme. Thirdly, the expansion of the nationalised routes was not sometimes possible due to a heavy rush in the Siliguri-Gangtok route. Vehicles purchased for other routes had often to be placed on this route to meet the tremendous increase in traffic.[34]

But in spite of these difficulties the nationalisation programme was carried on with satisfactory results as shown in the following table:

Routes, Route Mileage and Number of Vehicles under Operation in the Second Plan

Year	*S.No.*	*Route*	*Route Mileage*	*Number of vehicles*
1961-62	1.	Gangtok-Singtan - Rongpo	25	
	2.	Rongpo - Melli - Siliguri	46	
	3.	Gangtok - Tista - Ilalimpong	50	
	4.	Gangtok - Tista - Darjeeling	62	66
	5.	Melli - Naya Bazar	17	
	6.	Naya Bazar - Rishi	10	
	7.	Gangtok - Nathu La	37	
1962-63		As above (Excluding No. 7) &		
	8.	Rishi - Legship	6	
	9.	Naya Bazar - Sombare	17	94
	10.	Singtam - Makha	9	
1963-64		As Above &		
	11.	Legship - Geyzing	11	100
	12.	Naya Bazar - Namchi	12	
1964-65		As above &		
	13.	Nelli-Manpur-Namchi	23	109
1965-66		As above &		
	14.	Gangtok-Mangan	45	129

Source: Govt. of Sikkim, *Sikkim Through Figures* (Gangtok: Planning and Development Deptt., 1969), p. 30.

It may be mentioned in this connection that with the declaration of emergency in 1962, the vehicles of the Sikkim

Nationalised Transport were pressed into service of the Indian army and as a result the transport system was under severe strains. Transport services in the Gangtok-Nathu La route were completely suspended and the nationalisation of new routes in the subsequent years was dampened. Incidentally, an important event that took place towards the end of the Plan was that the Department gradually changed over to metric weights and measures. Financially, it proved to be a sound undertaking and the gross earning in the five years of the Second Plan amounted to Rs. 2,12,63,819 with a net profit of Rs. 66,77,108.[35]

The Third Plan commenced in 1966-67 vith a total outlay of Rs. 40,00,000 provided out of the development funds of the Government of Sikkim which was made available as a loan from the Government of India. Activities during the first two years of the Plan were on a very restricted scale awaiting finalisation of the details of this loan. The comparative lull of the preceding two years was, however, more than compensated in 1968-69 during which year some significant changes were introduced. A fleet of 4 tank lorries each of approximately 6 Kilolitre capacity were taken into use, and it eliminated almost entirely the use of barrels for the carriage of petroleum products for the Department and its clients.

By arrangement with the authorities of the Home (Transport) Department, West Bengal, the restriction imposed on the plying of 6-wheeler vehicles was removed. Pay-loads were thus increased from 3 to 5 tonnes; and the Sikkim Nationalised Transport was granted counter- signature for an additional 30 freight vehicles on the Siliguri-Rongpo axis.

Reorganisation of certain aspects of the Department was in the process of implementation with a view to meeting changed conditions and heavier demand. Nature, however, intervened, and the unprecedented landslides and floods of October, 1968, destroyed all major roads and bridges leading into Sikkim and left few of the nationalised routes in the country unscathed. For a little over a month the operations of the Sikkim Nationalised Transport were suspended.

The rehabilitation thereafter was speedy, limited only by the fact that round-about routes caused a set-back to time-schedules, and the extremely rough road surfaces brought about heavier costs of wear and tear. By the middle of November, 1968 with the restoration of an alternative route via Labha and Rishi—almost twice the distance of the former route along the National Highway No. 31A — the wheels began to roll again. Restoration of the former route which was the life-line of Sikkim was possible only after several months.

The gigantic task of reconstruction required the movement of huge quantities of construction material and essential commodities. Each agency involved in reconstruction assessing its own priorities created problems and placed resources of the Department under considerable strain. The Department, however, contributed effectively in maintaining the food supplies and reduced thereby the inevitable spiralling of prices and connected undesirable activities.[36]

As soon as the Department returned to normal routine the Rishi-Ranipul route was nationalised, passenger services introduced on the Gangtok-Rongli route and the district head-quarters of Namchi and Geyzing were linked with Gangtok by a daily 10-seater passenger bus service. Special charter services were introduced for students' excursions, recreation trips and tourists' visits to places of interest in the Gangtok area by providing some 20-seater mini-buses.

In May 1970 the carriage of petroleum products into Sikkim was made the exclusive responsibility of the Department, and the Gangtok Siliguri fleet of freight-carrying trucks was expanded to include 60 five-ton vehicles. Additional equipment, plant and machinery were procured to make the central workshops self-contained, and the staffing pattern was reorganised and expanded. To accommodate additional offices and staff as a result of increased traffic at Siliguri a three-storey building was acquired. The cottage annexe to the building served as a rest house for officials and visitors breaking journey at Siliguri. Successful negotiations with the Indian army resulted in a considerable increase in freight traffic on the Gangtok-Siliguri and Rongli-Daramdin routes. The gross earnings during the Third Plan period were estimated at Rs. 263.88 lakhs.[37]

The success of the state transport department in Sikkim can easily be gauged from the multitude of achievements in various fields mentioned above. From the point of view of revenue earning also the success can be measured; and it has proved to be a success there too. The following table will indicate the growth of gross revenue of the state transport department for the period under consideration.

Growth of Gross Revenue Earned by the State Transport Department of Sikkim

Years	*Total Gross Revenue (Rs. in lakh)*	*Yearly Average Gross Revenue (Rs. in lakh)*	*Percentage Rise in Yearly Average Gross Revenue*
1944-54	49.53	4.95	--
1954-61	143.62	20.52	315
1961-66	247.78	49.56	142
1966-71	263.88	52.78	7

Sources: As Cited Before.

The above table shows that there has been an upward trend in the average gross revenue per year since the inception of the state transport department and this indicates not only the supreme need of road transport facilities in a hilly state like Sikkim but also its potentiality and soundness as a commercial enterprise. Moreover, the table also indicates that the growth of transport facilities was closely linked with the overall economic development of the country — as the country developed, transport facilities also developed and vice versa.

From the above table we see that during the First Plan period the yearly average gross revenue increased by 315 per cent whereas in the Second Plan period it rose by 142 per cent. The decline in the rate of increase was perhaps the reflection of a secular trend. In the next 5 years the increase was quite moderate, at the rate of 7 per cent only, partly because of the devastating flood of 1968 which disrupted transport services for months and partly because of the secular decline in the rate of growth of the transport sector.

In fine, it must be admitted that the venture of the state transport department has proved to be a grand success — it is now the biggest internal source of revenue to the Government. Considering the state of affairs in Indian public undertakings it is no mean an achievement at all.

C. Development of Industries During the Plans

Sikkim being a hilly region inhabited by a traditional society the scope for development of industries is limited there not only by natural handicaps but also by social inhibitions. Before the commencement of the plans, Sikkim had no small or large-scale industries but there were a few cottage industries supported by household necessities and local trade, mostly barter. Under the developmental plans the State is, however, forging ahead with a strong urge for industrialisation and it has been successful in that respect to a great extent.

The traditional Sikkimese craftmanship dates back to several centuries. The Lepchas possessed expertise in bamboo-craft and wood-work and their creativity in this field received superlative plaudits under the penmanship of Dr. Hooker when he visited the country one and a half centuries ago. On the other hand, the Lepcha womenfolk were engaged in spinning and weaving traditional textures. The early Bhutia settlers who arrived in Sikkim more than 600 years ago brought with them the ancient Tibetan practice of carpet and rug weaving and this influence is alive even to-day in the carpets and rugs patterned to traditional design, alternating between muted shades and brilliant colours of pure vegetable dyes. Centuries later came the influx of the Nepalis bringing with them the celebrated craftsmanship of their metal-work, silverware and wood-work.

These handicrafts of Sikkim, particularly weaving and carpet- making, have survived the test of time as well as quality. The governmental patronage was no less important in this respect. The position towards the beginning of the 20th century may be noted in this connection:

"Carpets are still made at the palace factory, which since the death of the Maharani is maintained by the Maharaja, but outside orders are very few.

"The two weaving schools at Lachung and Lachen, which are managed by the ladies of the Scandinavian Alliance Mission stationed there, received aid from the State. The school buildings and looms are the property of the State and a small annual grant is given for their maintenance. In return the State receives 2 annas in the rupee on all sales. ... The value of the sales amounted during the year to Rs. 1,114 -3-0..."[38]

After the initiation of developmental plans the governmental patronage to cottage industries became much more pronounced and direct. Under the plans efforts were made to promote cottage industries as a subsidiary occupation which would be able to stabilise the economy of the rural population. During the First Plan period the Government spent a sum of Rs. 3.87 lakhs on the development of cottage industries.

At Gangtok a cottage industries institute was set up in 1957 and it provided the nucleus for the improvement of cottage industries in the State. This institute known as Palden Thondup Institute of Cottage Industries was started primarily to train the Sikkimese boys and girls in local handicrafts. It may be pointed out in this connection that the institute was started not to exploit the talents of the craftsmen for commercial gain, but to ensure that the traditional crafts of the country would not be lost to posterity.

During the First Plan 42 students successfully completed their courses in various arts and crafts at the institute. During the training period each student received a stipend of Rs. 25 per month. The 42 students vho successfully finished their training specialised in the following crafts: (i) Carpentry (7), (ii) Hand-made Paper (4), (iii) Carpet-making (11), (iv) Hand-loom and Lepcha-weave (11), and (v) Doll-making (9).[39]

It was felt that the institute should not merely train the Sikkimese young men and women in the traditional arts and crafts but should also produce various goods in these crafts to meet the demands of modern market and thereby add to the revenue of the State. Hence the basic mechanisation of the institute was undertaken during the Plan period and mechanised equipments like sewing machines, lathe machines and looms were introduced.

In 1959 the carpentry section attached to the institute was converted into a training-cum-production centre to meet the increasing demands from the public as well as the Government for furniture which till then had to be obtained at a considerable expense and difficult transportation from the adjoining areas of West Bengal like Kalimpong and Siliguri. Attempts were also made to introduce commercial production in other sections of the institute but they were not fruitful until the starting of the Second Plan.

In 1962 the institute was upgraded to include a full-fledged production unit with the newly qualified trainees now absorbed in the staffing programme. During the Second Plan period training and production went on side by side in all the sections.

According to the progress report of the Second Five-Year Plan 113 trainees completed their training in various arts and crafts during the Plan period. Training included the following arts and crafts:

(i) Carpentry (20), (ii) Hand-made Paper (4), (iii) Carpet-making (15), (iv) Hand-loom and Lepcha-weave (22), (v) Doll-making and Multicrafts (43) and (vi) Traditional Art (14). According to another source a total of 109 persons were trained in the above arts and crafts as well as in Ceramics, Batik work and Tailoring.[41] The trainees were given a stipend of Rs. 30 per month and depending upon the nature of the training the duration of the training course varied from one year to two years. As some of the trainees came from the distant parts of Sikkim two hostels, one for 20 boys and the other for 40 girls were constructed during the Plan.[42]

On completion of their training a good number of persons found employment in the combined production unit of the institute as paid labourers and workers. At the end of the Second Five-Year Plan there were 42 passed out trainees working as paid workers in the institute. Their wages varied from Rs. 35 to Rs. 200 per month depending upon their work output. The institute further maintained a close touch with the other passed out trainees with a view to encouraging and assisting them in their respective vocations.

In addition to the training programme that was conducted at Gangtok itself separate stipends were also given to selected candidates for undergoing vocational training in India. Seven persons were sent during the Second Plan period for specialised training in the following vocations: (i) Automobile Engineering (2), (ii) Hand-made Paper Course (2), (iii) Leather Work (1), (iv) Electrical Course (1), and (v) Tailoring (1).[43]

Apart from the attention paid to the expansion programme of the institute it was intended to open two new weaving centres in north Sikkim during the Second Plan period. At Lachung where the Khadi Commission had been running a small spinning and weaving centre a building was constructed and handed over to the Commission for the operation of a training-cum-production centre. Because of technical difficulties no such centre could be opened at Lachen, the other proposed site.

During the Third Plan period the institute of cottage industries continued to operate its usual functions and by the end of 1970 nearly 100 boys and girls, were receiving instructions at the institute, and some 85 qualified personnel were employed in the production unit. By the end of the Plan the institute's output was valued at Rs. 1.25 lakhs per year.[44]

The Palden Thondup Institute of Cottage Industries has been playing an important role in the regeneration and reinstatement of the traditional Sikkimese arts and crafts, particularly through its training programme. But so far as its production unit is concerned, it has proved to be unprofitable all along.[45]

There are many reasons for this financial set-back of the institute. First of all, the articles produced by the trainees of the institute are not generally as good and attractive as those made by the crafty village folk. The trainees are mostly young boys and girls who have little previous knowledge about the crafts. Consequently the articles produced by them during the training period are apt to be of inferior quality and fetch comparatively smaller price in the market.

Secondly, the labour cost of the articles produced is quite high compared to the labour cost of similar articles produced in villages. The village craftsman is generally a cultivator who spends his lean season in weaving, making of dolls or any other handicraft and whatever price the article fetches in the market becomes additional income for him. On the other hand, for the trainees and workers of the institute the price must cover their maintenance and consequently the cost price becomes higher.

Thirdly, some basic raw materials like cotton, wool, metals etc. are imported from other states of India and the import price which is higher than the price prevalent in the adjoining Indian territories, due to transport cost, enhances the cost of production of handicrafts. Naturally, these articles cannot compete on equal footing with similar goods produced elsewhere in India. Unless those materials are produced domestically or transport cost is reduced, there is little scope for any decrease in the cost of production of these articles on that account.

Lastly, Sikkim has a very insignificant domestic market for handicrafts and other articles of cottage industry. The small market in Gangtok does not provide a sufficient stimulus to the industry. There is, of course, one redeeming feature of the problem. Sikkim attracts a large number of foreign tourists and most of the sale proceeds of the institute is contributed by these foreigners. If more attention is paid to the modernisation and advertisement of the articles and arrangements are made for sales in foreign markets the chronic deficit may ultimatel turn into a surplus.

Let us now discuss about the "other industries" as referred to in the plan documents. By "other industries" is meant the Industries other than cottage industries, mainly small-scale. As mentioned earlier, there was no small or large-scale industry in Sikkim prior to the initiation of development plans. *Mining*, however, was already there but only on an experimental basis to be developed into a full-fledged industry in later years.

Comprehensive studies of the economic geology of Sikkim were carried out in the middle of the 19th century and led to the discovery of copper ore at no less than sixteen sites. Other minerals which were known to be found in Sikkim at that time were iron, lime and garnet. By the end of the 19th century at least two copper mines were being worked and several other ones had already been abandoned after experimental quarrying. Coming to the 20th century the first major attempt to assess the nature and extent of mineral resources was made by the Geological Survey of India in 1948-49 under the guidance of Mr. D. Kerr Cross, a mining Engineer.[46]

Investigations made by the Geological Survey of India have revealed that copper deposits are scattered all over the southern portion of the state. The most promising mine is at Bhotang in the Khanital area. It is also the most easily accessible as the main highway from Siliguri to Gangtok passes directly through it at Rangpo, the Indo-Sikkimese border town. Here the Tista river has eaten its way through a mountain of solid rocks and a rich seam of copper lies under the main highway. The total tonnage of probable ore is estimated by the Geological

Survey of India to be 41,000 tonnes.

Besides Bhotang there are also copper mines at Dikchu, Chakung, Rhotok, Rhenok and Chumbong. These were also examined by the Geological Survey of India. The probable ore at Dikchu was estimated to be about 2,300 tonnes. The Geological Survey of India recommended further work in respect of the copper deposits in the Chakung area along with the exploration of the Bhotang mine.[47]

Investigations made by the Geological Survey of India have revealed that coal deposits of fairly large magnitude exist in the Rangit valley near Naya Bazar. The total area of the coal field is estimated to be between 40 to 50 square miles. At a rough estimate the reserve amounts to 240 million tonnes. Detailed prospecting with the help of boring is required to determine the exact quantity of coal that can be recovered. The coal is reported to be non-coking.

The Geological Survey of India also found a deposit of graphite in the interior of western Sikkim. The quality and quantity are reported to be favourable. Minerals such as gypsum, kayanite, lime-stone, garnets and iron pyrites have also been found in various places of the State. However, no systematic mapping of mineral resources had been possible by the time the First Plan was introduced.

When the plans were introduced it was not mining but the distillation of wines and liquours that gained the first foothold in Sikkim. In 1955 a pioneering Indian entrepreneur ventured with Government approval to put up a still some distance out of Singtam. At the end of the Third Plan the *Sikkim Distilleries* gave, gainful employment to a managerial strength of 30 and to some 150 labourers. By that time the distilleries had been equipped with the most up-to-date silent spirit still and had an expansion programme fortified by a sales strategy that was finding larger markets from day to day. The distilleries' products had secured overseas markets and some shipments had already been made. In 1970-71 the progress of the Sikkim Distilleries' business was maintained at a high level with a turn-over of the order of Rs. 49.36 lakhs.[48]

Another undertaking that has been commercially rewarding is the *Government Fruit Preservation Factory* set up at Singtam in 1956. Orange is a major cash crop of Sikkim, but its market is outside the country. In addition to wastage in transit and market fluctuations, the orange growers were previously at the mercy of the middlemen which resulted in considerable loss to them as they were compelled to dispose of their produce at the rates offered, orange being a perishable commodity. The establishment of the factory not only relieved the growers of the losses which they suffered previously but also gave them incentive to bring additional areas under horticulture which has a vital role to play in the economy of a hilly state like Sikkim.[49]

Initially, however, the factory was not commercially sound. The First Technical Team which visited Sikkim at the end of the First Plan pointed out that its unremunerative condition was mainly due to the lack of proper planning and management. The Team also noted that the factory was well situated and housed and had the advantage of modern equipments; but it worked only for four months in a year during the apple and orange season. The Team recommended, therefore, that production should be diversified to make the factory work for a longer period and greater attention should be paid to the pooling of investment, proper planning, management and quality control. The authority followed these recommendations and within a few years the factory became profitable.[50]

Undoubtedly what has contributed most to the success of this factory is the superlative quality of the orange produced in Sikkim — a small, tight-skinned mandarin, both fleshy and sweet. The orange products, whether bottled as a squash, canned as juice, concentrate, marmalade or fruit segments, are the fast-selling items on the production range. The factory now preserves other fruits readily available in the country, such as apples, pears and guavas. Mangoes, pineapples, plums, peaches and lemons, all imported from the neighbouring states of India, are also in the production line thus providing a wide range of fruit products.

Efficient business management and specialised commercial marketing have been instrumental in bringing this enterprise to the affluent status that it enjoys today. It has a total fixed asset valued at about Rs. 8,00,000 and an annual gross sale valued at about Rs. 12,50,000. Year after year the factory has been showing better results and greater profit and so far as the quality is concerned, it has been able to secure certificates of international standard from many concerns of world repute such as the B.O.A.C.* that have been using its products.

During the First Plan considerable progress was made in the field of mining. Since 1956, with the full consent and co-operation of the Sikkim Durbar, the Indian Bureau of Mines had been surveying and investigating the deposits of copper ore in Sikkim. Zinc, lead and silver were also found in workable quantities in the overbody. Results were sufficiently encouraging for a mining corporation to be formed and consequently the *Sikkim Mining Corporation* — a joint undertaking of the Government of Sikkim and the Government of India — was constituted under a royal proclamation on February 27, 1960.

The Sikkim Mining Corporation was floated by the Government of Sikkim with an authorised capital of Rs. 1 crore. Fifty one per cent of the share capital was held by the Government of Sikkim and forty-nine per cent by the Government of India. The Sikkim Durbar has the option to acquire at face value and at any time the entire forty-nine per cent of shares held by the Government of India. Moreover, to make it possible for the Sikkim Government to supply share capital a loan was raised with the Indian Government. The Sikkim Mining Corporation was an autonomous body, its chairman being the Chogyal of Sikkim and two of its five directors were Sikkimese.

The Sikkim Mining Corporation was engaged in the exploitation of the Bhotang mines near Rongpo where the mineralisation of the ore deposits was claimed to be of a multi-metal nature containing-workable proportions of copper, lead, zinc and traces of silver. By the end of the First Plan the Corporation employed about 200 persons, some of them Sikkimese, but the majority were Indians. Technicians were almost entirely Indian but Sikkimese youths were being trained as the responsibility of running and developing the mines would ultimately be theirs.[51]

The Sikkim Mining Corporation, however, had to run at

* Currently it is renamed as British Airways.

a loss for several years after its commencement. An imported plant and equipment for the production of separate concentrates purchased in 1961 subsequently proved inadequate to yield the required concentrates. It took some time to recognise the shortcomings and difficulties and an experimental programme with suitable modifications in the equipment established good results in early 1967. The Corporation commenced production from April the same year and started to hold its own by competing against foreign companies having all the advantages of the advanced industrial countries.

Unpredictably, the efforts of the Corporation were suddenly brought to a standstill in October, 1968 when due to the devastating flood part of a hill collapsed on the mill area, buried the mill under 20 feet debris, and destroyed a large part of the mill, concentrates worth Rs. 5 lakhs, the water supply system, workshop, equipment and motor vehicles. With communications and electrical power cut, and all its units disrupted, it was no mean achievement that the Corporation was back in production within six months. By March, 1970 the Corporation claimed earnings to the value of Rs. 10 lakhs in foreign exchange out of its exports.[52]

It may be pointed out in this connection that *all the three above-mentioned industries were set up during the First Plan period. Surprisingly enough, these are also the only three commercial undertakings of the state that have established reputation for themselves abroad.* This shows that the tempo of industrialisation appreciably decreased during the subsequent plans.

During the Second Plan no new industry worth mentioning was set up except that a start was made in regard to the establishment of the *tea industry* and attempts were made for the establishment of private industrial estates through the provision of loans. The starting of the tea industry itself was, however, quite revolutionary for the economy of Sikkim. Considering the existence of a flourishing tea industry in Darjeeling which was similar in soil and climate and adjacent to Sikkim the potentiality of the industry was immense.

There was a late start in respect of the tea project and works were initially confined to the contour survey of the area at Kewzing in west Sikkim. Later on 700 seed-beds were prepared and about 3 lakh seeds were sown. By the end of the Second Plan all these seeds sprouted and in 1965-66, the last year of the Plan, tea estates were set up at Kewzing. At that time 50 Tibetan refugee families were working in the area. The Government of Sikkim provided them with accommodation and other facilities.[53]

During the Third Plan period there was further expansion of the industry. As part of the long-term planning towards developing a self-generating economy more tea estates were set up at Temi-Tarku in 1969. By the end of the Third Plan the capital investment in these tea estates had run to an expenditure of approximately Rs. 57 lakhs providing employment to some 16 administrative personnel and 900 labourers. The expenditure incurred in maintaining these estates has been assessed at Rs. 5.5. lakhs per year and it is anticipated that the first returns on this project will be forthcoming by the conclusion of the Fourth Plan.

The tea estates in Sikkim are located at altitudes and contained within climatic zones similar to the gardens in the Darjeeling District of West Bengal. Early experimental pickings carried out at Kewzing and Temi-Tarku have shown favourable results. Plans for furthering the tea industry, drawn up in consultation with the Indian Tea Board, include the extension of plantations and nurseries and the construction of buildings and a factory for processing tea.[54]

Another project initiated during the Second Five-Year Plan period was the encouragement to the establishment of *industrial estates* through providing industrial loans to private entrepreneurs. For the first time the Government accepted this programme as a matter of policy and from that point of view it was a landmark in the history of industrial development of the country. Even though it had a very bright prospect, no industrial estate could, however, be set up during the Plan period. Only Rs. 84,000 could be given as loans for the start of four small-scale industries. The progress was not satisfactory and the amount was quite small compared to the provision of Rs. 9.75 lakhs in the Plan. It has been pointed out in the progress report of the Plan that the delay in the formulation of loan rules in respect of this scheme was partly responsible for the very poor achievement.[55]

In the Third Plan period the Government provided substantial financial backing to the industries launched by the private sector. Among such units was the *Sikkim Tannery* set up near Rongpo in 1970 which commenced processing leather from indigenous hides by the end of the Plan. Other small-scale industries included a flour mill, a soap manufacturing unit and a factory manufacturing nails. Private entrepreneurs supported by Government loans also established an orchidarium, a dairy, a private press, a motor garage, an ice-cream factory, a distilled water processing unit, an umbrella manufacturing factory, blanket weaving centres, a goldsmithy and a unit engaged in specialised floriculture. Loans were also made available to the breeders to set up fisheries, piggeries, apiaries and poultry farms. While a certain amount of success was achieved by some small-scale industrialists, there were some units which had still to overcome the initial handicaps of breaking new ground.[56]

Apart from these small endeavours in the private sector no big project or industry was started in the public sector during the Third Plan period. Maintenance and expansion of old industries, however, continued. But it must be said that from the point of view of industrialisation of the country the Third Plan presented a poor show.

REFERENCES

1. R. N. Sharma, "Development of Electricity in Sikkim", *Sikkim Herald,* June 12, 1970.
2. Govt. of Sikkim, *Sikkim Development Plan,* (Gangtok: Sikkim Durbar Press, 1955), p. 18.
3. Sharma, *op. cit.*
4. Govt. of Sikkim, Seven Years of Progress: 1954-61 (Gangtok: Sikkim Darbar Press, 1962), p. 1. Hereafter referred to as — "Progress Report: First Plan."
5. Govt. of Sikkim, *Second Five Year Plan of Sikkim: Progress Report 1961-64, Review of Plan, Proposals for Revision of Plan* (Gangtok: Planning and Development Dept.), Critical Review Section, p. 4. Hereafter referred to as "Progress Report: 1961-64".
6. Sharma.
7. Talk with Chief Engineer, Sikkim Public Works Department on May 18, 1972.

8. Govt. of Sikkim, *The Second Five-Year Plan of Sikkim: Progress Report for the Period, April 1961-February, 1966*, Part I (Gangtok: Planning and Development Dept.), p. 16. Hereinafter referred to as "Progress Report: April, 1961-February, 1966".
9. Govt. of India, *Second Five-Year Plan of Sikkim: Report of the Technical Team* (New Delhi: Planning Commission, 1961), p. 52. Hereafter referred to as "First Team's Report."
10. Govt. of Sikkim, *Second Five-Year Plan: 1961-66* (Gangtok: Public Relations Officer), p. 11. Hereafter referred to as "Second Plan (Non-Detailed)".
11. P. P. Karan and W.M. Jenkins, *The Himalayan Kingdoms: Bhutan, Sikkim and Nepal* (New York: Van Nostrand Co., Inc., 1963), p. 73.
12. V.H. Coelho, *Sikkim and Bhutan* (New Delhi: Vikas Publications, 1971), p. 23.
13. *Ibid.*, p. 371.
14. Progress Report: First Plan, p. 32.
15. Govt. of India, *Progress Through partnership* (Gangtok: Office of the Political Officer in Sikkim), p. 24.
16. Govt. of Sikkim, *Second Five-Year Plan: 1961-66. Schemes in the Second Five-Year Plan* (Gangtok: Planning and Development Dept. 1962), p. 61. Hereafter referred to as "Second Plan (Detailed).
17. Govt, of India, *Progress Through Partnership*, p. 17.
18. *Ibid.*, p. 15.
19. Second Plan (Detailed), p. 62.
20. Progress Report, April, 1961—February, 1966, p. 19.
21. Second Plan (Detailed), p. 63.
22. Progress Report, April, 1961 — February, I960, p. 20.
23. Progress Report: First Plan, p. 21.
24. Progress Report: April, 1961 —February, 1966, p. 20.
25. *Ibid.*, p. 21.
26. *Ibid.*
27. Second Plan (Detailed), p. 64.
28. Progress Report, April, 1961— February, 1966, p. 21.
29. "The Process of Planned Development: Transport," *Sikkim Herald*, May 27, 1972, p. 1.
30. "Nationalised Transport," *The Statesman* (Calcutta), June 2, 1960, Sikkim: A Statesman Supplement, p. IV.
31. L. H. Harnett, "A Review of Nationalised Road Transport in Sikkim (1944-1969)", *Silver Jubilee*, A Souvenir Publication of Sikkim Nationalised Transport, 1969.
32. *The Statesman*, p. IV.
33. Harnett.

34. Govt. of India, *Mid-Term Appraisal of the Second Five-Year Plan of Sikkim: Report of the Technical Team* (New Delhi: Planning Commission, 1964), p. 62. Hereafter referred to as "Second Team's Report".
35. Harnett.
36. *Ibid.*
37. *Sikkim Herald,* May 27, 1972, p. 4.
38. Govt. of Bengal, *Administration Report of the Sikkim State for 1910-11* (Calcutta: Bengal Govt. Press), p. 4.
39. Progress Report, First Plan, p. 16.
40. Progress Report, April, 1961 — February 1966, p. 17.
41. "Palden Thondup Cottage Industries Institute," *Sikkim Herald,* 3, No. 1 (March, 1967), 13.
42. *Ibid.*
43. *Ibid.*
44. "The Process of Planned Development: Industries, Mining and Commerce", *Sikkim Herald,* June 1, 1972, p. 2.
45. Govt. of Sikkim, *Sikkim Through Figures* (Gangtok: Planning and Development Dept., 1969), pp. 19-25.
46. *The Statesman,* p. II.
47. First Plan, p. 20.
48. Address of Mr. I.S. Chopra, Sidlon of Sikkim, on April 4, 1972. Published by the Govt. of Sikkim, p. 7.
49. Govt. of Sikkim, *Second Development Plan (A Five-Year Plan 1961-62—1965-66),* unpublished Draft, Part I, 1960, p. 3.
50. First Team's Report, pp. 5-6.
51. *The Statesman,* p. II.
52. *Sikkim Herald,* June 1, 1972, pp. 1-2.
53. Progress Report, April, 1961 —February, 1966, p. 18.
54. *Silkkim Herald,* June 1, 1972, p. 2.
55. Progress Report, April, 1961—February, 1966, p. 18.
56. *Sikkim Herald,* June 1, 1972, pp. 2, 4.

7

Health Services and Education

As an economy develops, the people feel more and more the need for various types of services. That speaks for the inclusion of services in any developmental plan. The Services Sector assumes even greater significance in the case of Sikkim mainly because of the hilly nature of the terrain and extreme climatic conditions like severe winter in the north and prolonged monsoon in the south. In such a situation services can hardly be expected to come forth under private initiative without much governmental help. Considering this the Services Sector — which is also called the Tertiary Sector — should be given adequate consideration in any economic plan for Sikkim. In this chapter we shall be concerned with the two most essential services in the country — health and education.

A. Development of Health Services during the Plans

In early times shrouded in mystery the medical needs of the Sikkimese masses were satisfied by the village headmen or priests of local faiths who held that diseases were caused by evil spirits or gods as the punishment for wrong deeds. The treatment methods prescribed were prayers, sacrifices and the application of local herbs as directed by a particular deity in their dreams or visions. This is mostly the picture of the early Lepcha period.

Later on there came an era of reasoning with the advent of Buddhism along with the influx of the Bhutias. At that time local herbs and some medicines from animal sources began to be used without any magical or mystical association and solely on account of their medicinal properties. But even then there was hardly any serious attempt to enquire into the "cause and effect" relationship of the diseases, neither was there any statistics to guide the physician in that regard. The Lepchas gradually took to these new medicines but witchcraft and sorcery still continued to be taken resort to.[1]

Until the mid-nineteenth century the Lepchas and the Bhutias, apparently proved themselves to be quite self-sufficient in treating their diseases and wounds with indigenous medicines and when in risk of possible mortality a sorcerer was called in to dispel the spirit thought to have taken possession of the patient. But gradually there was a change in attitude. The early pioneers from the West appear to have popularised the use of allopathic medicines, because travellers through Sikkim in the middle of the 19th century have recorded local people's demands for medicines prescribed by Western physicians. At the same time the influence of the British rule in Sikkim in the ushering in of allopathic medicine was no less important.

At the beginning of the 20th century there was only one small dispensary in the country serving the people with allopathic drugs. By 1910-11 the number of dispensaries increased to six of which three were run by the Scottish Mission, two by the State Government and one by the Government of Bengal. The total expenditure incurred by the Government of Sikkim in regard to those dispensaries in the same year was roughly Rs. 5,500 only. The number of patients treated in those dispensaries in the same period was approximately 30,000. More detailed statistics is cited below:

Dispensaries in Sikkim: 1910-11

Dispensary	*No. of Patients Treated*	*State Expenditure/ Contribution (Rs.)*
A. State Dispensaries		
1. Gangtok	7,430	3,415
2. Chidam	8,267	1,719
3. Rongpo	6,109	*
B. Mission Dispensaries		
1. Rhenok	4,018	

2. Seryong	1,537	250
3. Dentam	N.A.	

*Maintained by the Public Works Department, Govt. of Bengal at a cost of Rs. 1,063.

Source: Govt. of Bengal, Administration Report of the Sikkim State for 1910-11 (Calcutta: Bengal Govt. Press), p. 23.

Adjacent to the Gangtok dispensary there was a small hospital for indoor patients. All other dispensaries afforded out-door relief except at Rongpo where a couple of beds was provided for very serious cases. The sub-assistant surgeons at Chidam and Rongpo visited the bazars at Namthang, Namchi, Manjitar, Pakyong and Singtam on *hat* days. At Lachen and Lachung, where there were no dispensaries, simple cases were treated by the members of the Scandinavian Alliance Mission who were supplied with drugs etc. from Gangtok for the purpose.[2]

The first hospital in Sikkim was started in 1917 at Gangtok when the First World War was in progress. It became the nucleus of further expansion of medical services in Sikkim and a few years after the World War two more hospitals were set up, one at Namchi and the other at Singtam. At the same time several dispensaries were established, particularly to cater to the needs of the village people. The position remained practically the same prior to the launching of the First Development Plan.

Just before the commencement of the First Plan Sikkim had a well-equipped hospital with 64 beds at Gangtok. There were also a hospital with 16 beds at Namchi and a 6- bed hospital at Singtam. The total bed strength of these hospitals was thus 86. Apart from these hospitals there were 8 dispensaries in Sikkim before the initiation of the plans. The Government of India had a dispensary at Rongpo for the Central Public Works Department. Previously that dispensary was run by the Government of Bengal for its ovn Public Works Department. This was aided by the Government of Sikkim and by arrangements with the Government of India the public could receive treatment there. There was also dispensaries at Mangan, Geyzing, Soreng and Rongli. These were run by the State Government and were in charge of compounders. The Scottish Mission ran three dispensaries at Rhenock, Dentam and Daramdin which were also in charge of compounders.

During the First Development Plan two more hospitals were built, one at Geyzing in west Sikkim and the other at Mangan in north Sikkim and the existing hospital at Singtam was renovated by building a new structure in the place of the old one. The number of hospitals during the Plan period, therefore, increased from 3 to 5 — an addition of 2 and an increase of about 67 per cent. The total bed strength also increased from 86 to 175 — an addition of 89 and an increase of about 104 per cent.[3]

During the First Plan period the total number of dispensaries increased from 8 to 18 — an addition of 10 and an increase of 125 per cent. What was more important, however, was not the number but the location of these dispensaries. The basic idea behind these dispensaries at the places where they were constructed was that they should serve the population within a 10-mile radius of their location so that they were within the reach of the local people in one day's journey.

The total number of patients treated in all the hospitals and dispensaries increased from the pre-Plan figure of 0.63 lakh in 1953-54 to 1.75 lakhs in 1960-61 — an addition of 1.12 lakhs and an increase of about 178 per cent. A big achievement indeed. It has been pointed out, however, that even though this was a great achievement, there was scope for better performance through the utilisation of idle capacity. The First Technical Team, in course of its visit to various institutions, observed that often the capacity of the newly expanded medical centres and facilities was not fully utilised.

Another important programme initiated during the First Plan period was the training of local people in medical services. Unless and until the local people are recruited in medical services, no broad-based and effective medical programme or campaign can be launched. It was deemed, therefore, that the Sikkimese should be trained and recruited as medical personnel. With a view to manning the health services by the Sikkimese 11 doctors, 5 sanitary inspectors, 1 nurse and 9 compounders were sent to India for training.[5] All, except 9 doctors and 3 compounders who were nearing completion of their training at the time of the commencement of the Second Plan, were fully trained by that time. In addition, one compounder was trained as a microscopist and two sanitary-inspectors as malaria inspectors. Locally, 17 midwives and 5 assistant compounders received training.[6]

An important achievement of the public health programmes in Sikkimese planning was that within a very short time of its inception the whole emphasis of the Medical and Public Health Department was shifted from a merely curative approach to a preventive one. Due to successful health campaigns malaria and kala azar, Sikkim's two greatest killers, had been almost completely eradicated by the end of the First Development Plan. Small-pox was now a thing of the past and tuberculosis, venereal diseases and intestinal worms, which were the other major diseases, were being contained.[7]

Health campaign formed an intrinsic part of the medical and public health programmes undertaken under the First Plan. Malaria and kala azar which used to take a heavy toll of the population were the first to receive the Government's attention and both these scourges were successfully controlled. The campaign against them was launched in 1956. Every roofed structure below an attitude of 5,000 ft. was sprayed with D.D.T. twice a year during the malaria season between April and November. The D.D.T. spraying was equally effective against the density of the kala azar vector, namely the sand flies.

The effect of Governmental efforts to rid the people of these two diseases can be gauged from the fact that the incidence of malaria was reduced from 18,000 in 1956 to only 3,000 in 1960-51. Similarly, kala azar was controlled and the incidence in 1960-61 was only 250 as compared to 4,500 in 1956. People in the rural areas, particularly in the Terai and the foot-hills, were the main beneficiaries of this programme.[8]

At the commencement of the First Plan vaccination against small-pox was carried out locally in and around the places where an outbreak was reported. During the First Plan systematic vaccination as a preventive measure was introduced. The success of this measure can be judged from the following table:

Progress in Small-Pox Vaccination during the First Plan

Year	*Persons Vaccinated*	*Cases of Small-Pox*
1954	14,632	86
1955	16,564	65
1956	18,141	142
1957	36,920	7
1958	21,395	4
1959	25,272	2
1960	30,113	1

Source: Progress Report: First Plan, p. 28.

It is evident from the table that by the end of the First Plan the disease of small-pox was almost completely eradicated from the State and that speaks for the unique achievement of the eradication programme. This conclusion is further supported by the fact that since 1958 the very few cases of small-pox were all imported into Sikkim from the neighbouring countries — there was no indigenous case of small-pox.

In order to find the incidence of T.B. a B.C.G. Team deputed by the Government of Bihar toured Sikkim in 1955 for about 4 months and tested over 12,000 children and nearly half of them were found to be positive cases. About 7,000 persons were vaccinated with B.C.G. The small T.B. hospital at Gangtok was greatly expanded at the same time.

A pilot survey was undertaken by a team deputed by the Government of West Bengal in 1956 to ascertain the incidence of venereal diseases and intestinal worms in Sikkim. The serological tests and microscopic examination of stools on a extensive scale revealed that the average incidence of V.D. was 58.3 per cent and as high as 87.9 per cent in certain localities in north Sikkim. About 95 per cent of the population was found to be suffering from helminthical infections.

A Mobile Eye Team toured Sikkim in 1957 and carried out medical and surgical treatment of eye diseases. Medical arrangements for school children were established consisting of (a) annual medical examination with follow-up, (b) monthly sanitary inspections by medical officers or compounders (c) regular vaccination against small-pox, (d) talks on first aid and hygiene by the Medical Officer, and (e) provision of 50 medicine chests to different schools. These arrangements were preventive in nature and infused a spirit of health-mindedness in the younger generation of the people.[9]

To cater to the increasing population in Gangtok a new reservoir was constructed and the old one was extended for the provision of good and sufficient drinking water supply to the town. Five water supply schemes were completed in north Sikkim, 6 in the west and 10 in the east covering a total population of 30,000. These schemes entailed the construction of the catchment areas, so that people outside Gangtok could also have good water supply for drinking purposes.

In the field of environmental sanitation, on which the Government laid particular stress, a trenching ground was established near Gangtok for the disposal of both wet and dry refuse including night soil. Sanitary inspectors were responsible for the proper sanitation in Gangtok and other areas and during their inspection visits they demonstrated and helped to build soakage and compost pits so that there was no cluttering up of the streets and roads.

The implementation of public health schemes during the Second Plan incurring an expenditure of about Rs. 46 lakhs aimed at the consolidation of the progress made under the First Plan. As before, the systematic expansion of medical facilities on the curative side of development and the simultaneous launching of various public health campaigns on the preventive side constituted the highlights of the progress made during the Second Plan.

During the Second Plan no new hospital was built. Much progress was, however, made in regard to the expansion programme of Sir Tashi Namgyal Memorial Hospital at Gangtok, the premier hospital of Sikkim. The entire building programme of that hospital was completed with the exception of the disinfection shed. After sustained efforts for over 4 years the services of one surgeon-cum-superintendent for the hospital was ultimately secured. With increasing stress laid on developing the surgical side the operation theatre was modernised and the blood transfusion centre organised. Opthalmic and dental sections were commissioned and facilities for the treatment of dental and eye diseases were provided by regular visits of a dental surgeon and an eye specialist. A new ward for children was also commissioned. The maternity section placed under the charge of a trained lady doctor became very popular with the public.

Expansions were made in other hospitals as well. At Namchi the old hospital was expanded by opening a new maternity section and by adding a new block for out-door patients, an operation theatre and a T.B. ward. Similar facilities had been provided at Singtam and Geyzing, but no progress was made at Mangan.[10]

At the beginning of the Second Plan there were 18 dispensaries out of which fifteen were functioning in the rural areas. Under the Plan 9 more had been added with a view to giving medical aid to the public in the interior within one day's journey. The dispensaries at Soreng and Rongli were upgraded by attaching a small detention ward for indoor patients. However, no progress was made at all regarding the establishment of mobile disnensaries.[11]

Training of medical personnel continued in the Second Plan also. During the Plan period 5 candidates had successfully completed the M.B.B.S. course and 8 were under training by the end of the Plan. Moreover, one candidate was sent for training in dental surgery. Also 12 candidates were trained as compounders and 24 candidates as midwives during the Second Plan period.[12]

Non-availability of technical personnel, however, continued and doctors and trained nurses, in particular, were in short supply. The post of the Deputy Chief Medical Officer remained vacant even at the end of the Second Plan.[13]

Although the difficulty to obtain the services of trained technical personnel or to select suitablc candidates for training made the position of manning the medical institutions and health campaigns rather weak, no hospital, dispensary or health campaign suffered seriously thereby. With improved medical facilities the hospitals and dispensaries as well as health campaigns grew in popularity and that accounts for the fact that in spite of the bottlenecks mentioned above the implementation of public health schemes was more or less satisfactory.

In the field of preventive measures like health campaigns special attention was placed towards the eradication of the problem diseases like malaria, kala azar, small-pox, tuberculosis, venereal diseases and intestinal worms.

Under the First Plan malaria had already been controlled, but later on its eradication was aimed at. The original Second

Plan allocation of Rs. 4 lakhs was, therefore, raised to Rs. 7.35 lakhs with a view to following the standard pattern laid down by the Government of India for the eradication programmes.[14] The total population covered under this scheme was 1.59 lakhs. Intensive D.T.T. spraying which was started in the First Plan continued in the Second Plan also along with the concurrent phase of searching fever cases from house to house. According to the progress report of the Plan both the spraying and surveillance operations were undertaken as scheduled. Along with malaria kala azar was also controlled to a great extent.

Regarding the eradication and prevention of small-pox the programme of systematic mass vaccination continued under the Second Plan. According to the progress report of the Second Plan about 80 per cent of the population was covered under the programme and there was no indigenous case of small-pox during the Plan period. A few out-breaks of small-pox, however, occurred due to imported infection brought by those who escaped vaccination. During the Plan every effort was made, therefore, to reduce the number of persons escaping vaccination.[15]

Regarding tuberculosis which was very wide-spread in Sikkim it was decided to launch an attack systematically with a view to eradicating it ultimately. For assessing the extent of the disease in the country it was originally proposed to undertake mass radiography. But on further investigations done with the help of Dr. T.L. Bordia, T. B. advisor to the Government of India, it was considered that mass radiography was not practicable in a hilly terrain like Sikkim at the prevailing stage. Instead of mass radiography as proposed in the original Plan the revised Plan envisaged mass collection of random samples of sputum, microscopic examination, hospital treatment of toxic cases and extension of domiciliary treatment. The Government recruited one Medical Officer experienced in T. B. and having organisational capacity to implement these measures.[16]

With a view to controlling the spread of tuberculosis the services of a B.C.G. team on deputation from the Government of India were obtained and a thorough coverage of the entire population was effected. At the same time facilities for the treatment of T.B. cases at all the hospitals were made available.

As regards venereal diseases and intestinal worms the pilot survey for the incidence of these diseases in north Sikkim conducted during the First Plan showed the necessity of undertaking a campaign for the diagnosis and treatment of these diseases in all the areas of Sikkim. In the Second Plan, therefore, with the help of a team of trained doctors and technicians, the entire population of the country was examined for systematic treatment. Moreover, facilities for the treatment of these diseases in all hospitals and dispensaries were made available to the public.[17]

In a hilly region like Sikkim water supply is a problem, not only because of the difficulty of transportation of water from the streams in the valleys to the human habitation at the hill-tops but also because of the difficulty of purifying the water which is full of unhygenic elements like mica, silica and other sorts of impurities. It is necessary therefore, on the part of the Government to provide this basic amenity to the people. Consequently, during the Second Plan period the Government undertook two programmes under the headings of "village water supply schemes" and "bazar water supply schemes."

The village water supply schemes were implemented through the Planning and Development Department. The schemes were undertaken with public co-operation and the government's contribution was in the form of supply of pipes, cement and transport cost of raw materials. As in the case of village roads the work on these schemes started only in 1964-65. Still it was possible to take up 91 such schemes in various parts of Sikkim. Of them 32 schemes had already been completed and the remaining 59 were nearing completion by the end of the Plan.

In the Plan it was envisaged to implement 21 bazar water supply schemes in various parts of Sikkim. The implementation was undertaken by the Sikkim Public Works Department in consultation with the Medical Department. Eight such schemes had been completed in all respects and the remaining ones were nearing completion by the end of the Plan.

It can be stated with regard to both the water supply schemes that the progress achieved was more or less satisfactory considering the brief span for their implementation. Much headway could not, however, be made in regard to the Gangtok Water Supply Scheme and due to the slow progress it was decided to continue it in the Third Plan. Regarding drainage and sewage nothing worth mentioning could be done and the master plan for the drainage and water-borne sewage system at Gangtok was only in the process of preparation by the end of the Second Plan.

Like the Second Plan the Third Plan was also a continuation of the programmes undertaken during the First Plan period. This will be clear from the objectives of the Third Five-Year Plan which were stated as:

"The objectives of the Third Plan are consolidation of the schemes already undertaken, strengthening of the staffing position of various hospitals and dispensaries, expansion of facilities for specialised treatments and investigations and to complete the unfinished water supply and sanitation projects".[18]

During the Third Plan, excepting one new dispensary, there was no increase in the number of medical institutions, but various expansion works were undertaken in the field of treatment as well as prevention of diseases. The total number of beds in hospitals was increased to 272. Hospitals at the district level were provided with facilities to treat general diseases including tuberculosis while the hospital at the capital was fully equipped to carry out modern and specialised treatment in various branches of medical science.

The Gengtok hospital provided treatment in surgery, radiology, ethology, ophthalmology, dentistry, midwifery and gynaecology, and tuberculosis. The hospital also ran ante-natal and post-natal clinics, a baby clinic, family planning centre and an up-to-date library. Classes were conducted for the training of auxiliary nurses and midwives and a private ward comprising six cabins and offering modern amenities was attached to the hospital.

With the object of providing speedy medical relief to the rural population 24 dispensaries and 4 sub-dispensaries were maintained by qualified compounders who referred all cases needing hospitalisation to the nearest district hospital. Moreover, for the benefit of the rural people these dispensaries were located strategically to provide a medical post within a radius of 10 miles which in Sikkim is generally regarded as a walking distance. Four mobile dispensaries were also provided to carry medical aid to the remote areas as well as in the cases where transportation of the patient to a hospital was needed.

Along with the curative medical services the health campaigns conducted during the Plan years received favourable response from the public as before and it was to the credit of the medical authorities that the once-dreaded malaria and kala azar were eradicated from the country by 1970-71. Mass vaccination against small-pox continued to be carried out to prevent any out-break of the disease which had already been eradicated excepting a few imported cases.

Tuberculosis was another disease of concern and while facilities were available to hospitalise and treat the disease, plans were under way to establish a separate and more commodious hospital providing patients with the benefits of a modern sanatorium. Curative and preventive measures against venereal diseases and intestinal worms were also strengthened during the Plan period.

The supply of safe, drinking water to the public was another important project of the health authorities. With regard to the drainage scheme for Gangtok a feasibility report was prepared and the engineers were engaged in working out the details of the scheme when the Third Plan ended.[19]

In reviewing the achievements of the plans in the field of public health we see that a total reorientation of the public health services occurred during the period under study. In fact, there was no co-ordinated medical and public health department prior to the launching of the plans. There was one Agency Civil Surgeon in the country who was also in charge of administration of the department. With his multifarious duties he could not, however, have much time to devote to the administrative and supervisory duties, particularly in the distant parts of the country. Incidentally, he was also the resident Medical Officer at the Gangtok hospital. It was necessary, therefore, to appoint a whole-time medical officer solely in charge of the organisation.[20] During the period of the Plans a Director of Health Services was appointed to meet the above requirements.

In the pre-Plan days the dearth of medical personnel was another great bottleneck. In those days there was no health inspector or lady doctor, nor was there any facility in the country-side for maternal cases. Vital statistics were not available though the village headmen were entrusted with the task of collecting them. All these shortcomings were removed in course of the Plans, and Sikkim can now boast of a modern and full-fledged medical service.

The growth of medical facilities in Sikkim during the plan period can be gauged from the few statistics given below:

Development of Health Services during the Plans

Head	*Pre-plan*	*First Plan*	*Second Plan*	*Third Plan*
Hospitals	3	5	5	5
Dispensaries	8	18	23*	24*
Beds	86	175	239	272

*Excluding 4 sub-dispensaries.

Source: As Cited Before.

It may be noted here that maximum growth of medical services occurred in the First Plan period. All the new hospitals and the majority of new dispensaries were established during that period. The increase in the number of beds was also maximum in the First Plan period. Beds went on increasing in the subsequent plans as well but that was solely due to the expansion of existing hospitals. In a word, the infrastructure of health services was laid down during the First Plan period.

Now let us discuss how far the plans were successful in the cure and prevention of diseases that are generally to be found in the State. In this connection it may be pointed out that Sikkim is blissfully free from many problem diseases. Diseases due to malnutrition are not noticed in Sikkim. Sikkim is also lucky to be free from indigenous cholera and enteric group of diseases. Epidemics of cholera— for that matter even an outbreak of it — are unknown. Stray cases of typhoid are reported but the infection appears to have been imported from outside. With improved internal road communications and increased traffic to and from the adjoining countries it is not unlikely, however, that these two diseases may creep into Sikkim in course of time. But during the period of planning no such thing happened as the public as well as the Government remained ever vigilant.

Diseases more common to children's age group viz. chickenpox, measles, diphtheria, poliomyelitis and whooping cough do occur but do not assume epidemic form as there are not many congested localities. The rising tempo of urbanization, however, may lead to develop such congested localities and slum areas. But up till now these diseases have posed no serious problem to the health authorities.

The seasonal outbreaks of gastro-enteritis, generally known as diarrhoea and dysentery, are common annual features during the monsoon. With the arrival of the monsoon drinking water supply is polluted, especially in the rural areas where water is taken directly from the springs or streams, and as a result gastro-enteritis spreads. The best preventive measure is to drink boiled water during that season, but unfortunately most of the village people are illiterate and unaware of its necessity. Public health authorities, therefore, laid a great emphasis during the plans to educate the people in such health practices.

The problem diseases in Sikkim, broadly speaking, may be grouped as malaria, kala azar, small-pox, tuberculosis, venereal diseases and intestinal worms. In combatting these diseases the Government laid equal emphasis on curative as well as preventive measures mainly through mass health campaigns. In course of the implementation of those health campaigns public participation and co-operation came forth quite spontaneously thereby making them a success.

Simultaneously, the age-old beliefs in local quacks and witchcrafts regarding prevention of diseases and their treatment soon gave way to the new methods. This was particularly true of maternity cases and as the health programmes flourished during the plans it was noticeable that more and more expectant mothers utilised the services of midwives in their areas or went to hospitals for their confinement.

The rate of hospital attendance in the beginning was low but as the plans progressed, it became clearly visible how treatment-minded the people had become and how they developed confidence in doctors and other medical staff qualified in modern medical science. The people also co-operated with the Government is providing accommodation for hospitals, dispensaries and their staff through donations and community subscriptions.[21] The Government in turn reciprocated by making treatment in hospitals and dispensaries absolutely free — and that was no mean an achievement for so small a State like Sikkim.

An important point to note in this connection is that health programmes are often inseparably linked with educational programmes — and the progress or retardation in one leads to similar repercussions in the other. Hence to make both the programmes more successful the Government should embark on an integrated scheme in which health and educational services would be complementary to each other. As has been pointed out :

"Of the handicaps militating against rapid progress in health matters, perhaps the most outstanding is the very considerable amount of illiteracy which still prevails. Not only is the imparting of health education made difficult thereby, but any attempt to require a satisfactory educational level of healthworker trainees at entry precludes their being recruited in sufficient numbers."[22] The Government of Sikkim was aware of these considerations and, as we shall see in the following section, there was remarkable development in the field of education during the plans.

B. Development of Education during the Plans

From the time of Bhutia establishment till the late 19th century education in Sikkim was confined to the study of scriptures in various monasteries of the country. Education at that time was intended for the benefit of those who were preparing for priesthood and was supervised by the great lamas of Tibet. In Sikkim as in Tibet the priests were made and not born. It was after severe tests in religious education in the scriptures of Buddhism that a young seeker of knowledge was admitted into the order.

The beginnings of modern education can be traced back to 1880 when the Finnish missionaries entered Sikkim. The missionaries opened up three primary schools — one each at Khamdong, Song and Mangan. Their pioneering efforts received further stimulus in 1884 with the advent of the Scottish missionaries who set up a chain of 10 primary schools during the subsequent years. The foundation of secondary education in Sikkim was laid by the tenth Chogyal, Thutob Namgyal, who in 1889 set up two boarding schools at Gangtok — one for the Bhutias and the other for the Nepalis.

The dawn of the 20th century witnessed the opening up of a number of primary schools both in the public and private sectors, and the setting up of middle schools by the Government. The position of education in 1910-11 is shown in the following table:

Education in Sikkim: 1910-11

Description of school	*No. of Schools*	*No. of Pupils*	*State Expenditure/ Contribution (Rs.)*
A. State Schools:			
Bhutia Boarding School	1	42	4,055
Nepali Boarding School	1	55	2,121
B. Schools maintained by the the Church of Scotland Mission:			
Lace School	3		
Day School	12	415	1,000
Night School	12		
C. Schools maintained by the Scandinavian Alliance Mission:			
Day School	N.A.	N.A.	436
Night School	N.A.	N.A.	
All Schools	29*	512*	7,612

*Excluding schools run by the Scandinavian Alliance Mission.
Source: Ad. Report for 1910-11, p. 23.

On the syllabi of the two secondary schools it has been said that English, history, geography, mathematics and drawing were the common subjects in both the Bhutia Boarding School and the Nepali Boarding School whereas Tibetan and Hindi were the special subjects taught in the two schools respectively. The benefits of these schools were being increasingly realised by the Kazis and the Nepali Thikadars. The number of their sons and relatives attending these schools increased gradually. The Nepalis showed particularly a greater desire for education.[24] In the year 1912-13, on the motion of the Maharajkumar the Sikkim State Council decided that all landlords should send at least half the number of their sons, of school-going age, to school for English education. The same year a school for the education of Kajis' daughters was opened.[25]

By the year 1913-14 Sikkim possessed 2 secondary and 25 primary schools. Of the primary schools 3 were maintained by the state, 14 by the Church of Scotland Mission, 2 by the Scandinavian Alliance Mission and 6 by the landlords in their own estates.[26]

In 1920-21 there were 20 schools in Sikkim of which 7 were state schools and 13 were missionary schools. The number of students as on 31st March, 1921 was 514. The state schools were the following: (i) Bhutia Boarding School, (ii) Nepali Boarding School, (iii) a girls school mostly for the daughters of the Kazis and the Thikadars, (iv) one village school at Lachen, (v) one village school at Lachung, (vi) Enchay Monastery School, and (vii) one industry school combined with the Jail Department where convicts were taught wicker works. There were 15 teachers in these state schools; but 10 out of them belonged to the first three schools, the remaining 5 belonging to the other 4 schools.

Of the 13 missionary schools 11 belonged to the Scotch mission and 2 to the Scandinavian mission. There were no private schools run by the landlords. We see, therefore, that in 1920-21 compared to 1910-11 the total number of schools decreased considerably despite the fact that the number of state schools increased. In Sikkim education was not a steady service and this type of fluctuation can be seen to happen quite frequently. Schools were started and closed depending on the conveniences or inconveniences of the founders, mostly the missionaries.

Moreover, the state of affairs in the schools was not very satisfactory. This is indicated by the number of teachers in the state schools. Condition does not seem to be better in the case of other schools.

An important reform in the education system was introduced in November, 1920 when the Maharaja of Sikkim reorganised the Education Department which was placed now under a "Director of Education, Sikkim State" to be assisted by a "Board of Education, Sikkim State". The above board was composed of the Maharajkumari as the president, Rhenock Kazi as the vice-president, and 9 other persons as members.

Excepting the president, all members of the board were expected to visit the state educational institutions occasionally and give report on their performance. Henceforth the Government had a control over the quality of instructions. The curriculum followed in the schools was the same as in the neighbouring province of Bengal.

By 1931-32 primary education became entirely free and a very modest scale of fees was charged for secondary education. An important point to note in this connection is that although secondary education started as early as in 1889 there was no high school in the state until 1925 when the Sir Tashi Namgyal High School was established in Gangtok.

This school became later on the premier educational institution in Sikkim. It sent its first batch of students for matriculation examination in March, 1931.[28] At present this institution is known as the Sir Tashi Namgyal Academy and is the only public school in Sikkim.

Coming to the era of planning we see a great change in the spirit as well as the system of education. Education now was viewed not as an auxiliary pursuit in human life but rather as an essential pre-requisite for material welfare. It was felt that the welfare of the people was closely linked up with education which provided an important means of tackling the problems generated by poverty and backwardness. It was also instrumental in modifying social customs which tended to hamper developmental process. In order to bring education nearer to the masses and offer them an opportunity of gaining its benefits so that they may play their proper role in the development of the country, the Government laid special emphasis on education during the plans.[29]

In this connection we may refer to a similar view expressed by the Education Ministers of the Asian Member States of UNESCO in a meeting held in April, 1962 on primary and compulsory education. There it was clearly said:

"...we have seen for the first time that education is not only the right of our peoples, not only a never-ending source of individual satisfaction, it is equally a factor which contributes directly, to the economic growth of our individual countries."[30]

During the plans a remodelling of the educational system was done in tune with the modern trend. Prior to the plans elementary education in Sikhim consisted of three stages: (i) lower primary school, (ii) upper primary school, & (iii) middle school; and secondary education was in two stages: (i) junior high school, & (ii) high or higher secondary school. Over the 17 years of planning the lower and upper primary schools have been amalgamated and the institution of middle schools abolished in favour of junior high schools. At the end of the Third Plan Sikkim had, therefore, three types of schools: (i) primary schools, (ii) junior high school, and (iii) high or higher secondary schools. The institution of high school was also in the process of liquidation being upgraded into higher secondary schools.

The position in 1954 and at the end of the three plans may be shown as below:

Growth of Schools in Sikkim 1954-71

S.No.	*Type of School*	*1954*	*1960-61*	*1965-66*	*1970-71*
1.	Lower Primary	70	117	117	164
2.	Upper Prinary	14	47	44	--
3.	Middle	2	13	13	--
4.	Junior High	-	1	5	21
5.	High/Higher Secondary	2	4	4	7

Source: 1. First Team's Report, p. 70.
2. Progress Report: April 1951-February 1966, pp. 29-31.
3. *Sikkim Herald,* May 20, 1972.

During the 17 years of planning Sikkim has advanced in the field of education in various respects. The number of students reading in primary schools in 1954 was about 1,800. By the end of 1970 the number increased to about 12,300. This shows a tremendous expansion of primary education in the country. Similar was the case with secondary education. In pre-1954 Sikkim there were only 600 students attending the middle schools, but at the end of 1971 it increased tenfold to about 6,000, though the middle schools were now upgraded to junior high schools. The statistics on the number of students reading in high or higher secondary schools is not available, but it is known that in 7 such schools at the end of the Third Plan students reading in higher classes numbered about 600. We can presume the number to be not more than 200 in the pre-1954 period when there were only 2 such schools.

Combining all these figures we see that during the 17 years of planning there was approximately a seven-fold increase in the number of school-going children which is quite significant for a small country like Sikkim.

During this period primary schools were established to cover all such areas which had been previously neglected. Junior high schools were established within a walking distance of 10 miles for every school-going child, and there was one higher secondary school at every district headquarter, apart from 3 such additional schools at Gangtok. Moreover, to obviate fatigue brought on by traversing long distances over difficult terrain hostel accommodation at selected places was provided. At each of the district headquarters provision was also made for establishing libraries which apart from being of service to the readers was intended to serve as centres for adult education.

Another important feature of educational development in Sikkim was financial assistance to the students. Prior to the plans education up to class IV was free but in course of the plans it was made free upto Class VI. Moreover, the Government of Sikkim through the generous assistance and co-operation of the Government of India arranged for the annual provision of 25 scholarships for the Sikkimese post-matriculate students to study in Indian institutions. Similarly 10 scholarships were provided each year for the Sikkimese students to study in Indian schools. The Government of Sikkim also on its own provided stipends to the poor students and arranged for the free supply of books to them.

The medium of instruction in Sikkimese schools is the mother tongue from Class I to Class IV, and English from Class V upwards. The teaching of English, however, begins from Class I. In order to facilitate instruction at the primary level, production of text-books in the regional languages was started in the Second Plan period when the First Lepcha Reader and the First, Second and Third Tibetan Primers were published.[32] In subsequent years publication of text-books in Nepali also was undertaken and it was intended to provide text-books in all regional languages for all classes at the primary level. By the end of the Third Plan a text-bock production unit was created within the Education Department for the purpose of publishing text-books in Sikkimese languages and to ensure that the fundamental reading material provided to the students was representative of the Sikkimese environment and culture.[33]

There was a scarcity of trained teachers in Sikkim before the commencement of the First Plan, and teachers in larger numbers were further required to man the schools opened under the plans. To cope with the situation a teachers' training centre was set up at Temi in western Sikkim in 1954. One hundred teachers were trained at the centre during the First Plan period. In course of the Second and Third Plans the number was increased to 40 teachers per session. In addition, language teachers were trained during the plans to provide instructions in primary schools in local languages.

Let us now have a review of the achievements in education during the plans. First of all, we note that after the plans there has been a definite change in the attitude of the Sikkimese masses regarding education. In place of the traditional religious education Sikkim is now placing more emphasis on modern education. No doubt, religious education is still being imparted, but that too is combined with modern education. The Enchay Monastery School at Gangtok is the principal institution in Sikkim imparting knowledge in Buddhist scriptures and philosophy to the young lamas. But there too modern subjects like English, geography and history are taught simultaneously with the religious studies which was not the case in the olden days. Students who pass out of this institution are now being absorbed as wholetime teachers in the areas where Buddhists predominate.

Coming to the growth of modern education in relation to the growth of population we find a notable upward trend during the plans. According to the Census report of 1960-61 the population of Sikkim was 1.67 lakhs and the provisional results published on the 1970-71 Census shows population of about 2 lakhs which means a 2 per cent @ per annum increase in copulation during the decade. Assuming this rate of increase to have held good in the 1950's also, we calculate the population of Sikkim in 1953-54 as 1.46 lakhs.

It has been calculated that the number of children in the age-group 6-17 years in 1960-61 was 41,400 which was about 25 per cent of the population.[34] Assuming the ratio of the children in that age-group to total population to be the same for other years as well, we calculate the number of children in the age-group of 6.17 years in 1953-54 and 1970-71 as 36.5 thousand and 50 thousand respectively.

We know that the number of children who attended schools in 1960-61 was 9,000.[35] The corresponding numbers for 1953-54 and 1970-71 were 2,600 and 18,900 respectively.[36] These were about 7, 22 and 38 per cent of the total number of children in the school-going age in 1953-54, 1960-61 and 1970-71 respectively. All these data can be assembled in the form of a table as below:

Growth of Population and Education during the Plans

Head	*Unit*	*1953-54*	*1960-61*	*1970-71*
Population	1,000	146	167	200
6-17 Age Group	1,000	36.5	41.4	50.0
Students	1,000	2.6	9.0	18.9
Students as per cent of 6-17 Age Group	-	7	22	38

Sources: Loc. cit.

The above table shows a great increase in literacy and education during the course of the plans, although scope for further increase still remains. What is specially gratifying in this regard is the increasing rate of growth of education compared to that of population.

Regarding female education it can be said that it is not very satisfactory even after the plans. Statistics are not available to show the rise or otherwise of female education in the state. But the position towards the end of the Third Plan may be noted as in the following table:

Sex and Community-wise Number of Students in 1968

Sex	*Nepali*	*Bhutia*	*Lepcha*	*Others*	*Total*
Boys	7,863	1,959	1,118	680	11,625
Girls	2,231	889	480	416	4,666
Total	10,749	2,848	1,598	1,096	16,291

Source: Govt. of Sikkim, *Sikkim Through Figure,* (Gangtok: Planning and Development Dept., 1969), p. 32.

The percentage of boys and girls in the student population of different communities as well as of the state as a whole is also quite interesting and worth noticing. The following table has been prepared for that purpose:

Percentage of Boy and Girl Students in 1968

Sex	*Nepali*	*Bhutia*	*Lepcha*	*Others*	*Total*
Boys	79	69	70	62	71
Girls	21	31	30	38	29
Total	100	100	100	100	100

Source: Loc. cit.

We see from the above table that female education was more or less restricted—about 29 per cent of the total number of students — even towards the end of the Third Plan. This is natural because in an educationally backward community education is more likely to be imparted to the male members of the society rather than to the females while in an advanced community a trend towards much more equal educational opportunities to both the sexes is evinced. And this holds good for Sikkim as well.

The proposition that the more backward a society is the less is the percentage of females attending educational institutions may also be corroborated by a study of educational attainments of the different communities of the state. From the above table it is seen that female education is highest among the section of the people classified as "others" mostly comprising the Indians (38%) while it is lowest among the Nepalis (21%). Female education is practically at par so far as the two Buddhist communities are concerned — the Bhutias (31%) and the Lepchas (30%).

The reason for this disparity in female education among the different communities is not very surprising considering the different factors involved therein. The Indians are educationally much more conscious and generally tried to educate their daughters, at least up to the primary standard. The Nepalis, on the other hand, are a hard-working people most of whom employed their daughters at work at an early age thereby preventing them from getting any education. Female education among the Bhutias and the Lepchas was at par and higher than that among the Nepalis, mainly due to the influence of Buddhism which requires a certain minimum education for all and some special monastic training for the future monks.

One point is worth mentioning in assessing the achievements of educational programmes during the plans. It is the multitude of difficulties in a small state like Sikkim which pose serious obstacles to the implementation of any educational programme. Some of these difficulties may be mentioned as follows:

(i) lack of communicational facilities in a hilly terrain full of gorges, forests and untractable hill slopes which prevent children from attending even nearby schools.

(ii) diversity of languages which leads to the difficulty of introducing a uniform medium of instruction, and also to the more difficult problem of teaching in a primary school where there are one or two teachers knowing only their mother tongues but the students come from various linguistic groups.

(iii) diversity of educational norms, chiefly as regards modern and monastic education;

(iv) lack of qualified and trained teachers in adequate numbers;

(v) illiteracy and poverty among the parents and the consequent inability on the part of the students to continue their studies;

(vi) lack of realistic and detailed planning, as in the case of the "craftsman training" scheme which could not be implemented at all during the first three years of the Second Plan in the absence of properly worked out details;[37]

(vii) difficulties of timely procurement and supply of furniture, equipments and building materials like G.C.I. sheet and cement which hindered the building of schools, hostels and other educational institutions;[38]

(viii) low standard of school education which itself hindered the growth of higher education as in the case of the scheme "technical and professional scholarships" in the Second Plan period which could not be fully utilised due to the very insignificant number of students who passed the matriculation examination with credit.[39]

In the context of these difficulties the achievements of the Sikkimese authorities in the field of education assume special significance which must not be overlooked. One can hope, therefore, that in course of economic development when most of the difficulties would be resolved, educational progress would be much more widespread and rapid.

REFERENCES

1. L. Dadul, "Medical Services in Sikkim", *Sikkim Herald*, 3, No. 1 (March, 1967), 11.
2. Govt. of Sikkim, *Administration Report of the Sikkim State for 1910-11* (Calcutta: Bengal Govt. Press), p. 6. Hereafter referred to as "Ad. Report for (Year)".
3. Govt. of Sikkim, *Seven Years of Progress: 1954-61* (Gangtok: Sikkim Durbar Press, 1962), p. 27. Hereafter referred to as "Progress Report: First Plan".
4. Govt. of India, *Second Five-Year Plan of Sikkim: Report of the Technical Team* (New Delhi: Planning Commission, 1961), p. 76. Hereafter referred to as "First Team's Reports".
5. *Ibid.*, pp. 76-7.
6. Govt. of Sikkim, *Second Five-Year Plan: 1961-66* (Gangtok: Public Relations Officer), p. 22.
7. "Crusade Against Disease", *The Statesman* (Calcutta), June 2, 1960, "Sikkim: A Statesman Supplement," p. II.
8. Progress Report: First Plan, p. 23.
9. First Team's Report, p. 76. See also, Progress Report: First Plan, p. 29.
10. Govt. of Sikkim. *The Second Five-Year Plan of Sikkim: Progress Report for the Period April, 1961—February, 1966, Part I* (Gangtok: Planning and Development Dept.), pp. 33-4, Hereafter referred to as "Progress Report: April, 1961 — February 1966".
11. *Ibid.*, p. 34. Also see, S. V. Garde, "Medical and Public Health: Achievements of Second 5-Year Plan, Progress and Prospects of Third 5-Year Plan", *Sikkim Herald*, 3, No. 1 (March, 1967), p. 7.
12. Garde, p. 8.
13. Progress Report: April, 1961-February, 1966, p. 33.
14. Govt. of India, *Mid-Term Appraisal of the Second Five-Year Plan of Sikkim: Report of the Technical Team* (New Delhi: Planning Commission, 1964), p. 71. Hereafter referred to as "Second Team's Report."
15. Progress Report: April, 1961-February, 1966, p. 35.
16. Second Team's Report, pp. 71-72.

17. Garde, p. 8.
18. Govt. of Sikkim, *The Third Five-Year Plans 1966-71, Final Draft, Vol. 1* (Gangtok: Planning and Development Dept., 1966), Section on Health.
19. "The Process of Planned Development--Health," *Sikkim Herald*, May 23, 1972.
20. Govt. of Sikkim, *Sikkim Development Plan* (Gangtok: Sikkim Durbar Press, 1955), p. 34.
21. Progress Report: First Plan, p. 30.
22. United Nations, *Problems of Social Development Planning with Special Reference to Asia and the Far East: Report of a Group of Experts*, Development Programming Techniques Series No. 4 (New York: 1964), p. 23.
23. "The Process of Planned Development — Education", *Sikkim Herald*, May 20, 1972.
24. Ad. Report for 1910-11, pp. 6-7.
25. Ad. Report for 1912-13, p. 9.
26. Ad. Report for 1913-14, p. 7.
26. Ad. Report for 1920-21, pp. 18-19.
27. Ad. Report for 1931-32, pp. 45-6.
29. Progress Report: First Plan, p. 25.
30. United Nations, *Problems of Social Development Planning*, p. 1.
31. *Silkkim Herald*, May 20, 1972.
32. Progress Report: April, 1961-February, 1966, pp. 29-30.
33. *Sikkim Herald*, May 20, 1972.
34. Govt. of Sikkim, *Second Five-Year Plan, 1961-66*, p. 20.
35. Progress Report: First Plan, p. 26.
36. *Sikkim Herald*, May 20, 1972.
37. Govt. of Sikkim, *Second Five-Year Plan of Sikkim Progress Report 1961-64: Review of the Plant Proposals for Revision of Plan* (Gangtok: Planning and Development Dept.), Critical Review Section, p. 8. Hereafter referred to as "Progress Report: 1961-64".
38. Progress Report: April, 1961-February, 1966, p. 31.
39. Progress Report: 1961-64, Critical Review Section, p. 8.

8

A Review of the Sikkimese Plans

Introduction, of economic planning in Sikkim may be regarded as a historical phenomenon considering its great impact on the age-old economy. It is to be seen now whether and to what extent the plans fitted into the economic fabric of the country and whether they require to be modified in the future.

A. Plan Preparation, Supervision and Implementation

Let us begin with the preparation of the plans. In the preparation of a plan the starting point should always be the enunciation of *objectives*. In fact, the objectives are the *raison d' etre* of planning. The determination of objectives depends on national preferences as well as economic conditions of the country prevailing at a particular time.

If objectives were chosen on the basis of existing conditions alone, there should never be any conflict between them. But often conflicts ensue because of incompatibility between national preferences and existing conditions. In order to avoid such conflicts it is advisable, first of all, to restrict the number of objectives to the minimum because larger the number of objectives the greater is the possibility of a conflict taking place; and secondly, even after minimising the objectives if a conflict becomes unavoidable, it is necessary to proceed in terms of *priorities,* laying more emphasis on one and less on the other ones.

A similar notion was expressed in the progress report of Sikkim's First Plan, though in a different language: "Priorities, in a Plan are predetermined by the existing conditions in the country like terrain, climate, social and economic institutions and traditions of the people, level of economic development, availability of resources both natural and human and the objectives and aims set out for achievement."[1] It is clear, therefore, that the Sikkimese planners tried to set up priorities among the different objectives taking into account "the existing conditions in the country."

But what were the objectives and priorities in the Sikkimese plans? Though they have not been clearly stated, two broad objectives seem to have dominated the planners' mind while formulating the plans. These were: (i) an increase in the revenue-earning capacity of different projects with the long-run aim of self-sustaining growth, and (ii) provision of some basic necessities and social services in the context of the hilly and underdeveloped nature of the country.

Of the above two objectives the first was given priority over the second as can be gleaned from different plan documents. It was stated that:

"The Development Projects like schools, hospitals, roads etc., after their completion place a burden on the State's resources on their maintenance to meet the expenditure. To enable the State to bear this burden to the extent possible, revenue-earning schemes and programmes like nationalised transport, development of forests, fruit preservation factory etc., have also been given priority".[2]

The Draft First Plan had also expressed a similar opinion: "It has been estimated that maintenance of the projects provided in the Plan will entail a minimum recurring expenditure of Rs. 10 lakhs per year. An effort has, therefore, been made to plan quick revenue-earning projects and to give them top priority so that funds will automatically become available for maintenance before the period of Plan expires. In order to provide for increasing expenditure even afterwards, an attempt has been made to find additional revenue amounting to Rs. 12 lakhs per year."[3]

In the Second Plan the same objectives and priorities seem to have been retained. At the very beginning of the first chapter the Draft Second Plan enunciates the objectives as follows:

"In formulating schemes for the Second Plan, attempts have been made, taking the success achieved in the First Plan as the starting point, to ensure more sustained efforts in a planned manner towards, larger increase in production with the help of modern science and technology, both in the fields of agriculture and industry, and also to achieve progressive advancement in the different fields of social services like education, medical facilities, health and sanitation, safe drinking water, communication, transport, community development etc., in keeping with the traditional cultural pattern of the country."[4]

In the above statement we can clearly see the twin objectives of revenue-earning and social services as in the First Plan. Likewise, the first objective was given priority. The following extract is worth mentioning in this connection:

"Though for the balanced growth of a country it is necessary, to provide better facilities in regard to agriculture, communications, education, health etc., yet in order to maintain and expand the various welfare activities undertaken it becomes necessary to undertake projects which would be of revenue-earning value and would meet, in the long run, the financial requirements of the various projects to be maintained on internal resources only.

"In the Second Plan greater emphasis has, therefore, been laid on revenue-earning projects like power projects, paper, carpentry, bamboo and other industries, 'ham, sausage and bacon factory', timber floating, plantation of commercial timber and valuable medicinal herbs. These projects would, to a considerable extent, meet the financial requirements of the country and thus be able to achieve, to a greater degree, the long-range objective of a self-reliant economy."[5]

The First Technical Team which visited Sikkim in early 1961 observed that the principal considerations in fixing the outlay of the Second Plan were the following:

(i) utilisation of assets already created,
(ii) development of resources in productive sectors,
(iii) assurance of minimum amenities, and
(iv) regional balance in development.

We can point out that while the first two considerations

fall under the category of revenue-earning projects, the latter two constitute social services. Moreover, the team also observed that "in the allocation of outlays among the different heads of development an attempt was made to reconcile the competing demands of productive sectors and social services."[6] Obviously, that reconciliation was in the form of priority fixation as pointed out earlier.

The basic objectives in the Third Plan remained the same as before, but now they were classified under four heads: (i) agriculture, (ii) industry, (iii) power and transport, and (iv) social services, as in the following:

"1. To increase agricultural production, both of food and cash crops.
2. Industrialisation based on agricultural and fresh raw materials and specialised skills.
3. Improvement and extension of transport and power facilities already existing.
4. Investment on producers, i.e. expansion and development of social services and amenities."[7]

It can easily be shown that these objectives were nothing but further elaboration of the earlier two basic objectives. Two important changes in the approach may, however, be noted. First, in the field of agriculture a mere "increase in agricultural production" was envisaged while the Second Plan had hoped "to effect an appreciable increase in agricultural production so as to achieve, to a considerable extent, self sufficiency in food-grains".[8]

That self-sufficiency is unattainable in the agricultural sector was, however, ultimately admitted in the Final Draft of the Third Plan. There it was pointed out that:

"Sikkim imports about 20,000 maunds of rice per month at present. It is not possible for Sikkim to be self-sufficient in food in the near future, even if per acre yields are raised substantially."[9]

Instead of self-sufficiency in food-grains —which was the objective of the Second Plan—the new objective of the Third Plan became simply to increase agricultural production as much as possible.

Secondly, another change in attitude in the Third Plan objectives was that provision of basic amenities and social services was no longer looked upon as an end in itself but rather as a factor in the economic uplift of the country. This is evident from the enumeration of the Third Plan objectives where we find the expression. "Investment on producers, i.e. expansion and development of social services and amenities."

The above expression clearly suggests the view that social services are not only necessary for their own sake but they are also conducive to economic growth. 'The quantity and quality of labour, for example, is directly related to the conditions of health prevailing in any country. The spread and standard of education is likewise related to the technical and managerial efficiency of the people. Similar observations may be made as regards other types of social services.

The rationale of the two broad objectives of revenue-earning and provision of basic amenities throughout the plans can be found in the peculiar position that Sikkim holds. The fact that Sikkim is a protectorate of India has prompted the latter, under a sense of moral responsibility, to help usher in the process of economic development in Sikkim and as a result India has been generously helping the country. But apart from the intrinsic value of the plan projects both the countries must see that ultimately Sikkim is to stand on her own feet without any further assistance from India, because if the assistance remains perennial, there is hardly any justification for planning. Grants and loans are needed initially for the launching of planned economic programmes in a virgin land, but ultimately the country must be in a position to repay the debts or at least not to incur further debts.

This idea seems to have prompted the planners in Sikkim to lay great emphasis on revenue-earning projects in all development plans. As the planners have stated:

"...but a stage has to come when the people and the Government of Sikkim must shoulder all these commitments from their own resources. One of the objectives of planning is that the assets created by the first two and subsequent plans will make Sikkim dependent on its own resources."[10]

As regards the other objective, viz. provision of basic amenities, it may be pointed out that its purpose is more social than economic. This objective is a very general one and can be found in the planning of many countries but it has assumed greater significance in Sikkim not only due to the backwardness of the people but also to the hilly and river-strewn terrain of the country. In such a situation the people and the Government cannot rely on private enterprises and institutions for the provision of the amenities and as such the Government must come forward.

It should be borne in mind that objectives alone do not constitute any plan. They must be concretised into specific *targets* and arrangements made to achieve them. Target determination is, therefore, the next step to the formulation of the plan objectives.

Objectives and targets are not, in fact, separate entities—when an objective is quantified, it is transformed into a target. For example, the objective of the plan may be to increase the per capita income of the country. If the planners now quantify it and lay down that the per capita income is to increase at the rate of 5 per cent per annum, then it is transformed into a target. Objectives should be transformed into targets because the latter act as guidelines for the determination of required amounts of different factors of production like raw materials, manpower etc., as well as for the preparation of effective policy instruments for the execution of the plan.

It is clear, therefore, that the specification of targets is an important ingredient of planning. In Sikkimese planning, however, targets are not generally specified and only projects are mentioned. That is why Sikkimese plans have often been called *project-oriented.*

There were, of course, some targets associated with the projects, but there was hardly any "national" target included in the plans, except in the Second Plan where it was intended "to secure during the Plan period a rise in national income of approximately 10 per cent".[11] In the absence of appropriate data we do not know whether that single national target* was realistically set or really achieved.

The primary reason for the lack of specification of targets is the acute deficiency of statistical data on which targets are to be based. Even after three successive plans Sikkim has no statistical cell in the Planning and Development Department.

---

* Interestingly, in the Plan document it was stated as an "objective", not a target.

The few data available are often conflicting and not systematically arranged. The official attempt at the compilation of data is miserably faulty. *Sikkim Through Figures* a book of compilation of statistical data published in 1969 by the Government of Sikkim, is full of errors. A more astonishing fact is that nobody cared to see whether the figures were all right and when the high officials were told about the errors they simply pleaded ignorance.

We may point out here that the setting up of a strong, competent and reliable *statistical organisation* should precede the formulation of a plan. In this context the views expressed by the United Nations experts are worth mentioning. They have laid great stress on the need and desirability of setting up of a central statiscal organisation which should be made responsible for the collection, co-ordination and standardisation of statistics. They have further recommended that this organisation should remain in constant touch with the planning authority so that it can be aware of the specific requirements of data for the purposes of planning.[12] The Sikkimese planning authority should have borne this in mind while preparing the plans.

Along with the determination of objectives and targets the planning authority should attempt to secure, as far as possible, the internal consistency of the plan through a number of balances to ensure the smooth and successful implementation of the plan. If this is not done, there is every possibility of a plan ending up in fiasco, with gluts or shortages in different sectors of the economy thereby frustrating all the targets. In fact, it is advisable to draw up the various balances even before the financial production targets are laid down. It is the duty of the planners to see that the targets are synchronised with those balances so that they can actually be achieved.

We may here refer to some very important balances in planning and see whether they were maintained in Sikkimese planning. The first is known as *cross-wise balance* which attempts to secure equilibrium between aggregate output targets and total resources available in the country. This balance attempts to avoid both non-utilisation and mal-utilisation of resources. If the aggregate output target is too modest then the resources available will not be fully utilised and if it is too ambitious the latter nay not stand the pressure of demand leading ultimately to the partial execution of the plan which means mal-utilisation of resources. In Sikkim no such balance was ever prepared and as such we do not know whether the targets were too modest, too ambitious or appropriate.

The second important balance known *as backward balance* is an attempt to establish equilibrium between every final physical target and its numerous components which enter into its production. This balance ensures that a particular target is feasible. It may be pointed out in this connection that though the preparation of backward balance for a particular target is not so difficult, the preparation of such balances for all the targets is a very complex job requiring technical knowledge as well as planning prudence. This is because the output of one industry is the input of another industry and all the inputs and outputs are to be considered simultaneously. As Frisch has said:

"Scientific planning means co-ordinating everything in one simultaneous (and integrated) piece of analysis and doing it on some optimum basis. It is solving the whole nexus as one simultaneous problem where everything determines everything else."[13]

A thorough *knowledge of the resources* of the country and a comprehensive *input-output analysis* based on those resources can provide both the crosswise and backward balances in a plan. But unfortunately, in Sikkim we do not find either of them to be operative in plan formulation. The reason again is the lack of statistical data. One pre-requisite for the establishment of those balances is the availability of detailed statistical data regarding existing or potential resources as well as *technical relationships between the inputs and outputs* of every type of industry; but in Sikkim it is still lacking.

Though the Sikkimese authority was not very keen on maintaining those balances it was conscious of one balance: the *regional balance*. This balance implies that less developed areas of the country should come up as far as possible to the level of development of other areas to ensure integrity and unity of the nation and economic equality for the people living in different regions. This aspect, however, should not be over-emphasised as different regions have different growth potentialities and as such require differential treatment. There should be a compromise between economic and social considerations to resolve this problem. We find the following statement in the report of the First Technical Team:

"For various reasons during the First Plan the development of the northern areas was not adequately attended to. The opening up of these areas by means of the highways under construction, will bring about a virtual transformation in the economy and the social life of the area. The Second Plan projects and programmes will promote development of the resources of this region and cater for its social and cultural needs."[14]

Regarding the Second Plan the Team also said: "... there is a fair balance in the allocation of investment and current outlays for projects and programmes which will benefit the three broad regions."[15]

After discussing some physical and spatial balances let us now come to the problem of *monetary balance*. The purpose of this balance is to assure monetary equilibrium by maintaining equality between the expenditure in different sectors and the value of goods produced in these sectors at current prices so that neither inflation nor deflation may grip the country.

So far as this balance is concerned Sikkimese planners have very little to do because there is free trade between Sikkim and India and the same currency, i.e. Indian rupee, prevails in both the countries. It is not so much a problem of Sikkim as of India which is much larger than the former. Sikkim, therefore, can do very little to solve this problem without a concurrent move by Indian.

There is, however, one redeeming feature of the problem. So long Sikkim has experienced price-rise along with India but it is very difficult to say whether that price-rise can really be called inflation. It is because the large amounts of grants and other expenditures by the Government of India have increased the money as well as real income of all sections of the Sikkimese people. *If we mean by inflation "a decrease in real wage-income", it has perhaps not been the case in Sikkim.*

The main beneficiaries during an inflation are the private investors, but in Sikkim almost the entire development expenditure is carried on by the Government so that *there is no scope of one section of the people being more benefited than another.* Moreover, there are many indications that the real income of the Sikkimese fixed-income group has gone up, at least not down. This is mainly because of a high demand for labour for developmental works which pushes the wage rate upwards. To meet the excess demand sometimes workers are even hired from India. At the same time there are various amenities benefiting the poorer sections of the people. The people get food-stuff and other daily necessities at rationed and subsidised rates. Medical facilities are free. Education upto a certain stage is also free. All these have contributed to a *high real income of the working people* which means that the hardship of high prices has hardly hit them.

After discussing the objectives, targets and balances which are all problems of preparation of a plan, let us now probe into the question of *implementation* of the plans in Sikkim. Implementation is no less important or difficult than preparation of a plan. According to Professor W.A. Lewis: *"Implementing a Plan is more difficult than making it. Making a Plan is an exercise of the imagination, while implementation is a struggle with reality. Before crossing the Atlantic, the pilot of an aircraft plots his course in relation to expected weather and winds. Once aloft, reality is found to differ from expectations; the plan must be modified continually to cope vith changing facts."*[16]

At the same time we must remember that preparation and implementation of the plan are inextricably related to each other — any defect in the preparation of the plan is apt to lead to difficulties in its implementation and any lacuna in the implementation of the plan is apt to frustrate the preparation of the next plan. A proper link between preparation and implementation of the plan is, therefore, the *sine qua non* for the success of the plan.

The expert group on social development planning held under the auspices of the ECAFE was very much concerned about the problem of link between planning and implementation. The group observed that:

> *"In some countries, planners do not have effective means of knowing fully what has actually happened to the plans in the course of implementation. In this connection, the question was raised as to whether planners or the central planning agency might not have a more direct association in terms of inspection or control with implementing agencies.*

> *Moreover, the annual plans can also be used as instruments of indirect control over implementation. It was generally agreed that the planning agency should sound evaluation machinery giving continuous and comprehensive information on performance and implementation."*[17]

In Sikkim *annual plans* were introduced only from the time of the Second Plan. These were intended to smooth out the unforeseen bottlenecks and tailor the plan programmes according to the changing circumstances. The annual plan splits up the various plan targets into annual targets for the purpose of implementation. It is the controlling plan in Sikkim in the sense that this is the only document which, when passed by the State Council, authorises the concerned departments to spend money for development; the Government of India also releases money on the basis of the annual plans.

Annual planning is an important feature of the medium-term plans in the Soviet and East European countries. There a typical annual plan starts with an evaluation of the progress of the medium-term plan in the previous year. The achieved targets are compared with the planned targets and the reasons for deviations, if any, are analysed. The projects which are to be carried out in the current year along with the estimates of costs and resources are described in detail. The plan also describes the steps to be taken to correct deficiencies and make up for shortfalls of the earlier years.[18]

In Sikkim annual plans do not show any such deep analysis. *They show only the financial aspect of the plans— the budget estimates for the next year, revised estimates for the current year and actuals for the previous year.* The supervisory and corrective nature of annual planning is, therefore, very much restricted in Sikkim.

Regarding other kinds of control there is practically very little in Sikkim. Supervision of the progress of the plan is one of the fundamental pre-requisites of planning. Molotov observes that "planning cannot be considered good unless it takes into account the course of the fulfilment of the plan". In the Soviet Union the Gosplan is empowered to send its authorised representatives to watch the fulfilment of the plan in the various regions and republics of the country.

There is no such supervisory body in Sikkim. To evaluate the plan progress the Planning Commission of India sent expert bodies only thrice in 1961, 1964 and 1970. Apart from the fact that there was no regular visit of the Planning Commission teams, the assessments made by them were very brief and not so critical.

So far as the Government of Sikkim is concerned, it occasionally prepares reports on the achievements of the plans but these point out very little of the drawbacks or non-fulfilments. A more or less comprehensive report was published after the completion of the First Plan. At the end of the Second Plan the Government prepared a very brief report but did not publish it. None has so far been prepared or published on the achievements of the Third Plan. The irregularity and inadequacy in the preparation and publication of the *achievement reports* is a major drawback in Sikkimese planning.

In Sikkim plans are not only prepared by the various departments, but they are also executed by them, so that some sort of *internal supervision* is already there. This certainly helps to make a synchronization between the preparation and execution of the plans. But at the same time it is also prone to breed inefficiency, dishonesty and collusion among the planning and executing authorities.

It seems that the supervision of the plans in Sikkim calls for an *independent body* of experts, technicians and accountants unconnected either with plan formulation or its execution. This body should evaluate plan fulfilment in a strictly impartial manner. It should boldly bring to the notice of the Government the failures and drawbacks which it detects in course of its evaluation. To perform the evaluation function properly, it should prepare regular reports like quarterly, half-yearly and yearly evaluations of the plan progress.

Now coming to the execution of the plans we may record some of the experiences during the period under study. First of all, the need for *streamlining the executing mechanism* was gradually being felt as the plans progressed. Initially there was a great deal of confusion with respect to the powers, functions, responsibilities and liaison among the different executing agencies. But in the light of past experiences the organisational set-up was later on streamlined to meet the exigencies of development planning. Attempts were made to assign definite objectives, powers and responsibilities to each section of the executing authorities which eliminated much of the former confusion. To quote the Draft Second Plan:

"... steps are already being taken up for gearing up the administrative machinery so as to meet the challenge of the changing and complex needs and administrative requirements. The creation of the Development Blocks in the Revenue Divisions and putting them under the Magistrates in charge of those divisions would not only effectively associate the revenue authorities with the development programmes but would also be a great step in laying larger emphasis on the development activities of the Welfare State."[20]

Moreover, it was also decided that, "... the administration has to be *decentralised* in order to effectively and speedily implement the Plan projects with higher efficiency."[21] The decision was the outcome of the plan experience that often development projects, particularly the agricultural ones, could not be executed effectively due to the lack of management by the local people. It was decided, therefore, that a greater responsibility should henceforth devolve on the panchayats or village councils for implementing local projects.

Under the decentralisation policy the most important function of the panchayats would be to execute and maintain village development programmes and formulate new schemes in their own areas. The beneficiaries had to contribute 50% of the project cost and a matching grant was made by the Government. The panchayats had also the power to levy taxes and tap other sources of revenue for the maintenance of utility schemes.

In course of the implementation of the plans the Government also realised the *suitability* or otherwise of particular projects in a country like Sikkim. For example, in the, case of agricultural projects it was realised during the Third Plan period that "impact package programmes" were more suitable than the creation of an expensive agricultural research wing or demonstration farms, as had been done during the first two plans. The programmes were entrusted to some selected progressive farmers who provided exemplary diligence and industry and the Government provided technical knowhow, improved seedlings and fertilizers. The farmers were expected to create model farms in their respective localities which could encourage others to follow suit.[22]

In fact, as planning proceeds, a country becomes wiser by experience and the trial and error process in course, of execution of the plans ultimately settles down to a more appropriate approach to plan execution. The same happened in the case of Sikkim.

B. Plan Achievements and Prospects

The general impression of anyone who visits Sikkim today is that after all this tiny country has found quite well in her developmental programmes. Dr. V.K.R.V. Rao, former member of the Planning Commission of India and Dr. P. S. Lokanathan, former Director-General of the National Council of Applied Economic Research, who were in Gangtok towards the end of 1965 shared this view — and it may be taken to hold good by the end of 1970-71 as well.[23]

After the three plans the average Sikkimese now consumes more food and clothing than he did a generation ago. Gangtok has acquired a number or beautiful buildings. Agricultural production has shown a steady rise. The mountain kingdom has been opened up by means of roads and communication. Where there was practically nothing before, the kingdom has now a workable health and educational set-up.

There is no reliable estimate of Sikkim's national income and as such it is difficult to assess the rise or otherwise of national income during the plan period. An estimate of the country's net domestic product was made for the year 1965-66 but it was more or less a guess-work and no subsequent attempt was made towards that direction.*[24]

According to the estimate of the Durbar Sikkim's per capita annual income in 1965-66 was nearly Rs. 900 which was about three times as high as that in India. By the end of the Third Plan the figure is believed to have crossed the Rs. 1,000 mark. Some feel, however, that this is rather exaggerated. But even then, according to all available evidences the per capita income

---

* The net domestic product for the year 1965-66 was estimated as Rs. 9 crores approximately.

of Sikkim seems to be higher than that of India.

But the most comprehensive and reliable yardstick of economic growth in Sikkim is internal revenue. Between 1950 and 1965 Sikkim's annual revenue increased tenfold— from Rs. 10 lakhs, to nearly Rs. 100 lakhs—and by 1970-71 it has jumped to Rs. 266 lakhs as estimated in the 1970-71 budget. A phenomenal increase indeed. Certainly the value of money has fallen because of inflation triggered off by the presence of the army and development expenditures on projects having long gestation period. This means that the rise in real internal revenue will be less than that in money internal revenue as stated above.

Granted that the fall in the value of money has not been as much as the rise in money revenue—and this assumption seems to be quite reasonable under the Sikkimese circumstances—the high increase in money revenue is an indicator of an increase in real revenue, though not so high. As the rate of taxation has increased very little during the period, the rise in real revenue also indicates a rise in real income of the people.[25]

There are also other indicators. Sikkim has no unemployment. This is because it is mainly an agricultural country and population is quite small compared to the availability of land. In Sikkim there is still the scope of further reclamation of land which is a potential source of employment. Moreover, the development plans have absorbed a large number of labourers — and indeed, modern Sikkim is faced not so much with the problem of unemployment as with the problem of labour shortage. The Sikkimese boast that there is no native beggar in their country. The few beggars found in the Gangtok bazar and other market places are all of Indian origin, according to them. This is a strikingly different picture compared to what one finds in India.

Another comfortable feature of the Sikkimese economy is that it is *fairly stable* and there have been little vissicitudes in her path of progress. This again can be compared with the neighbouring economy of India where sharp rise and fall in economic activities have caused much headache to the planners. This is due to a steady flow of Government expenditure coupled with a negligible share of the private sector in the gross national expenditure of Sikkim. There have been unforeseen circumstances like the emergency arising out of the Sino-Indian conflict of 1962 or the unprecedented flood of 1968, but on all such occasions the Sikkimese economy has shown extraordinary resilience.

Coming to further comparative economic aspects of Sikkim and India it may be noted that India has been very generous to Sikkim in the matter of economic aid. *India's per capita annual aid to Sikkim was about Rs. 100 in 1965 whereas in the neighbouring state of West Bengal the per capita expenditure on developmental projects was barely a quarter of that amount.*[26]

This was the picture when Sikkim was completing her Second Plan and India, her Third Plan. In the subsequent years the gap seems to have widened still further. As revealed by Mr. Siddhartha Sankar Ray, Chief Minister of West Bengal, *during 1967-68 and 1968-69, the last two years of the plan holiday, the per capita outlay for developmental purposes in West Bengal was the lowest in India. The Fourth Plan allocation for West Bengal, again, was not high—it was only Rs. 16 crores more than the Third Plan allocation, while for most other states it was double the Third Plan allocation. On the other hand, the plan expenditures in Sikkim continued to increase substantially during the period.* It can be presumed, therefore, that after the three plans in Sikkim the gap in the per capita outlay as between Sikkim and West Bengal has widened still further.[27]

There is yet another channel through which Indian money flows into Sikkim—the *refund of excise duty* on exports from India. According to Article V of the Indo-Sikkimese treaty no duty can be imposed on the exports of either country. As there is free trade between India and Sikkim Indian goods flow into Sikkim and are sold as in India at a price including excise duty. The amount of excise duty on all such commodities is computed by the end of the year and the money is refunded to the Government of Sikkim. The amount appears in the revenue side of the Sikkimese budget. As Sikkim imports more than she exports it is India who has to make the refund. The annual refund by the end of 1970-71 was more than Rs. 1 crore and constituted a major share of the state revenue.[28]

In addition to plan aid and excise duty refund India spends a sizeable amount of money on public works like the maintenance of some *strategic roads*. She also spends a large amount for the stationing of the *army* and other defensive measures. If all these are considered, the per capita Indian aid to Sikkim will be very high.

Still, what one finds in Sikkim is not a sense of gratitude, but of resentment towards India. Thus in an interview with Mr. Sunanda K. Datta Ray, Mr. Ashoke Tsering of the Sikkim National Party chastised India for "heaping tax upon tax for the benefit of the Indian public and to the detriment of the Sikkimese consumer".[29] Obviously he was referring to the excise duty on Indian goods, hut apparantly oblivious of the refund of the same based on Sikkimese calculations.* The reason behind this type of charge seems to be more political than economic.

Interestingly, the political consciousness and a distinct sense of national identity have only intensified with the economic progress which owes so much to India. The Sikkimese argue that they would as easily have found donors elsewhere. In their view the small countries like Switzerland and the Netherlands would be better able to appreciate their problems. Consciously or unconsciously the Sikkimese compare themselves with those countries and the result is frustration and disappointment.

Sometimes frictions in economic interests occur, but there also political solution is sought after. For example, Sikkim's annual output of about 50,000 maunds of cardamom is sold in Gangtok for Rs. 460 per maund whereas, according to Mr. Madan Mohan Rasaily, the Secretary for Trade, Industries and Commerce, the Indian price is nearly double that and the West Asian markets, including Pakistan, can offer as much as Rs. 2,000 per maund. Among the Sikkimese it is a moot point whether economic and financial relations with foreign powers, which are in New Delhi's sole charge, also include trade.

A political status similar to that of Nepal and Bhutan lies at the heart of the Sikkimese elite and they think that it can

* The other taxes that the Sikkimese paid were not imposed by India, but by the Government of Sikkim and were spent for the people of Sikkim.

be achieved through the building up of a strong economic base as well as political movements. Thus they are in favour of big industries. On the other hand, the Government of India's general preference has so far been in favour of agriculture, transport, small industries and social services. In the opinion of New Delhi Sikkim's bias towards what is termed "prestige projects" in preference to the basic needs of the country is detrimental to its interests. But it has often been interpreted otherwise in Sikkim. One Secretary to the Government of Sikkim, for example, expressed to the present author in confidence that the Government of India does not really want that Sikkim becomes industrialised.

The above controversy is pointless. What is important is to determine whether a particular project is suitable to Sikkim taking into consideration the resources of the country, feasibility of production and marketing prospects. If these are considered with care a sound and sure path of progress is not very difficult to find out.

In this context it appears to the present author that there should be some sort of tying of the Sikkimese economy with that of India. The Sikkimese economy should be deemed as complementary to that of India and the principle of regional planning should be followed in its developmental efforts. In fact, economically speaking, Sikkim is part of India, and there is no reason why she should be developed independent of what is happening in India. Dr. V.K.R.V. Rao, a former member of the Planning Commission of India, expressed the opinion in 1965 while he was touring Sikkim that the country should relate its economic development to that of the northern districts of West Bengal. Unfortunately uptill now no such step has been taken.[30]

A joint Indo-Sikkimese programme for economic development is imperative. A vast country with diversified resources can produce all the goods and services that are necessary but a small country handicapped by limited resources can hardly do that. Self-reliance in the sense of self-sufficiency in every direction within the framework of a closed econony is therefore, not a very good proposition for a country like Sikkim.

Sikkim should rather develop herself as complementary to the Indian economy which means that she should be able to produce some commodities at a cost of production which is lower than that in India so that those could be sold to India at a profit. The earnings thus acquired could then be used for the import of commodities which Sikkim cannot produce economically. In order to do that, account should be taken of the resources of the country and effective measures adopted for their utilisation.

Unfortunately emotion sometimes takes precedence of rational thinking. In recent years, for example, Sikkim has launched some "prestigious projects" like transistor factory and jewel-bearing plant. Sikkim had been clamouring for these projects for a pretty long time but they could not materialise due to the reluctance of the Government of India. At long last after much hesitation the latter has agreed to these projects. But it does not seem to the present author that these projects would be complementary to the Indian economy. Rather, they are competitive in nature and Sikkim does not possess any special advantage, resources or technical know-how which can make the projects more economical then those in India.

It may however, be argued that along with those projects skill formation will take place and when the skills are formed Sikkim will be placed at a better position. But it is a mere presumption to think that the Sikkimese can excel in skill to such an extent as to make similar Indian projects less economical. Moreover, skill formation takes time. Switzerland's example may be cited, but it is an exception and not a rule. The Sikkimese people who till very recently were hunters, gatherers, agriculturists and small traders, and are largely so even today, cannot be expected to turn overnight into skillful watchmakers. It may be pointed out in this connection that the Swiss watchmakers have more than hundred years of experience in modern watchmaking whereas the Sikkimese have yet to acquire any such experience.

It is also not true that the utilisation of natural resources has reached a saturation point in Sikkim and the prospect of economic development lies solely in skill formation. There still remains a vast amount of untapped resources. Some progress has been made during the plans in this direction but much more awaits to be done. A few such prospective lines of development may be mentioned in this connection.

Apart from the traditional items of exports like potatoes, cardamom, fruits, medicinal herbs, timber, hides and skins, handicrafts and tourism a few new ventures were initiated during the period 1954-71. These are fruit products, liquor, copper, power and tea. While power and tea are yet to be exported other items have already appeared prominently in the export list.

Though not in the export list at present, power and tea seem to be the most promising of all ventures. The Lagyap Power Complex to which reference has already been made earlier will be a major foreign exchange earner of the country. Sikkim having similar geographical and climatic conditions like Darjeeling might one day be one of the principal tea exporting countries of the world.

In this connection some prospective lines of development which have not yet been undertaken may be mentioned. Sikkim exports a sizeable amount of medicinal herbs. There is, therefore a good scope for the development of pharmacy. The industry requires specialists, technicians and skilled workers which the country lacks at present. But there are the resources and if Sikkim can endeavour to launch a transistor or watch factory, why not pharmacy?

There is also scope for the development of dairy and allied industries. The hill section of the Darjeeling district is a surplus area of dairy products and Sikkim being situated adjacent to it and having more or less similar climatic and geographical conditions should also be able to produce dairy products in sufficient quantities Side by side a leather goods industry can be launched as Sikkim is an exporter of hides and skins. Already there is a tannery and a factory can easily be established for the production of footwear, leather bags suitcases etc.

So far as mining is concerned, Sikkim is exporting copper at present, but no attempt has yet been made for the extraction of coal the deposit of which exists in fairly large magnitude in the Rangit valley near Nayabazar. There is a considerable demand for coal in Darjeeling. Recently an aerial ropeway has been constructed between Darjeeling and Singla Bazar in the Rangit valley. With the help of this ropeway the demand for coal in Darjeeling can be met.

Sikkim is one of the world's largest suppliers of cardamom and it is the country's major cash crop. There is a good possibility of increasing the production of this crop as well as development of an allied industry like extraction of cardamom oil.

At present Sikkim produces about 50,000 maunds of cardamom every year. But this production can still be increased with appropriate prophylactic and pesticidal measures. The main enemies of the crop are hail and "purkhey". Purkhey is a virus disease which often causes the cultivator severe losses. While little can be done against hail the disease can be controlled to a great extent. Actually, in 1955 a small experimental nursery was established near Gangtok for the purpose and disease-free cardamom sedlings were distributed among the cultivators.

The export market of cardamom is, however, erratic as consumption is largely in Pakistan and the Middle East, and very often export restrictions and unforeseen circumstances lead to sharp fall in prices. It was suggested by the First Technical Team that an industry be set up for the extraction and refinement of cardamom oil for which there is demand in many parts of the world. It would help to stabilise the market and thereby increase exchange earnings.[31]

Sikkim abounds in forest wealth which should be explored and exploited. Setting up of some wood-based industries is a natural corrollary. Some of the local species of forest trees are useful for railway sleepers, tea chests, packing boxes, matches, furniture and construction work. Fir and spruce found abandantly in Sikkim are excellent raw materials for paper pulp, specially for the production of newsprint. The present paper and newsprint crisis in India offers a very good market for paper pulp. The Sikkimese planners should pay special attention in this matter.

At the same time it would be good if the Government of India establishes a paper mill somewhere near Sikkim. The Second Technical Team proposed the setting-up of a paper mill of about 60-100 tons a day capacity in North Bengal where the raw materials from Sikkim could be supplied.[32]

No such mill has yet been established and the nearest paper mill where the raw materials can be sent now is in Bihar and the transport cost is quite high. It is urgent, therefore, that the proposed paper mill is established with due care and earnestness.

Assuming an open economy and taking into account all the resources, prospects and requirements of the country we can envisage an ideal export-import chart for Sikkim as follows:

An Ideal Export-Import Chart for Sikkim

Exports	*Imports*
A. Items Already Explored: Potato, Cardamom, Fruits, Fruit Products, Liquor, Medicinal Herbs, Timber, Hides & Skins, Copper, Handicrafts, Tourism, Power, Tea.	**A. Household Requirements:** Food. Other Household Requirements.
B. Items Yet Unexplored: Pharmacy, Dairy Products, leather Goods, Coal, Cardamom Oil, Paper Pulp.	**B. Other Requirements:** Transport Materials, Raw Materials, Equipments, Skill & Technical Know-how, Other Imports

Note: During the current Fourth Plan a transistor factory and a water-making (initially jewel-bearing) plant are being constructed the possibilities of which do not seem to be very bright to the present author.

If the items in the export side are properly developed, it is hoped there would be no adverse balance of payment (in the accounting sense, as trade is free between Sikkim and India) so that Sikkim would be able to stand on her own feet. It is, in fact, as we have seen, the prime objective of development planning in Sikkim. When that stage is reached thete will be no further need for Indian aid. If that day really comes, it would not only be a thing of joy to the Sikkimese but also a thing of gratification to the people of India.

REFERENCES

1. Govt. of Sikkim, *Seven Years of Progress: 1954-61*(Gangtok: Sikkim Darbar Press, 1962), p. ii. Hereafter referred to as "Progress Report: First Plan."
2. *Ibid.*
3. Govt. of Sikkim, *Sikkim Development Plan* (Gangtok: Sikkim Darbar Press, 1955), p. 1.
4. Govt. of Sikkim, *Second Development Plan (A Five Year Plan 1961-62 - 1963-66)*, Unpublished Draft, Part I. 1960, p. 1. Hereafter deferred to as "Second Plan (Unpublished)".
5. *Ibid.*, p. 8.
6. Govt. of India, *Second Five-Year Plan of Sikkim: Report of the Technical Team* (New Delhi: Planning Commission, 1961), p. 2. Hereafter referred to as "First Team's Report".
7. Govt. of Sikkim, *Third Five Year: 1966-71*, Final Draft, Vol. I (Gangtok: Planning and Development, Dept., 1966), p. 1. Hereafter referred to as "Third Plan (final), Vol. 1".
8. Second Plan (Unpublished), pp. 1-2.
9. Third Plan (Final) Vol. II, Introduction.
10. Second Plan (Unpublished) p. 4.
11. *Ibid.*, pp. 1-2.
12. United Nations, *Economic Bulletin for Asia and the Far East*, November, 1955, pp. 63-70.
13. R. Frisch, *Planning for India* (Asia, 1960), p. 2.
14. First Team's Report, p. 2.
15. Ibid.
16. W.A. Lewis, *Development Planning: The Essentials of Economic Policy* (Nev York: Harper & Row, 1966), p. 264.
17. United Nations, *Problems of Social Development Planning With Special Reference to Asia and the Far East: Report of a Group of Experts*, Development Programming Techniques Series No. 4 (New York: 1964), p. 66.
18. M.L. Seth, *Theory and Practice of Economic Planning*, 5th ed. (New Delhi: S. Chand & Co., 1971), p. 117.
19. V. Molotov, *The Third Five-Year Plan for the Development of the National Economy of the U.S.S.R.*, (Moscow: Foreign Languages Publishing House), pp. 20-21.
20. Second Plan (Unpublished) Ch. 3, p. 12.
21. *Ibid.*
22. D. Bose, "Rapid Progress with Help from India: But Diversion of Manpower to Defence is a Drawback," *The Statesman*, Calcutta, September 21, 1965.
23. A. Bhandari, "Indian Planning Team for Sikkim", *Indian Express*, December 9, 1965.

24. Govt. of Sikkim, *Sikkim Through Figures* (Gangtok: Planning and Development Dept, 1969), p. 1.
25. Bhandari, See also Sikkim's Budget for 1970-71.
26. Bose.
27. *The Statesman* (Calcutta), Dak Edition, August 28, 1973, p. 1.
28. S.K. Datta-Ray, "Voting in the Himalayas—III: Time to Review Indo-Sikkimese Relations", *The Statesman* (Calcutta), February 9, 1973.
29. *Ibid.*
30. Bhandari.
31. First Team's Report.
32. Govt. of India, *Mid-Term Appraisal of the Second Five Year Plan of Sikkim: Report of the Technical Team* (New Delhi: Planning Commission, 1964), p. 48.

Bibliography

Aitchison, Sir Charles Umpherston, Comp. *A Collection of Treaties, Engagements and Sanads Relating to India and Neighbouring Countries,* Calcutta: Office of the Superintendent of Govt. Printing, 1892. I, 151-71. Vol. II, India, 1909.

Alexandrowicz, C. H. "Indian Himalayan Dependencies", *Year Book of World Affairs,* 1956, London: 1958, pp. 128-43.

Allewein, Eugen. "The Passanran and Talung Valleys, Sikkim", *Himalayan Journal,* 5(1933), pp. 58-64.

Armstrong, Hamilton Fish. "Where India Faces China", *Foreign Affairs,* 37 July, 1959, 617-25.

Ashton, T.S. "The Relation of Economic History to Economic Theory". *Economica,* May, 1946, pp. 81-96.

Baden-Powell. *The Land System of British India,* 3 vols. London: 1896.

Bakewell, Anderson, "The Himalaya: Retrospect and Prospect", *The Journal of the Swiss Foundation for Alpine Research,* 1 (1956).

Banderji, S. "Sikkim: Land of Peaks and Beauties", *United Nations World,* 6(Feb. 1952), 24-27.

Bell, C. *The People of Tibet.* Oxford: Clarendon Press, 1928.

Bhandari, A. "Indian Planning Team for Sikkim", *Indian Express,* Dec. 9, 1965.

Bhanja, K.C. *Mystic Tibet and the Himalaya,* Darjeeling: Gilbert & Co., 1948. pp. 115-60.

Bhanja, K. C. *Wonders of Darjeeling and the Sikkim Himalaya (Accounts All Authentic),* Darjeeling: Published by the Author, 1943, 163p.

Biswas, P.C. "The Lepchas of Sikkim", *Indian Culture, I* (1934-35), 483-86.

Blanford, W.T. "Journey through Sikkim", *Journal of the Asiatic Society of Bengal,* 40, pt 2 (1871), 367.

Bose, D. "Rapid Progress with Help from India: But Diversion of Manpower to Defence is a Drawback", *The Statesman* (Calcutta), September 21, 1965.

Bose, P.N. "Extracts from the 'Journal of a Trip to the Glaciers of Kabru, Pandim & C' and the Geology and Mineral Resources of Sikkim", *Records, Geological Survey of India,* vol. 24, Parts I and IV.

Bose, Saradindu. "The Bhot of Northern Sikkim", *Man in India* 46, No. 2 (April-June, 1966).

Brown, Percy. *Tours in Sikkim and the Darjeeling District,* 4th ed. Calcutta: W. Newman & Co., 1944. pp. 3-67.

Buchanan, W.H. "A Journey in Sikkim", *Blackwood's Edinburgh Magazine,* No. 191 (1912).

Buchanan, Daniel Houston. *Development of Capitalistic Enterprise in India,* London: Frank Cass & Co. Ltd., 1966.

Buchanan, W.J. *Notes on Tours in Darjeeling and Sikkim Darjeeling,* Darjeeling Improvement Fund, 1916, 41p.

Buchanan, W.J. "Some Tours in Sikkim", *The Calcutta Review,* No. 275 (Jan., 1914), 21-55, and No. 276 (April, 1914), 191-213.

Bulger, George E. *Notes of a Tour from Bangalore to Calcutta: Thence Delhi and Subsequently to British Sikkim.* Secunderabad: 1869.

Burrard, S. G. and Hayden, H. H. *A Sketch of the Geography and Geology of the Himalayan Mountains and Tibet,* Delhi: Manager of Publications, 1933.

Cammann, S. *Trade Through the Himalayas,* Princeton: 1951.

Campbell, A. "Diary of a Journey through Sikkim to the Frontier of Tibet", *Journal of the Asiatic Society of Bengal,* 21 (1852), 407-28, 477-501, 563-75.

Campbell, A. "Journal of a Trip to Sikkim in December 1848 with a Sketch Map", *Journal of the Asiatic Society of Bengal,* 18 (1849), 482-541.

Campbell, A. "Papers on the Relations with Sikkim and Nepal", *The Oriental,* Jan., 1874.

Campbell, A. *Papers on the Sikkim Morung, Bengal,* Selection No. 5, Calcutta: Military Orphan Press, 1851.

Campbell, A. "Routes from Darjeeling to Thibet", *Journal of the Asiatic Society of Bengal,* 17, pt. 2 (1848), 488-94.

Caroe, Sir Olaf. "The Geography and Ethnics of India's Northern Frontiers: Sikkim", *United Asia,* 12, No. 4 (1960).

Carrasco, Pedro. *Land and Polity in Tibet,* Seattle: University of Washington Press, 1959.

Chattopadhyay, Gouranga. "Lepchas of Kalimpong and of Sikkim: A Comparison", *Vanyajati,* 10 (July 1962), 99-109.

Chief Secretary's Report: January 21, 1971, *Sikkim Herald,* April 4, 1971.

Chopra, I.S. Address on April 4, 1972. Published by the Govt. of Sikkim.

Choudhury, Rabijit. "Changing Pattern of NEFA Economy", *Amrita Bazar Patrika* (Calcutta), Feb. 8, 1971. NEFA Supplement.

Clark, C. *The Conditions of Economic Progress,* 3rd od. New York: St. Martin's, 1957.

Coelho, Vincent Herbert. *Sikkim and Bhutan,* New Delhi: Vikas Publications, 1971.

Colomb, F.C. *Routes in Sikkim,* Simla: Govt. Central Printing Office, 1894. 38p., bibl.

Cooper. T.T. *Travels of a Pioneer of Commerce,* London: 1871.

Crocker, H.E. "The Northern States of India", *Quarterly Review* 298 (Jan., 1960), 50-58.

"Crusade against Disease", *The Statesman* (Calcutta), June 2, 1960. Sikkim: A Statesman Supplement, p. II.

Dadul, L. "Medical Services in Sikkim", *Sikkim Herald,* 3, No. 1 (March, 1967).

Das, S.C. *Journey to Lhasa and Central Tibet,* London: J. Murray, 1902.

Dash, Arthur Jules, ed. *Bengal District Gazetteers: Darjeeling,* Calcutta: Bengal Govt. Press, 1947.

Datta-Majumdar, Niharendu. *The Sikkim Diary,* October, 1948, Calcutta: Superintendent of Govt. Printing, 1951. 14p.

Datta-Ray, S.K. "Voting in the Himalayas—III: Time to Review Indo-Sikkimese Relations", *The Statesman* (Calcutta), February 9, 1973.

Doig, Dasmond. "Sikkim: Enmity between Giant Neighbours, India and Red China, Threatens the Independence of a Tiny Kingdom in the Clouds", *National Geographic Magazine,* 123 (3 March, 1963), 398-429.

Donaldson, Florence. *Lepcha Land, or Six Weeks in the Sikkim Himalayas,* London: Sampson Low Marston & Co., 1900. xil, 213p.

Dorji, Kazi Lhendup. "Sikkim Today", *United Asia,* 14 (July, 1962), 388-89.

Dozey, E.C. *Darjeeling: Past and Present,* Calcutta: 1933.

Earl, A. "On Polyandry in Sikkim and Tibet", *Census of India, 1901.*

Calcutta: Bengal Secretariat Press, vol. vi, (Bengal), Pt. I (Report), Appendix V, pp. 27-30.

The Earl of Ronaldsky. *Lands of the Thunderbolt,* 1923.

Easton, John. *An Unfrequented Highway through Sikkim and Tibet to Chunolaori,* London: Scholaris Press, 1928. 133p.

Eden, Ashley. *Report of the State of Bhootan,* 1865.

Edgar, Sir J. Ware. *Report on a Visit to Sikkim and the Tibetan Front in Oct.-Dec., 1873,* Calcutta: Bengal Secretariat Press, 1874, vi, 103p.

"Education in Sikkim", *Sikkim Herald,* Feb. 23 and 25, 1971.

Elwin, Verrier. *A Philosophy for NEFA,* 2nd rev. ed. Shillong: Adviser to the Governor of Assam, 1964.

Elwin, Verrier and Coverley-Price, Victor. *The Hill People of North-East India,* London: Oxford University Press, 1959.

"Every Day is a Request Day", *The statesman* (Calcutta), June 2, 1960. Sikkim: A Statesman Supplement, p.III.

"Expeditions: Northern Sikkim, 1932", *The Himalayan Journal,* 5(1933), 108-09.

Feer, M.C. "India's Himalayan Frontier: Progress in Sikkim", *Far Eastern Survey,* 22 (Oct., 1953), 139.

Fisher, A.G.B. "Primary, Secondary and Tertiary Production", *Economic Record,* June, 1939.

Forest Manual. A Treatise on the Forestry of Sikkim Compiled in 1909 and Supplemented from Time to Time.

"Forest Wealth", *The Statesman* (Calcutta), June 2, 1960, Sikkim: A Statesman Supplement, p. III.

Frank, A.G. *Capitalism and Underdevelopment in Latin America,* New York: Monthly Review Publication.

Frisch, R. *Planning for India,* Bombay: Asia Publishing House, 1960.

Garde, Dr. S.V. "Public Participation & Positive Health with Special Reference to Sikkim", *Sikkim Herald,* June 3, 1970.

Gawler, J.C. *Sikkim: With Hints on Mountain and Jungle Warfare, Exhibiting Also the Facilities for Opening Commercial Relations through the State of Sikkim with Central Asia, Thibet and Western China,* London: Edward Standard, 1874. viii, 105 p.

The Gazetteer of Sikkim, Calcutta: Bengal Secretariat Press, 1894. With an Introduction by H.H. Risley.

Ghosh, Alak. *Indian Economy: Its Nature and Problems,* 7th ed., rev, and enlarged, Calcutta: The World Press Private Ltd., 1963.

Gorer, Geoffrey. *Himalayan Village: An Account of the Lepchas of Sikkim,* London: Michael Joseph, 1938, 510p.

Gould, B.J. *The Jewel in the Lotus*, 1957.

Graham, J.A. *On the Threshold of Three Closed Lands: The Guild Putpost in the Eastern Himalayas*, Edinburgh: R & R. Clark Ltd., 1897, 166p.

Hagen, Everett E. *On the Theory of Social Change: How Economic Growth Begins*, Homewood, Illinois: The Dorsey Press Inc., 1962.

Hakluyt, Richard: *The Principal Navigations* (1599) vol. 2.

Halder, Hem Chandra, "India's Neighbour: Sikkim", *Modern Review*, 107 (June, 1960), 479-85.

Haldipur, R.N. "Address of Shri R.N. Haldipur", Principal Administrative Officer, Government of Sikkim at the Darbar on the occasion of Losar (New Year Day), February 21, 1966, Published by the Govt. of Sikkim.

Hamilton, W. *The East India Gazetteer*, London: 1815.

Harnett, L.H. "A Review of Nationalished Road Transport in Sikkim (1944-1969)," *Silver Jubilee*, A Souvenir Publication of Sikkim Nationalised Transport, 1969.

Hastings. *Encyclopaedia of Religion*, VII, 784-89.

Hathorn, J.G. *A Hand-book of Darjeeling*, Calcutta: 1863.

Hertslet, G.E.P. *Treaties between Great Britain and China*, 2 vols. London: 1908.

Holt, E. "Worship of the Snowy Range", *Holiday*, 27(March, 1960), 25.

Hooker, Sir Joseph Dalton. *Himalayan Journals or Notes of a Naturalist in Bengal, the Sikkim and Nepal Himalayas, the Khasia Mountains*, London: Ward, Lock, Bowden & Co., 1891, xxx, 574p.

Hoselitz, Bert F. "Entrepreneurial Element in Economic Development", *The Economic Weekly*, 15 (February, 1963), Annual Number.

Hunter, Sir W.W. *A Statistical Account of Bengal*, X. London: 1876.

Imperial Gazetteer of India, New Edition, XXII. London: Oxford University Press, 1908.

Govt. of Bengal. Proceedings of the Hon'ble The Lieutenant- Governor of Bengal during (Month, Year). Political Department, Calcutta: Bengal Secretariat Press.

Govt. of Bengal. *Report on the Administration of Bengal During 1889-90*, Calcutta: Bengal Secretariat Press, 1890.

Govt. of India, Dept. of Statistics. *Report on the Internal Trade of Bengal for the Year 1877-78*, Calcutta: 1878.

Govt. of India, Dept. of Statistics. *Reports on the Trade between Assam and the Adjoining Foreign Countries: 1878 to 1905*. Calcutta: Bengal Secretariat Book Depot.

Govt. of India, Dept. of Statistics. *Report on Trade of Bengal with Nepal. Sikkim and Bhutan, 1880-81 to 1912-13,* Calcutta: Bengal Secretariat Book Depot.

Govt. of India, Dept. of Statistics. *The Frontier Trade of Bengal, 1913-14, etc., to 1920-21,* Calcutta: Bengal Secretariat Book Depot.

Govt. of India, Dept. of Statistics. *The Trade of Bengal with Nepal, Tibet, Sikkim and Bhutan in 1921-22,* Calcutta: Bengal Secretariat Book Depot.

Govt. of India, *Census of India, 1931,* Calcutta: Central Publication Branch. 1933, Vol. V (Bengal and Sikkim), Pt. II (Report), Pt. II (Tables).

Govt. of India. *Census of India, 1951,* Delhi: Manager of Publications, 1953. Vol. VI (West Bengal, Sikkim and Chandernagore), Pt. I - A & Pt. I-C (Report by A. Mitra), Pt II (Tables), Pt V (West Bengal, Sikkim and Calcutta: Administrative Report Enumeration).

Govt. of India. *Census of India, 1961.* Delhi: Manager of Publications, 1963-64, Vol. XVI, (West Bengal and Sikkim), Pt II (General Population Tables), Pt VIII (Administrative Report), Pt VIIIA (Enumeration), Ref. Pt VIII (Census of Sikkim, pp. 40-46).

Govt. of India. *Bhutan and Sikkim,* Gangtok: Office of the Political Officer in Sikkim.

Govt. of India. Ministry of Information and Broadcasting, Gazetteer of India: Indian Union. Delhi: Publications Division, 1965.

Govt. of India. *Progress Through Partnership.* Gangtok: Office of the Political Officer in Sikkim.

Govt. of India, Ministry of Information and Broadcasting. *Sikkim Looks Ahead,* Delhi: Publications Division, 1956.

Govt. of India, Ministry of External Affairs. *Treaty Between India and Bhutan 1949,* Gangtok: Govt. of India Press.

Govt. of India: Ministry of External Affairs. *Treaty Between India and Sikkim 1950,* Gangtok: Govt. of India Press.

Govt. of India. *Second Five-Year Plan of Sikkim: Report of the Technical Team,* New Delhi: Planning Commission, 1961.

Govt. of India. *Mid-Term Appraisal of the Second Five-Year Plan of Sikkim,* Report of the Technical Team, New Delhi: Planning Commission, 1964.

Govt. of India: Ministry of External Affairs, *Annual Reports.*

Govt. of Sikkim. *Administration Report of the Sikkim State for (Year),* Calcutta: Superintendent of Govt. Printing, Bengal Govt. Press.

Govt. of Sikkim. *Sikkim Development Plan*, Gangtok: Sikkim Darbar Press, 1955.

Govt. of Sikkim. *Seven Years of Progress: 1954-61*, Gangtok: Sikkim Darbar Press, 1962.

Govt. of Sikkim. *Second Development Plan (A Five-Year Plan 1961-62 — 1965-66)*. Unpublished Draft, Part I, 1960. Part II not prepared.

Govt. of Sikkim. *Second Five-Year Plan: 1961-66*, Gangtok: Public Relations Officer.

Govt. of Sikkim. Second Five-Year Plan: 1961-66. Schemes in the Second Five-Year Plan. Gangtok: Planning and Development Dept., 1962.

Govt. of Sikkim. *Second Five-Year Plan of Sikkim. Budget Proposals for Annual Plan (Next Year) and Revised Estimates (Current Year)*. 5 vols, containing Revised Estimates for the years 1961-62 to 1965-66, also containing Budget Proposals for those years except 1965-66; Gangtok: Planning and Development Deptt.

Govt. of Sikkim. *Second Five-Year Plan of Sikkim: Progress Report 1961-64 (Review of Plan, Proposals for Revision of Plan)*, Gangtok: Planning and Development Dept.

Govt. of Sikkim. *The Second Five-Year Plan of Sikkim: Progress Report for the Period April, 1961—February, 1966*, Part I. Part II not published. Gangtok: Planning and Development Dept.

Govt. of Sikkim. *The Third Flve-Year Plan: Draft Proposals 1966-71*, 3 vols. Gangtok: Planning and Development Dept., 1965.

Govt. of Sikkim. *The Third Five-Year Plan 1966-71: Final Draft*, 2 vols. Gangtok: Planning and Development Dept., 1966.

Govt. of Sikkim. *The Third Five-Year Plan of Sikkim: Mid-Term Proposals and Revised Outlays 1965-71*. Gangtok: Planning and Development Dept., 1969.

Govt. of Sikkim. *Third Five-Year Plan of Sikkim: Budget Proposals for Annual Plan (Next Year) and Revised Estimates (Current Year)*, 5 vols., containing Revised Estimates for the years 1966-67 to 1970-71; also containing Budget Proposals for those years except 1970-71, Gangtok: Finance Dept.

Govt. of Sikkim. *Mid-Term Progress Report of the Third Five-Year Plan for the Period April, 1966 to September, 1968*, Gangtok: Planning and Development Dept.

Govt. of Sikkim. *Progress Report of the Third Five Year Plan for the Period October, 1968—March, 1969*, Gangtok: Planning and Development Dept.

Govt. of Sikkim. *Progress Report of the Third Fiver Year Plan for the Period April, 1969—June, 1969,* Gangtok: Planning and Development Dept.

Govt. of Sikkim. *The Third, Five-Year Plan Progress Report April, 1969-March, 1970,* Gangtok: Planning and Development Dept.

Govt. of Sikkim. *Sikkim: A Concise Chronicle,* Gangtok: Publicity Dept.

Govt. of Sikkim. *Sikkim: Her Faith and Future,* Gangtok: Dept. of Information and Publicity.

Govt. of Sikkim. *Sikkim: The Land and Its People,* Gangtok: Publicity Dept.

Govt. of Sikkim. *Sikkim through Figures,* Gangtok: Planning and Development Dept.

Jackson, W.B. *Report on Darjeeling: Selections from the Records of the Bengal Govt.,* No. 17, Calcutta: 1854.

Johri, Sitaram, Retd. Major. *Our Borderlands,* Lucknow: Himalaya Publications, 1964.

Kakodkar, Avadhuth. *Bhutan and Sikkim,* Gangtok: Office of the Political Officer in Sikkim, 1965.

Kapur, B.K. "Sikkim and Bhutan", *Commonwealth Journal,* 5 (Nov. 1962), 275-77.

Karan, Pradyumna P. "Bhutan and Sikkim: Himalayan Shangrila, Now Darkened by Communist China's Shadow, Faces up to 20th Century", *Canadian Geographical Journal,* 65 (Dec. 1962), 200-09.

Karan, Pradyumna P. "Geographic Patterns in the Himalayas." *Bulletin of Tibetology* (Gangtok), 3, No. (July 21, 1966), 5-25, bibl.

Karan, P.P. & Jenkins, W.M. *The Himalayan Kingdoms: Bhutan, Sikkim and Nepal,* New York: Van Nostrand Company Inc., 1963.

Kellas, A.M. "The Mountains of Northern Sikkim and Garwal", *Alpine Journal,* 26 (1912).

Kosambi, D. D. *An Introduction to the Study of Indian History,* Bombay: Popular Book Depot, 1956.

Lamb, A. *Britain and Chinese Central Asia.*

"Land of the Uphill Devils", *Time,* 73 (Jan. 12, 1959), 28.

"Lessons in Prosperity", *The Statesman* (Calcutta), June 2, 1960, Sikkim: A Statesman Supplement, p. III.

Letter No. 386 dated April 10, 1863 from the Superintendent of Darjeeling to the Secretary to the Govt. of Bengal.

Levi, W. "Bhutan and Sikkim: Two Buffer States", *World Today* 15(Dec. 1959), 492-500.

Levi, W. "India's Himalayan Border", *Contemporary Review,* 188 (July, 1955), 43-44.

Lewis, Arthur W. *The Theory of Economic Growth,* London: George Allen & Unwin, 1964-65.

Lewis, Arthur W. *Development Planning: The Essentials of Economic Policy,* New York: Harper & Row, 1966.

Louis, J.A.H. *The Gates of Tibet: A Bird's Eve View of Independent Sikkim British Bhootan and the Dooars,* Calcutta: 1894, 183p.

Macaulay, Colman. *Report of a Mission to Sikkim and the Tibetan Frontier: With a Memorandum on Our Relations with Tibet,* Calcutta: 1885.

Macdonald, David. *Touring in Sikkim and Tibet,* Kalimpong: 1930. 142p.

McCarty, H.H. "An Approach to a Theory of Economic Geography", *Professional Geographer,* 10, No. 4 (1958), 2-10.

McNee, Robert B. "The Changing Relationships of Economics and Economic Geography", *Economic Geography* 35(1959), 189-198.

Maharaj Kumar of Sikkim. Text of Address by the Maharaj Kumar of Sikkim at the XXV International Congress of Orientalists, Moscow, 12 August, 1960. Gangtok: Namgyal Institute of Tibetology.

Maine. *Early Law and Custom.* Murray: 1883. See Paper on "Theories of Primitive Society."

Mainwarring, Col. G.B. *A Grammar of the Rong (Lepcha) Language As It Exists in the Darjeeling and Sikkim Hills,* Calcutta: Baptist Mission Press, 1876.

Markham, Sir C. *Narratives of the Mission of George Bogle to Tibet and of the Journey of Thomas Manning to Lhasa.* London: 1876.

Markham, C. J. *Report on the Sikkim Expedition from January, 1888 to January, 1890,* Calcutta: Superintendent of Govt. Printing, 1890. 90p.

Mathai, John. *Village Government in British India,* Adelphi Terrace, London: Fisher Unwin Ltd., 1915.

Mehra, P. *Younghusband Expedition.*

Minney, Rebeigh James. *Midst Himalayan Mists,* Calcutta: Butterworth & Co., 1920, 80p.

Molotov, V. *The Third Five-Year Plan for the Development of the National Economy of the U.S.S.R.,* Moscow: Foreign Languages Publishing House.

Mookerji, Radha Kumud. "Indian Land System: Ancient, Mediaeval and Modern (with Special Reference to Bengal)", *Report of the*

Land Revenue Commission Bengal by Govt. of Bengal, II. Calcutta: Bengal Govt. Press, 1940.

Morris, C. John. *Living with Lepchas: A Book about the Sikkim Himalayas*, London, William Heinemann, 1938. xiii, 312p. bibl.

Myrdal, G. *International Economy: Problems and Prospects*, London: Routledge & Kegan Paul Ltd., 1959.

Nakane, Chi. "A Plural Society in Sikkim: A Study of the Inter-Relations of Lepchas, Bhotias and Nepalis," *Caste and Kin in Nepal, India and Ceylon*, ed. C.V. Furer-Haimendorf, Bombay: Asia Publishing House, 1966.

Namgyal, Gyalmo Hope. "Sikkim", *Asia Magazine*, 5, No. 9 (Feb. 28, 1956), 4-8.

Namgyal, Gyalmo Hope. "The Sikkimese Theory of Land-holding and the Darjeeling Grant", *Bulletin of Tibetology* (Gangtok), 3, No. 2 (July 21, 1966).

Namgyal, Thutob and Dolma, Jeshay. *History of Sikkim*, trans. Lama Dawa Kazi Samdup. MSS, 1908.

National Council of Applied Economic Research. Socio-Economic Conditions of Primitive Tribes in Madhya Pradesh. New Delhi: 1963.

"Nationalised Transport", *The Statesman* (Calcutta), June 2, 1960. Sikkim: A Statesman Supplement, p. IV.

O'Connor, Sir William Frederick Travers. On the Frontier and Beyond: A Record of Thirty Years' Service. London: John Murray, 1931. xiv, 355p.

O'Malley, L.S.S., ed., *Bengal District Gazetteer: Darjeeling*, Calcutta: Bengal Secretariat Book Depot, 1907.

"Orchids and Citrus Fruits", *The Statesman* (Calcutta), June 2, 1960, Sikkim: A Statesman Supplement, p. IV.

"Palden Thondup Cottage Industries Institute", *Sikkim Herald* 3, No. 1 (March, 1967).

Pant, S.D., *The Social Economy of the Himalayans*, London: George Allen and Unwin, 1935.

Papanek, G.F., "The Development of Entrepreneurship", *American Economic Review* 52(1962), 48-58.

Parkhurst, C.A., *Sikkim*, London: Macmillan & Co, Ltd., 1946, 40p.

Parsons, Kenneth H., et al, ed, *Land Tenure*, Wisconsin, The University of Wisconsin Press, 1956. Proceedings of the International Conference on Land Tenure and Related Problems in World Agriculture Held at Madison, Wisconsin, 1951.

Pascoe, Edwin H., *A Manuel of the Geology of India and Burma*, Delhi: Manager of Publications, 1950.

Pavlov, V.J., *The Indian Capitalist Class*, New Delhi: People's Publishing House, 1964.

Pemberton, Captain R. Boileau, Envoy to Bootan. *Report on Bootan* (With an Appendix and Maps 1838) Calcutta: Bengal Military Orphan Press, 1839, Reprinted in *Indian Studies: Past and Present* (Calcutta), 2, No, 4 and 3, No. 1.

Peter, Prince of Greece and Denmark, "The Peoples of the Himalayas," *Geographical Magazine*, 33 (Sept., 1960), 295-308.

Plaisted, B. "An Account of the Countries Adjacent to Bengal", *Bengal Past and Present*, IV, Calcutta: 1909.

"Portrait of a Country", *The Statesman* (Calcutta), June 2, 1960, Sikkim, A Statesman Supplement, p. I.

Pradhan, K.R. "Whither Sikkim?", *United Asia*, 12, No. 4 (1960), 488-92.

"The Process of Planned Development — Agriculture", *Sikkim Herald*, May 13, 1972.

"The Process of Planned Development — Animal Husbandry," *Sikkim Herald*, May 17, 1972.

"The Process of Planned Development — Education," *Sikkim Herald*, May 20, 1972.

"The Process of Planned Development — Forests", *Sikkim Herald*, May 18, 1972.

"The Process of Planned Development — Health", *Sikkim Herald*, May 23, 1972.

"The Process of Planned Development — Industries", Mining and Commerce." *Sikkim Herald*, June 1, 1972.

"The Process of Planned Development — Power", *Sikkim Herald*, June 22, 1972.

"The Process of Planned Development— Transport", *Sikkim Herald*, May 27, 1972.

Rahul Ram. *Himalaya as a Frontier.*

Rai, Chandra Das. "Sikkim", *United Asia*, 12, No. 4 (1960), 356-62.

Ramsbotham, R.B. *Studies in the Land Revenue History of Bengal, 1769-87*, London: Oxford University Press, 1926.

Rao, P.R. *Sikkim: The Story of Its Integration with India.*

Rasaily, M.M. "Landslides and Floods in Sikkim with Reference to Forestry", *Sikkim Herald*, June 9, 1970 (Part I), and June 10, 1970 (Part II).

Rasaily, M.M. "Sikkim: Its Flora and Fauna", (Part I) *Sikkim Herald,* May 29, 1970.

Rawlings, E.H. "The Buffer States of Sikkim and Bhutan", *Eastern World.* 16 (November, 1962), 12-13.

Rennie, D.F. *Bhotan and the Story of the Door War,* London, J. Murray.

"Rich Copper Mines", *The Statesman* (Calcutta), June 2, 1960, Sikkim: A Statesman Supplement, p.II.

Rock, Joseph F. "Excerpts from a History of Sikkim," *Anthropos,* 48(1953) 925-948.

Ronaldsay, *Himalayan Bhutan.*

Rose, L.E. "Himalayan Border States: Buffers in Transition", *Asian Survey* 3(Feb., 1963), 116-22. bibl.

Roy, Sarat Chandra. "Kinship Organisation among the Managers of Sikkim", *The Journal of the Bihar and Orrissa Research Society,* 7(1921), 81-89.

Roy Choudhuri, K.C. (Deputy Conservator of Forests, Sikkim), *A Plan for Forest Development,* Gangtok; Sikkim Darbar Press, 1951.

Schumpeter, J.A. "The Creative Response in Economic History", *Journal of Economic History,* November, 1947, pp. 149-59.

Schumpeter, J.A. *The Theory of Economic Development,* New York: Oxford University Press, 1961.

Sen, Bhawani, *The Evolution of Agrarian Relations in India,* New Delhi: People's Publishing House, 1962.

Seth, M.L. *Theory and Practice of Economic Planning,* 5th ed. New Delhi: S. Chand & Co., 1971.

Shakabpa, Tsepon W.D. *Tibet: A Political History,* Yale University Press, 1967.

Sharma, R.N. "Development of Electricity in Sikkim", *Sikkim Herald,* June 12, 1970.

Shen, Tsung-Lien and Liu, Shen-Chi. *Tibet, and the Tibetans,* Stanford University Press, 1953.

Shepherd, G. "Where India Meets China High in the Himalayas", *Reporter,* 19(Sept. 4, 1958), 29-31.

Sherwill, J. L."Journal of a Trip Undertaken to Explore the Glaciers of the Kinchinjunga Group in the Sikkim Himalaya", *Journal of the Asiatic Society of Bengal,* Vol. 31.

Sherwill, W.S. "Notes upon a Tour in the Sikkim Himalayan Mountains", *Journal of the Asiatic Society of Bengal,* 22 (1853), 540-70, 611-38.

"Sikkim", *The Times* (London), June 13, 1963, p. 13, col. 6; Correction June 27, p.10, col. 5.

"Sikkim and Bhutan", Govt. of Australia: Dept. of External Affairs. *Current Notes on International Affairs,* 33, No.12 (Dec. 1962), 5-13.

"Sikkim: Trade with Tibet to be Restricted", *The Times* (London), 17 (1954), 8, col. 4.

Simons, Henry C. *Economic Policy for a Free Society,* Chicago, 1948.

Sinha, J.C. *The Economic Annals of Bengal,* London: 1927.

Snellgrove, D. *Buddhist Himalaya,* Oxford: Bruno Cassier & Co. Ltd., 1957.

Stamp, J. C. "Geography and Economic Theory," *Geography,* 22(1937), 1-13.

Stocks, C. De Beauvoir. "Folk-lore and Customs of the Lapchas of Sikkim", *The Journal and Proceedings, Asiatic Society of Bengal,* N.S., 21, No. 4 (1925), 325-505.

Sweezy, Paul M. *Theory of Capitalist Development,* London: Dennis Dobsoh Ltd., 1946.

Sweezy, Paul M. et al. *The Transition from Feudalism to Capitalism,* Patna: People's Publishing House, 1957.

Tandon, P.D. "Spotlight on Sikkim: An Interview with the Maharajkumar", *Vigil,* 11, No. 23 (June 25, 1960), 353-56.

Temple, Sir Richard. *Journals Kept in Hyderabad, Kashmir. Sikkim and Nepal.* London: W. H. Allen & Co., 1887, II, 151-73, 179-220.

Thoman, Richards S. *The Geography of Economic Activity: An Introductory World Survey,* McGraw-Hill Book Company Inc., 1962.

Thorner, D. *Land and Labour in India,* New Delhi: Asia Publishing House, 1962.

Turner, S. *Account of an Embassy to the Court of the Tashi Lama in Tibet 1783,* London: W. Bulmer, 1800.

United Nations. *Economic Bulletin for Asia and the Far East,* November, 1955.

United Nations. *Planning for Economic Development,* New York: Dept. of Economic and Social Affairs, 1963.

United Nations. *Problems of Social Development Planning: With Special Reference to Asia and the Far East: Report of a Group of Experts,* Development Programming Techniques Series, No. 4. New York 1964.

Varma, S.P. *Struggle for the Himalayas,* 1965.

Vasu, Pramatha Nath. *Notes on the Geology and Mineral Resources of Sikkim,* Calcutta, 1891.

Waddel, L.A. *Among the Himalayas,* Westminister: Archibald Constable & Co., 1899, xvi, 452p.

Waddel, L.A. *The Buddhism of Tibet: Or Lamaism with Its Mystic Cults, Symbolism and Mythology and Its Relation to Indian Buddhism,* 2nd ed. Cambridge: W. Heffer & Sons Ltd., 1934.

---, *Lhasa and Its Mysteries with a Record of the Expedition of 1903-04.*

----, *Tribes of the Brahmputra.*

Waddel, L.A. "Place and River Names in the Darjeeling District and Sikkim", *Journal of the Asiatic Society of Bengal,* 60 Pt. I, No. 2 (1891), 53-79.

Weber, Max. *From Max Weber: Essays in Sociology,* London: Kegan Paul, 1948.

Weber, Max. *Protestant Ethic and the Spirit of Capitalism,* London: George Allen & Unwin, 1948.

Weber, Max. *The Sociology of Religion,* trans. Ephraim Fischoff, London: Methuen & Co. Ltd., 1965.

White, J. Claude. *Sikkim, and Bhutan: Twenty Years on the North-East Frontier 1887-1908,* London: Edward Arnold, 1909, xx, 332p.

Younghusband, Sir Francis. *India and Tibet,* 1910.

Zetland, Lawrence John Lumlay Dundas, 2nd Marquis of, 1876. *Lands of the Thunderbolt: Sikkim, Chumbi and Bhutan.* London: Constable & Co., 1923. xxii, 267p.

Appendix I

Treaty between India and Bhutan 1949

The Government of India on the one part, and His Highness the Druk Gyalpo's Government on the other part, equally animated by the desire to regulate in a friendly manner and upon a solid and durable basis the state of affairs caused by the termination of the British Government's authority in India, and to promote and foster the relations of friendship and neighbourliness so necessary for the well-being of their peoples, have resolved to conclude the following treaty, and have, for this purpose named their representatives, that is to say Sri Harishwar Dayal representing the Government of India, who has full powers to agree to the said treaty on behalf of the Government of India, and Deb Zimpon Sonam, Tobgye Dorji, Yang-Lop Sonam, Chho-Zim Thondup, Rin-Zim Tandin and Ha Drung Jigmie Palden Dorji, representing the Government of His Highness the Druk Gyalpo, Maharaja of Bhutan, who have full powers to agree to the same on behalf of the Government of Bhutan.

Article 1. There shall be perpetual peace and friendship between the Government of India and the Government of Bhutan.

Article 2. The Government of India undertakes to exercise no interference in the internal administration of Bhutan. On its part the Government of Bhutan agrees to be guided by the advice of the Government of India in regard to its external relations.

Article 3. In place of the compensation granted to the Government of Bhutan under Article 4 of the Treaty of Sinchula and enhanced by the treaty of the eigith day of January 1910 and the temporary subsidy of Rupees one lakh per annum granted in 1942, the Government of India agrees to make an annual payment of Rupees five lakhs to the Government of Bhutan. And it is further hereby agreed that the said annual payment shall be made on the tenth day of January every year, the first payment being made on the tenth day of January 1950. This payment shall continue so long as this treaty remains in force and its terms are duly observed.

Article 4. Further to mark the friendship existing and continuing between the said Governments, the Government of India shall, within one year from the date of signature of this treaty, return to the Government of Bhutan about thirty-two square miles of territory in the area known as Dewangiri. The Government of India shall appoint a competent officer or officers to mark out the area so returned to the Government of Bhutan.

Article 5. There shall, as heretofore, be free trade and commerce between the territories of the Government of India and of the Government of Bhutan; and the Government of India agrees to grant the Government of Bhutan every facility for the carriage, by land and water, of its produce throughout the territory of the Government of India, including the right to use such forest roads; as may be specified by mutual agreement from time to time.

Article 6. The Government of India agrees that the Government of Bhutan shall be free to import with the assistance and approval of the Government of India, from or through India into Bhutan, whatever arms, ammunition, machinery, warlike material or stores may be required or desired for the strength and welfare of Bhutan, and that this arrangement shall hold good for all time as long as the Government of India is satisfied that the intentions of the Government of Bhutan are friendly and that there is no danger to India from such importations. The Government of Bhutan, on the other hand, agrees that there shall be no export of such arms, ammunition, etc., across the frontier of Bhutan either by the Government of Bhutan or by private individuals.

Article 7. The Government of India and the Government of Bhutan agree that Bhutanese subjects residing in Indian territories shall have equal justice with Indian subjects, and that Indian subjects residing in Bhutan shall have equal justice with the subjects of the Government of Bhutan.

Article 8.

(1) The Government of India shall, on demand being duly made in writing by the Government of Bhutan, take proceedings in accordance with the provisions of the Indian Extradition Act, 1903 (of which a copy shall be furnished to the Government of Bhutan), for the surrender of all Bhutanese subjects accused of any of the crimes specified in the first schedule of the said Act who may take refuge in Indian territory.

(2) The Government of Bhutan shall, on requisition being duly made by the Government of India, or by any officer authorised by the Government of India in this behalf, surrender any Indian subjects, or subjects of a foreign power, whose extradition may be required in pursuance of any agreement or arrangements made by the Government of India with the said power, accused of any of the crimes, specified in the first schedule of Act XV of 1903, who may take refuge in the territory under the jurisdiction of the Government of Bhutan and also any Bhutanese subjects who, after committing any of the crimes referred to in Indian territory, shall flee into Bhutan, on such evidence of their guilt being produced as shall satisfy the local court of the district in which the offence may have been committed.

Article 9. Any differences and disputes arising in the application or interpretation of this treaty shall in the first instance be settled by negotiation. If within three months of the start of negotiations no settlement is arrived at then the matter shall be referred to the Arbitration of three arbitrators, who shall be nationals of either India or Bhutan, chosen in the following manner:—

(1) One person nominated by the Government of India;
(2) One person nominated by the Government of Bhutan;
(3) A Judge of the Federal Court, or of a High Court in

India, to be chosen by the Government of Bhutan, who shall be Chairman.

The judgment of this Tribunal shall be final and executed without delay by either party.

Article 10. This treaty shall continue in force in perpetuity unless terminated or modified by mutual consent.

Done in duplicate at Darjeeling this eighth day of August, one thousand nine hundred and forty-nine, corresponding with the Bhutanese date the fifteenth day of the sixth month of the Earth-Bull year.

HARISHWAR DAYAL Political Officer in Sikkim.	DEB ZIMPON SONAM TOBGYE DORJI YANG-LOP SONAM CHHO-ZIM THONDUP RIN-ZIM TANDIN HA DRUNG JIGMIE PALDEN DORJI

Instruments of Ratification

Whereas a Treaty relating to the promotion of, and fostering the relations of friendship and neighbourliness was signed at Darjeeling on the 8th day of August 1949 by representatives of the Government of India and of the Government of His Holiness the Druk Gyalpo, Maharaja of Bhutan, which Treaty is, word for word, as follows :—

* * * * * *

The Government of India, having considered the treaty aforesaid, hereby confirm and ratify the same and undertake faithfully to perform and carry out all the stipulations therein contained.

In witness whereof this instrument of ratification is signed and sealed by the Governor-General of India.

Done at New Delhi, the 22nd day of September 1949.

(Sd.) C. RAJAGOPALACHARI,
Governor-General of India.

Whereas a Treaty relating to the promotion of, and fostering, relations of friendship and neighbourliness was signed at Darjeeling on the eighth day of August 1949 by Representatives of my Government and of the Government of India which Treaty is, word for word, as follows:—

* * * * * *

My Government, having considered the treaty aforesaid, hereby confirm and ratify the same and undertake faithfully to perform and carry out all the stipulations therein contained.

In witness whereof I have signed this instrument of ratification and affixed hereto my seal.

Done at Tongsa the fifteenth day of September, 1949.

(Sd.) J. WANGCHUK
Druk Gyalpo.

SEAL.

Appendix II

Treaty between India and Sikkim 1950

The President of India and His Highness the Maharaja of Sikkim being desirous of further strengthening the good relations already existing between India and Sikkim, have resolved to enter into a new Treaty with each other, and the President of India has, for the purpose, appointed as his plenipotentiary Shri Harishwar Dayal, Political Officer in Sikkim, and His Highness the Maharaja having examined Shri Harishwar Dayal's credentials and found them good and in due form, the two have agreed as follows:—

Article I

All previous treaties between the British Government and Sikkim which are at present in force as between India and Sikkim are hereby formally cancelled.

Article II

Sikkim shall continue to be a Protectorate of India and, subject to the provisions of this Treaty, shall enjoy autonomy in regard to its internal affairs.

Article III

(1) The Government of India will be responsible for the defence and territorial integrity of Sikkim. It shall have the right to take such measures as it considers necessary for the defence of Sikkim or the security of India, whether preparatory or otherwise, and whether within or outside Sikkim. In particular, the Government of India shall have the right to station troops anywhere within Sikkim.

(2) The measures referred to in paragraph (1) will as far as possible be taken by the Government of India in consultation with the Government of Sikkim.

(3) The Government of Sikkim shall not import any arms, ammunition, military stores or other warlike material of any description for any purpose whatsoever without the previous consent of the Government of India.

Article IV

(1) The external relations of Sikkim, whether political, economic or financial, shall be conducted and regulated solely by the Government of India; and the Government of Sikkim shall have no dealings with any foreign power.

(2) Subjects of Sikkim travelling to foreign countries shall be treated as Indian protected persons for the purpose of passports, and shall receive from Indian representatives abroad the same protection and facilities as Indian nationals.

Article V

The Government of Sikkim agrees not to levy any import duty, transit duty or other impost on goods brought into, or in transit through, Sikkim; and the Government of India agrees not to levy any import or other duty on goods of Sikkimese origin brought into India from Sikkim.

Article VI

(1) The Government of India shall have the exclusive right of constructing, maintaining and regulating the use of railways, aerodromes and landing grounds and air navigation facilities, posts, telegraphs, telephones and wireless installations in Sikkim; and the Government of Sikkim shall render the Government of India every assistance in their construction, maintenance and protection.

(2) The Government of Sikkim may, however, construct, maintain, and regulate the use of, railways and aerodromes and landing grounds and air navigation facilities to such extent as may be agreed to by the Government of India.

(3) The Government of India shall have the right to construct and maintain in Sikkim roads for strategic

purposes and for the purpose of improving communications with India and other adjoining countries; and the Government of Sikkim shall render the Government of India every assistance in the construction, maintenance and protection of such roads.

Article VII

(1) Subjects of Sikkim shall have the right of entry into, and free movement within, India, and Indian nationals shall have the right of entry into, and free movement within, Sikkim.

(2) Subject to such regulations as the Government of Sikkim may prescribe in consultation with the Government of India, Indian nationals shall have:—

(a) the right to carry on trade and commerce in Sikkim; and

(b) when established in any trade in Sikkim, the right to acquire, hold and dispose of any property, movable or immovable, for the purposes of their trade or residence in Sikkim.

(3) Subjects of Sikkim shall have the same right—

(a) to carry on trade and commerce in India, and to employment therein; and

(b) of acquiring, holding and disposing of property, movable and immovable, as Indian nationals.

Article VIII

(1) Indian nationals within Sikkim shall be subject to the laws of Sikkim and subjects of Sikkim within India shall be subject to the laws of India.

(2) Whenever any criminal proceedings are initiated in Sikkim against any Indian national or any person in the service of the Government of India or any foreigner, the Government of Sikkim shall furnish the Representative of the Government of India in Sikkim (hereinafter referred to as the Indian Representative) with particulars of the charges against such person.

If in the case of any person in the service of the Government of India or any foreigner it is so demanded by the Indian Representative, such person shall be handed over to him for trial before such court as may be established for the purpose by the Government of India either in Sikkim or outside.

Article IX

(1) The Government of Sikkim agrees to seize and deliver up any fugitive offender from outside Sikkim who has taken refuge therein on demand being made by the Indian Representative. Should any delay occur in complying with such demand, the Indian police may follow the person whose surrender has been demanded into any part of Sikkim, and shall, on showing a warrant signed by the Indian Representative, receive every assistance and protection in the prosecution of their object from the Sikkim officers.

(2) The Government of India similarly agrees, on demand being made by the Government of Sikkim, to take extradition proceedings against, and surrender, any fugitive offender from Sikkim who has taken refuge in the territory of India.

(3) In this article, "fugitive offender" means a person who is accused of having committed an extradition offence as defined in the #(First Schedule to the Indian Extradition Act, 1903) or any other offence which may hereafter be agreed upon between the Government of India and the Government of Sikkim as being an extradition offence. {See appendix 1).

Article X

The Government of India, having in mind the friendly relations already existing between India and Sikkim and now further strengthened by this Treaty, and being desirous of assisting in the development and good administration of Sikkim, agrees to pay the Government of Sikkim a sum of rupees three lakhs every year so long as the terms of this Treaty are duly observed by the Government of Sikkim.

The first payment under this Article will be made before the end of the year 1950, and subsequent payments will be made in the month of August every year.

Article XI

The Government of India shall have the right to appoint a Representative to reside in Sikkim; and the Government of Sikkim shall provide him and his staff with all reasonable facilities in regard to their residential and office accommodation and generally in regard to their carrying out their duties in Sikkim.

Article XII

If any dispute arises in the interpretation of the provisions of this Treaty which cannot be resolved by mutual consultation, the dispute shall be referred to the Chief Justice of India whose decision thereon shall be final.

Article XIII

This Treaty shall come into force without ratification from the date of signature by both the parties.

Done in duplicate at Gangtok on this 5th day of December, 1950.

(Sd.) HARISHWAR DAYAL
Political Officer in Sikkim.

(Sd.) TASHI NAMGYAL
His Highness the Maharaja of Sikkim

Appendix I (Ref. Art. IX para (3))

(LETTERS EXCHANGED BETWEEN THE POLITICAL OFFICER AND THE MAHARAJA OF SIKKIM REGARDING ARTICLE IX, PARA (3) OF THE INDO-SIKKIM TREATY OF 1950)

Copy of Political Officer's letter No. 1(7)-NS/63 dated 24 December, 1963 addressed to His Highness the Maharaja of Sikkim.

As a result of negotiations which took place in Gangtok between us on the question of extradition of fugitive offenders, under Article IX paragraph (3) of the Treaty of 1950, it was agreed to modify Article IX paragraph (3) so as to substitute reference to Second Schedule to the Extradition Act of 1962 (Act 34 of 1962) thereto for the First Schedule to the Indian Extradition Act of 1903 respectively.

Accordingly it was agreed that Article IX, paragraph (3) will read as follows:— "In this Article 'fugitive offender' means a person who is accused of having committed an extradition offence as defined in the Second Schedule to the Indian Extradition Act of 1962 (Act of 1962) or any other offence which may hereafter be agreed upon between the Government of India and the Government of Sikkim as being an extradition offence."

I shall be grateful if you will please confirm that the above sets out correctly the understanding reached between us.

Please accept, Your Highness, the assurances of my highest consideration.

Copy of letter No. LCA/91 dated 12 March, 1964 from His Highness the Maharaja of Sikkim addressed to the Political Officer in Sikkim, Gangtok.

I acknowledge the receipt of your letter No. 1 (7)-NS/63 of 24th December 1963 which reads as follows:—

"As a result of negotiations which took place in Gangtok between us on the question of extradition of fugitive offenders, under Article IX paragraph (3) of the Treaty of 1950, it was agreed to modify Article IX paragraph (3) so as to substitute reference to Second Schedule to the Extradition Act of 1962 (Act 34 of 1962) thereto for the First Schedule to the Indian Extradition Act of 1903 respectively.

Accordingly it was agreed that Article IX paragraph (3) will read as follows:— In this Article 'fugitive offender' means a person who is accused of having committed an extradition offence as defined in the Second Schedule to the Indian Extradition Act of 1962 (Act 34 of 1962) or any other offence which may hereafter be agreed upon between the Government of India and the Government of Sikkim as being an extradition offence."

It is confirmed that the above sets out correctly the understanding reached between us.

Please accept, Excellency, the assurances of my highest consideration.

Index

■■■